W9-CTY-885

The Great Books Reading & Discussion Program

THIRD SERIES · VOLUME THREE

The Great Books Foundation

A Nonprofit Educational Corporation

Designed by Don Walkoe Design, Chicago

Handmade marbled paper, photographed on cover,
courtesy of Skycraft Designs, Gresham, Oregon.

9   8   7   6   5   4   3   2

Published and distributed by

The Great Books Foundation
A Nonprofit Educational Corporation
40 East Huron Street
Chicago, Illinois 60611

Acknowledgments

"Habits and Will" from *Human Nature and Conduct* in Volume 14 of *The Middle Works, 1899–1924* by John Dewey, edited by Jo Ann Boydston. Reprinted by permission of the publisher, Center for Dewey Studies, Southern Illinois University at Carbondale.

"History of the Peloponnesian War" from *History of the Peloponnesian War* by Thucydides, translated by Rex Warner. Copyright 1954 by Rex Warner. Reprinted by permission of the publisher, Penguin Books, Ltd.

"What is War?" from *On War* by Karl von Clausewitz, translated by O. J. Matthijs Jolles. Copyright 1943 by Random House, Inc. Reprinted by permission of the publisher.

"Uncle Vanya" from *Chekhov: The Major Plays,* translated by Ann Dunnigan. Copyright 1964 by Ann Dunnigan. Reprinted by permission of the publisher, The New American Library, Inc.

"On Evil" from *The Guide of the Perplexed,* Vol. II, Part III, by Moses Maimonides, translated by Shlomo Pines. Copyright 1963 by The University of Chicago. Reprinted by permission of the publisher, The University of Chicago Press.

"The Iliad" from *The Iliad* by Homer, translated by Robert Fitzgerald. Copyright 1974 by Robert Fitzgerald. Reprinted by permission of the publisher, Doubleday & Company, Inc.

"Principles of Government" from *The Spirit of the Laws* by Baron de Montesquieu, translated by Thomas Nugent. Copyright 1949 by Hafner Publishing Company. Reprinted by permission of the publisher, Macmillan Publishing Company, Inc.

"The Canterbury Tales" from *The Canterbury Tales* by Geoffrey Chaucer, translated by Nevill Coghill. Copyright 1952 by Nevill Coghill. Reprinted by permission of the publisher, Penguin Books, Ltd.

"Agamemnon" from *The Oresteia* by Aeschylus, translated by Robert Fagles. Copyright 1977 by Robert Fagles. Reprinted by permission of the publisher, Viking Penguin Inc.

"The Prince" from *The Prince, A Bilingual Edition* by Niccolò Machiavelli, translated and edited by Mark Musa. Copyright 1964 by St. Martin's Press, Inc. Reprinted by permission of the publisher, St. Martin's Press, Inc.

"The Death of Ivan Ilych" from *The Death of Ivan Ilych and Other Stories* by Leo Tolstoy, translated by Louise and Aylmer Maude. Reprinted by permission of the publisher, Oxford University Press, Inc.

A source note appears, together with biographical information about the author, opposite the opening page of each work in this series. Footnotes by the author are not bracketed; footnotes by GBF or a translator are [bracketed].

CONTENTS

*

GEOFFREY CHAUCER was born in about 1340 in
London, England. At one time, the Chaucers may have
been shoemakers, but Chaucer's father and grandfather
were prosperous wine merchants. Chaucer, though a
poet, conducted a lifelong career as a diplomat, civil
servant, and businessman which began in 1357 with his
service in the household of Elizabeth, countess of Ulster
and daughter-in-law of King Edward III. Chaucer's
appointments included a position as Esquire of the
Royal Household of Edward III; Controller of Customs
and Subsidy of Wools, Skins, and Hides in the port
of London; Knight of the Shire in Parliament; and
Clerk of the King's Works. For his labors, Chaucer was
rewarded with a yearly pension and an annual hogshead
of wine. His travels to Italy on secret missions for the
crown were also fruitful for Chaucer as a writer, since
he discovered the works of Dante, Petrarch, and Boc-
caccio there and learned enough Italian to read them.
Chaucer's first published book was *The Book of the
Duchesse,* a poem. Others include *Troilus and Criseyde,*
The Canterbury Tales, and *The House of Fame.* Chaucer
died in 1400 in London and was buried in Westminster
Abbey.

A selection from *The Canterbury Tales,* translated by
Nevill Coghill. Publisher: Penguin Books, Ltd., 1952.
A portion of the "General Prologue," and "The Wife of
Bath's Tale" and "The Clerk's Tale."

The Canterbury Tales

THE PROLOGUE

When the sweet showers of April fall and shoot
Down through the drought of March to pierce the root,
Bathing every vein in liquid power
From which there springs the engendering of the flower,
When also Zephyrus with his sweet breath
Exhales an air in every grove and heath
Upon the tender shoots, and the young sun
His half-course in the sign of the *Ram* has run,
And the small fowl are making melody
That sleep away the night with open eye
(So nature pricks them and their heart engages)
Then people long to go on pilgrimages
And palmers long to seek the stranger strands
Of far-off saints, hallowed in sundry lands,
And specially, from every shire's end
In England, down to Canterbury they wend
To seek the holy blissful martyr, quick
In giving help to them when they were sick.
  It happened in that season that one day
In Southwark, at *The Tabard,* as I lay
Ready to go on pilgrimage and start
For Canterbury, most devout at heart,
At night there came into that hostelry
Some nine and twenty in a company

Of sundry folk happening then to fall
In fellowship, and they were pilgrims all
That towards Canterbury meant to ride.
The rooms and stables of the inn were wide;
They made us easy, all was of the best.
And shortly, when the sun had gone to rest,
By speaking to them all upon the trip
I was admitted to their fellowship
And promised to rise early and take the way
To Canterbury, as you heard me say. . . .

[The pilgrims are described individually; then Chaucer tells how the host of the inn proposes a story-telling contest to amuse them as they travel. The host will be referee, the teller of the best tale will win a free dinner, and any who break the rules will pay expenses for the trip. They all agree, and in the morning begin their journey and their stories, which Chaucer promises to recount word for word.]

THE WIFE OF BATH'S TALE

*

The Wife of Bath's Prologue

"If there were no authority on earth
Except experience, mine, for what it's worth,
(And that's enough for me) all goes to show
That marriage is a misery and a woe;
For let me say, if I may make so bold,
My lords, since when I was but twelve years old,
Thanks be to God Eternal evermore,
Five husbands have I had at the church door;
Yes, it's a fact that I have had so many,
All worthy in their way, as good as any.

"Someone said recently for my persuasion
That as Christ only went on one occasion
To grace a wedding—in Cana of Galilee—
He taught me by example there to see
That it is wrong to marry more than once.
Consider, too, how sharply, for the nonce,
He spoke, rebuking the Samaritan
Beside the well, Christ Jesus, God and man.
'Thou hast had five men husband unto thee
And he that even now thou hast,' said He,
'Is not thy husband.' Such the words that fell;
But what He meant thereby I cannot tell.
Why was her fifth—explain it if you can—
No lawful spouse to the Samaritan?
How many might have had her, then, to wife?
I've never heard an answer all my life
To give the number final definition.
People may guess or frame a supposition,
But I can say for certain, it's no lie,
God bade us all to wax and multiply.
That kindly text I well can understand.
Is not my husband under God's command
To leave his father and mother and take me?
No word of what the number was to be,
Then why not marry two or even eight?
And why speak evil of the married state?

"Take wise King Solomon of long ago;
We hear he had a thousand wives or so.
And would to God it were allowed to me
To be refreshed, aye, half so much as he!
He must have had a gift of God for wives,
No one to match him in a world of lives!
This noble king, one may as well admit,
On the first night threw many a merry fit

With each of them, he was so much alive.
Blessed be God that I have wedded five!
Welcome the sixth, whenever he appears.
I can't keep continent for years and years.
No sooner than one husband's dead and gone
Some other christian man shall take me on,
For then, so says the Apostle, I am free
To wed, o' God's name, where it pleases me.
Wedding's no sin, so far as I can learn.
Better it is to marry than to burn.

    "What do I care if people choose to see
Scandal in Lamech for his bigamy?
I know that Abraham was a holy man,
And Jacob too, for all that I can scan,
Yet each of them, we know, had several brides,
Like many another holy man besides.
Show me a time or text where God disparages
Or sets a prohibition upon marriages
Expressly, let me have it! Show it me!
And where did He command virginity?
I know as well as you do, never doubt it,
All the Apostle Paul has said about it;
He said that as for precepts he had none.
One may advise a woman to be one;
Advice is no commandment in my view.
He left it in our judgment what to do.

    "Had God commanded maidenhood to all
Marriage would be condemned beyond recall,
For clearly, if the seed were never sown,
How ever could virginity be grown?
Paul did not dare command, let matters rest,
His Master having given him no behest.
There's a prize offered for virginity;
Catch as catch can! Who's in for it? Let's see!

"It is not everyone who hears the call;
On whom God wills He lets His power fall.
The Apostle was a virgin, well I know;
Nevertheless, though all his writings show
He wished that everyone were such as he,
It's all mere counsel to virginity.
And as for being married, he lets me do it
Out of indulgence, so there's nothing to it
In marrying me, suppose my husband dead;
There's nothing bigamous in such a bed.
Though it were good a man should never touch
A woman (meaning here in bed and such)
And dangerous to assemble fire and tow
—What this allusion means you all must know—
He only says virginity is fresh,
More perfect than the frailty of the flesh
In married life—except when he and she
Prefer to live in married chastity.

"I grant it you. I'll never say a word
Decrying maidenhood although preferred
To frequent marriage; there are those who mean
To live in their virginity, as clean
In body as in soul, and never mate.
I'll make no boast about my own estate.
As in a noble household, we are told,
Not every dish and vessel's made of gold,
Some are of wood, yet earn their master's praise,
God calls His folk to Him in many ways.
To each of them God gave His proper gift,
Some this, some that, and left them to make shift.

"Virginity is perfect, unforsaken,
Continence too, devoutly undertaken.
But Christ, who of perfection is the Well,
Bade not that everyone should go and sell

All that he had and give it to the poor
To follow in His footsteps, that is sure.
He spoke to those that would live perfectly,
And by your leave, my lords, that's not for me.
I will bestow the flower of life, the honey,
Upon the acts and fruit of matrimony.

   "Tell me to what conclusion, or in aid
Of what, were generative organs made?
And for what profit were those creatures wrought?
You take my word they were not made for naught.
Gloze as you will and plead the explanation
That they were only made for the purgation
Of urine, little things of no avail
Except to know a female from a male,
And nothing else. Did somebody say no?
Experience knows well it isn't so.
The learned may rebuke me, or be loath
To think it so, but they were made for both,
That is to say both use and pleasure in
Engendering, except in case of sin.
Why else the proverb written down and set
In books: 'A man must yield his wife her debt'?
What means of paying her can he invent
Unless he use his silly instrument?
It follows they were fashioned at creation
Both to purge urine and for propagation.

   "But I'm not saying everyone is bound
Who has such harness as you heard me expound
To go and use it breeding; that would be
To show too little care for chastity.
Christ was a virgin, fashioned as a man,
And many of his saints since time began
Were ever perfect in celibacy.
I'll speak no evil of virginity.

Let them be pure wheat loaves of maidenhead
And let us wives be known for barley-bread;
Yet Mark can tell that barley-bread sufficed
To freshen many at the hand of Christ.
In that estate to which God summoned me
I'll persevere; I'm not pernickety.
In wifehood I will use my instrument
As freely as my Maker me it sent.
If I turn difficult, God give me sorrow!
My husband, he shall have it eve and morrow
Whenever he likes to come and pay his debt,
I won't prevent him! I'll have a husband yet
Who shall be both my debtor and my slave
And bear his tribulation to the grave
Upon his flesh, as long as I'm his wife.
For mine shall be the power all his life
Over his proper body, and not he,
Just as St Paul has given it out to me
In bidding husbands love their wives, I say.
That's an opinion suits me every way."

    The Pardoner, as she was going on,
Started and said, "By God and by St John,
Madam, that's preaching no one could surpass!
I was about to marry, but alas
If I shall have to pay for it so dear
There'll be no marrying for me this year!"

    "You wait," she said, "my story's not begun.
You'll taste another brew before I've done;
You'll find it isn't quite so nice as beer.
For while the tale is telling you shall hear
Of all the tribulations man and wife
Can have; I've been an expert all my life,
That is to say myself have been the whip.
So please yourself whether you want to sip

At that same cask of marriage I shall broach.
Be cautious before making the approach,
For I'll give instances, and more than ten.
And those who won't be warned by other men
By other men shall suffer their correction.
So Ptolemy has said in this connection.
You read his *Almagest;* you'll find it there."
    "Madam, I put it to you as a prayer,"
The Pardoner said, "go on as you began!
Tell us your tale, spare not for any man.
Instruct us younger men in your technique."
"Gladly," she answered, "if I am to speak.
But still I hope the company won't reprove me
Though I should speak as fantasy may move me,
And please don't be offended at my views;
They're really only offered to amuse.
    "Now, gentlemen, I'll on and tell my tale
And as I hope to drink good wine and ale
I'll tell the truth. Those husbands that I had,
Three of them were good and two were bad.
The three that I call 'good' were rich and old.
They could indeed with difficulty hold
The articles that bound them all to me;
(No doubt you understand my simile).
So help me God, I have to laugh outright
Remembering how I made them work at night!
And, faith, I set no store by it; no pleasure
It was to me. They'd given me their treasure,
I had no need to do my diligence
To win their love or show them reverence.
They loved me well enough, so, heavens above,
Why should I make a dainty of their love?
    "A knowing woman's work is never done
To get a lover if she hasn't one,

But as I had them eating from my hand
And as they'd yielded me their gold and land,
Why then take trouble to provide them pleasure
Unless to profit and amuse my leisure?
I set them so to work, I'm bound to say;
Many a night they sang, 'Alack the day!'
Never for them the flitch of bacon, though,
That some have won in Essex at Dunmow!
I governed them so well and held the rein
So firmly they were rapturously fain
To go and buy me pretty things to wear;
They were delighted if I spoke them fair.
God knows how spitefully I used to scold them.
  "Listen, I'll tell you how I used to hold them,
You knowing women, who can understand.
First put them in the wrong, and out of hand.
No one can be so bold—I mean no man—
At lies and swearing as a woman can.
This is no news, as you'll have realized,
To knowing ones, but to the misadvised.
A knowing wife if she is worth her salt
Can always prove her husband is at fault,
And even though the fellow may have heard
Some story told him by a little bird
She knows enough to prove the bird is crazy
And get her maid to witness she's a daisy,
With full agreement, scarce solicited.
But listen. Here's the sort of thing I said:
  " 'Now, sir old dotard, what is that you say?
Why is my neighbor's wife so smart and gay?
She is respected everywhere she goes.
I sit at home and have no decent clothes.
Why haunt her house? What are you doing there?
Are you so amorous? Is she so fair?

What, whispering secrets to our maid? For shame,
Sir ancient lecher! Time you dropped that game.
And if I see my gossip or a friend
You scold me like a devil! There's no end
If I so much as stroll towards his house.
Then you come home as drunken as a mouse,
You mount your throne and preach, chapter and verse
—All nonsense—and you tell me it's a curse
To marry a poor woman—she's expensive;
Or if her family's wealthy and extensive
You say it's torture to endure her pride
And melancholy airs, and more beside.
And if she has a pretty face, old traitor,
You say she's game for any fornicator
And ask what likelihood will keep her straight
With all those men who lie about in wait.
     " 'You say that some desire us for our wealth,
Some for our shapeliness, our looks, our health,
Some for our singing, others for our dancing,
Some for our courtesy and dalliant glancing,
And some because our hands are soft and small;
By your account the devil gets us all.
     " 'You say what castle wall can be so strong
As to hold out against a siege for long?
And if her looks are foul you say that she
Is hot for every man that she can see,
Leaping upon them with a spaniel's airs
Until she finds a man to buy her wares.
Never was goose upon the lake so gray
But that she found a gander, so you say.
You say it's hard to keep a girl controlled
If she's the kind that no one wants to hold.
That's what you say as you stump off to bed,
You brute! You say no man of sense would wed,

That is, not if he wants to go to Heaven.
Wild thunderbolts and fire from the seven
Planets descend and break your withered neck!

" 'You say that buildings falling into wreck,
And smoke, and scolding women, are the three
Things that will drive a man from home. Dear me!
What ails the poor old man to grumble so?

" 'You say we hide our faults to let them show
Once we are safely married, so you say.
There's a fine proverb for a popinjay!

" 'You say that oxen, asses, hounds and horses
Can be tried out on various ploys and courses;
And basins too, and dishes when you buy them,
Spoons, chairs and furnishings, a man can try them
As he can try a suit of clothes, no doubt,
But no one ever tries a woman out
Until he's married her; old dotard crow!
And then you say she lets her vices show.

" 'You also say we count it for a crime
Unless you praise our beauty all the time,
Unless you're always poring on our faces
And call us pretty names in public places;
Or if you fail to treat me to a feast
Upon my birthday—presents at the least—
Or to respect my nurse and her gray hairs,
Or be polite to all my maids upstairs
And to my father's cronies and his spies.
That's what you say, old barrelful of lies!

" 'Then there's our young apprentice, handsome
  Johnny;
Because he has crisp hair that shines as bonny
As finest gold, and squires me up and down
You show your low suspicions in a frown.
I wouldn't have him, not if you died to-morrow!

" 'And tell me this, God punish you with sorrow,
Why do you hide the keys of coffer doors?
It's just as much my property as yours.
Do you want to make an idiot of your wife?
Now, by the Lord that gave me soul and life,
You shan't have both, you can't be such a noddy
As think to keep my goods and have my body!
One you must do without, whatever you say.
And do you need to spy on me all day?
I think you'd like to lock me in your coffer!
"Go where you please, dear wife," you ought to offer,
"Amuse yourself! I shan't give ear to malice,
I know you for a virtuous wife, Dame Alice."
We cannot love a husband who takes charge
Of where we go. We like to be at large.
    " 'Above all other men may God confer
His blessing on that wise astrologer
Sir Ptolemy who, in his *Almagest,*
Has set this proverb down: "Of men the best
And wisest care not who may have in hand
The conduct of the world." I understand
That means, "If you've enough, you shouldn't care
How prosperously other people fare."
Be sure, old dotard, if you call the bluff,
You'll get your evening rations right enough.
He's a mean fellow that lets no man handle
His lantern when it's just to light a candle;
He has lost no light, he hasn't felt a strain;
And you have light enough, so why complain?
    " 'And when a woman tries a mild display
In dress or costly ornament, you say
It is a danger to her chastity,
And then, bad luck to you, start making free
With Bible tags in the Apostle's name;

"And in like manner, chastely and with shame,
You women should adorn yourselves," said he,
"And not with braided hair or jewelry
With pearl or golden ornament." What next!
I'll pay as much attention to your text
And rubric in such things as would a gnat.

" 'And once you said that I was like a cat,
For if you singe a cat it will not roam
And that's the way to keep a cat at home.
But when she feels her fur is sleek and gay
She can't be kept indoors for half a day
But off she takes herself as dusk is falling
To show her fur and go a-caterwauling.
Which means if I feel gay, as you suppose,
I shall run out to show my poor old clothes.

" 'Silly old fool! You and your private spies!
Go on, beg Argus with his hundred eyes
To be my bodyguard, and try his skill!
But yet he shan't, I say, against my will.
I'll pull him by the beard, believe you me!

" 'And once you said that principally three
Misfortunes trouble earth, east, west and north,
And no man living could endure a fourth.
My dear sir shrew, Jesu cut short your life!
You preach away and say a hateful wife
Is reckoned to be one of these misfortunes.
Is there no other trouble that importunes
The world and that your parables could condemn?
Must an unhappy wife be one of them?

" 'Then you compared a woman's love to Hell,
To barren land where water will not dwell,
And you compared it to a quenchless fire,
The more it burns the more is its desire
To burn up everything that burnt can be.

You say that just as worms destroy a tree
A wife destroys her husband and contrives,
As husbands know, the ruin of their lives.'
  "Such was the way, my lords, you understand
I kept my older husbands well in hand.
I told them they were drunk and their unfitness
To judge my conduct forced me to take witness
That they were lying. Johnny and my niece
Would back me up. Lord, how they longed for peace,
Poor dears! I tortured them without remorse,
For I could bite and whinney like a horse
And launch complaints when things were all my fault;
I'd have been lost if I had called a halt.
First to the mill is first to grind your corn;
I attacked first and they were overborne,
Glad to apologize and even suing
Pardon for what they'd never thought of doing.
  "I'd tackle one for wenching, out of hand,
Although so ill the man could hardly stand,
Yet he felt flattered in his heart because
He thought it showed how fond of him I was.
I swore that all my walking out at night
Was just to keep his wenching well in sight.
That was a dodge that made me shake with mirth;
But all such wit is given us at birth.
Lies, tears and spinning are the things God gives
By nature to a woman, while she lives.
So there's one thing at least that I can boast,
That in the end I always ruled the roast;
Cunning or force was sure to make them stumble,
And always keeping up a steady grumble.
  "But bed-time above all was their misfortune;
That was the place to scold them and importune
And balk their fun. I never would abide

In bed with them if hands began to slide
Till they had promised ransom, paid a fee;
And then I let them do their nicety.
And so I tell this tale to every man,
'It's all for sale and let him win who can.'
No empty-handed man can lure a bird.
His pleasures were my profit; I concurred,
Even assumed fictitious appetite
Though bacon never gave me much delight.
And that's the very fact that made me chide them.
And had the Pope been sitting there beside them
I wouldn't have spared them at their very table,
But paid them out as far as I was able.
I say, so help me God Omnipotent,
Were I to make my will and testament
I owe them nothing, paid them word for word
Putting my wits to use, and they preferred
To give it up and take it for the best
For otherwise they would have got no rest.
Though they might glower like a maddened beast
They got no satisfaction, not the least.
    "I then would say, 'My dear, just take a peep!
What a meek look on Willikin our sheep!
Come nearer, husband, let me kiss your cheek;
You should be just as patient, just as meek;
Sweeten your heart. Your conscience needs a probe.
You're fond of preaching patience out of Job,
And so be patient; practice what you preach,
And if you don't, my dear, we'll have to teach
You that it's nice to have a quiet life.
One of us must be master, man or wife,
And since a man's more reasonable, he
Should be the patient one, you must agree.

" 'What ails you, man, to grumble so and groan?
Just that you want my what-not all your own?
Why, take it man! It's yours all said and done.
St Peter! How you like your bit of fun!
Well, if I were to sell my *belle chose*,
I could go walking fresher than a rose;
But I will keep it for your private tooth.
By God, you are to blame, and that's the truth.'
    "That's how my first three husbands were undone.
Now let me tell you of my last but one.
    "He was a reveler, was number four;
That is to say he kept a paramour.
And I was young, ah, ragery's the word,
Stubborn and strong and jolly as a bird.
Play me the harp and I would dance and sing,
Believe me, like a nightingale in spring,
If I had had a draught of sweetened wine.
    "Metellius, that filthy lout—the swine
Who snatched a staff and took his woman's life
For drinking wine—if I had been his wife
He never would have daunted me from drink.
Whenever I take wine I have to think
Of Venus, for as cold engenders hail
A lecherous mouth begets a lecherous tail.
A woman in her cups has no defense,
As lechers know from long experience.
    "But Christ! Whenever it comes back to me,
When I recall my youth and jollity,
It fairly warms the cockles of my heart!
This very day I feel a pleasure start,
Yes, I can feel it tickling at the root.
Lord, how it does me good! I've had my fruit,
I've had my world and time, I've had my fling!
But age that comes to poison everything

Has taken all my beauty and my pith.
Well, let it go, the devil go therewith!
The flour is gone, there is no more to say,
And I must sell the bran as best I may;
But still I mean to find my way to fun. . . .
Now let me tell you of my last but one.

"I told you how it filled my heart with spite
To see another woman his delight,
By God and all His saints I made it good!
I carved him out a cross of the same wood,
Not with my body—just by breaking jokes
And flirting, making up to other folks.
I fried him properly in his own grease
Of jealously and rage; he got no peace.
By God on earth I was his purgatory,
For which I hope his soul may be in glory.
God knows he sang a sorry tune, he flinched,
And bitterly enough, when the shoe pinched.
And God and he alone can say how grim,
How many were the ways I tortured him.

"He died when I came back from Jordan Stream
And he lies buried under the rood-beam,
Albeit that his tomb can scarce supply us
With such a show as that of King Darius
—Apelles sculped it in a sumptuous taste—
But costly burial would have been a waste.
Farewell to him, God give his spirit rest!
He's in his grave, he's nailed up in his chest.

"Now of my fifth, last husband let me tell.
God never let his soul be sent to Hell!
And yet he was my worst, and many a blow
He struck me still can ache along my row
Of ribs, and will until my dying day.

"But in our bed he was so fresh and gay,

So coaxing, so persuasive. . . . Heaven knows
Whenever he wanted it—my *belle chose*—
Though he had beaten me in every bone
He still could wheedle me to love, I own.
I think I loved him best, I'll tell no lie.
He was disdainful in his love, that's why.
We women have a curious fantasy
In such affairs, or so it seems to me.
When something's difficult, or can't be had,
We crave and cry for it all day like mad.
Forbid a thing, we pine for it all night,
Press fast upon us and we take to flight;
We use disdain in offering our wares.
A throng of buyers sends prices up at fairs,
Cheap goods have little value, they suppose;
And that's a thing that every woman knows.
   "My fifth and last—God keep his soul in health!—
The one I took for love and not for wealth,
Had been at Oxford not so long before
But had left school and gone to lodge next door,
Yes, it was to my godmother's he'd gone.
God bless her soul! *Her* name was Alison.
She knew my heart and more of what I thought
Than did the parish priest, and so she ought!
She was my confidante, I told her all.
For had my husband pissed against a wall
Or done some crime that would have cost his life,
To her and to another worthy wife
And to my niece, because I loved her well,
I'd have told everything there was to tell.
And so I often did, and Heaven knows
It used to set him blushing like a rose
In very shame, and he would blame his folly
In letting out his secrets to poor Polly.

"And so one time it happened that in Lent,
As I so often did, I rose and went
To see her, ever wanting to be gay
And go a-strolling, March, April and May,
From house to house for chat and village malice.
  "Johnny (the boy from Oxford) and Dame Alice
And I myself, into the fields we went.
My husband was in London all that Lent;
All the more fun for me—I only mean
The fun of seeing people and being seen
By cocky lads; for how was I to know
Where or what graces Fortune might bestow?
And so I made a round of visitations,
Went to processions, festivals, orations,
Preachments and pilgrimages, watched the carriages
They use for plays and pageants, went to marriages,
And always wore my gayest scarlet dress.
  "These worms, these moths, these mites, I must
    confess
Got little chance to eat it, by the way.
Why not? Because I wore it every day.
  "Now let me tell you all that came to pass.
We sauntered in the meadows through the grass
Toying and dallying to such extent,
Johnny and I, that I grew provident
And I suggested, were I ever free
And made a widow, he should marry me.
And certainly—I do not mean to boast—
I ever was more provident than most
In marriage matters and in other such.
I never think a mouse is up to much
That only has one hole in all the house;
If that should fail, well, it's good-by the mouse.
  "I let him think I was as one enchanted

(That was a trick my godmother implanted)
And told him I had dreamt the night away
Thinking of him, and dreamt that as I lay
He tried to kill me. Blood had drenched the bed.
    " 'But still it was a lucky dream,' I said,
'For blood betokens money, I recall.'
It was a lie. I hadn't dreamt at all.
'Twas from my godmother I learnt my lore
In matters such as that, and many more.
    "Well, let me see . . . what had I to explain?
Aha! By God, I've got the thread again.
    "When my fourth husband lay upon his bier
I wept all day and looked as drear as drear,
As widows must, for it is quite in place,
And with a handkerchief I hid my face.
Now that I felt provided with a mate
I wept but little, I need hardly state.
    "To church they bore my husband on the morrow
With all the neighbors round him venting sorrow,
And one of them of course was handsome Johnny.
So help me God I thought he looked so bonny
Behind the coffin! Heavens, what a pair
Of legs he had! Such feet, so clean and fair!
I gave my heart, I put it in his cage.
    "He was, I think, some twenty years of age
And I was forty then, to tell the truth.
But still I always had a coltish tooth.
Yes, I'm gap-toothed; it suits me well I feel,
It is the print of Venus and her seal.
So help me God I was a lusty one,
Fair, young and well-to-do, and full of fun!
And truly, as my husbands said to me,
I had the finest *quoniam* that might be.
Venus had sent me feeling from the stars

And my heart's boldness came to me from Mars.
Venus gave me desire and lecherousness
And Mars my hardihood, or so I guess,
Born under Taurus and with Mars therein.
Alas, alas, that ever love was sin!
And so I followed natural inclination
In virtue of my natal constellation;
I couldn't refuse, seeing what stars I had,
My chamber of Venus to a likely lad.
The mark of Mars is still upon my face
And also in another privy place.
For as I may be saved by God above,
I never used discretion when in love
But ever followed on my appetite,
Whether the lad was short, long, black or white.
Little I cared, if he was fond of me,
How poor he was, or what his rank might be.
  "What shall I say? Before the month was gone
This gay young student, my delightful John,
Had married me in solemn festival.
I handed him the money, lands and all
That ever had been given me before;
This I repented later, more and more.
He stopped my gadding round, my hide-and-seek,
By God, he smote me once upon the cheek
Because I tore a page out of his book,
And that's the reason why I'm deaf. But look,
Stubborn I was, just like a lioness;
In argument and wrangling, pitiless.
I went off gadding as I had before
From house to house, however much he swore.
Because of that he used to preach and scold,
Drag Roman history up from days of old,
How one Simplicius Gallus left his wife

Deserting her completely all his life,
Only for poking out her head one day
Without a hat upon the public way.

"Some other Roman—I forget his name—
Because his wife went to a summer's game
Without his knowledge, left her in the lurch.

"And he would take the Bible up and search
For proverbs in Ecclesiasticus,
Particularly one that has it thus:
'Suffer no wicked woman to gad about.'
And then would come the saying (need you doubt?)

> *A man who seeks to build his house of sallows,*
> *A man who spurs a blind horse over fallows,*
> *Or lets his wife make pilgrimage to Hallows,*
> *Is worthy to be hanged upon the gallows.*

But all for naught. I didn't give a hen
For all his proverbs and his wise old men.
I wouldn't be rebuked at any price;
I hate a man who points me out my vice,
And so, God knows, do many more than I.
That drove him raging mad, you may rely.
No more would I forbear with him, I promise.

"Now let me tell you truly by St Thomas
About that book and why I tore the page
And how he smote me deaf in very rage.

"He had a book, he kept it on his shelf,
And night and day he read it to himself
And laughed aloud, although it was quite serious.
He called it *Theophrastus and Valerius.*
There was another Roman, much the same,
A cardinal; St Jerome was his name.
He wrote a book against Jovinian,
Bound up together with Tertullian,
Chrysippus, Trotula and Heloise,

(An abbess, lived near Paris). And with these
Were bound the parables of Solomon,
With Ovid's *Art of Love* another one.
All these were bound together in one book
And day and night he used to take a look
At what it said, when he had time and leisure
Or had no occupation but his pleasure.
    "It was a book that dealt with wicked wives;
He knew more legends of them and their lives
Than there are good ones mentioned in the Bible.
For take my word for it, there is no libel
On women that the clergy will not paint,
Except when writing of a woman-saint,
But never good of other women, though.
Who called the lion savage? Do you know?
By God, if women had but written stories
Like those the clergy kept in oratories,
More had been written of man's wickedness
Than all the sons of Adam could redress.
Children of Mercury and we of Venus
Keep up the contrariety between us;
Mercury stands for wisdom, thrift and science,
Venus for revel, squandering and defiance.
Their several natures govern their direction;
One rises when the other's in dejection.
And thus the works of Mercury are halted
In *Pisces,* just where Venus is exalted,
And Venus falls where Mercury is raised,
And women therefore never can be praised
By learned men, old scribes who cannot do
The works of Venus more than my old shoe.
These in their dotage sit them down to frowse
And say that women break their marriage-vows!

"Now to my purpose as I told you; look,
Here's how I got a beating for a book.
One evening Johnny, glowering with ire,
Sat with his book and read it by the fire.
And first he read of Eve whose wickedness
Brought all mankind to sorrow and distress,
Root-cause why Jesus Christ Himself was slain
And gave His blood to buy us back again.
Aye, there's the text where you expressly find
That woman brought the loss of all mankind.

"He read me then how Samson as he slept
Was shorn of all his hair by her he kept,
And by that treachery Samson lost his eyes.
And then he read me, if I tell no lies,
All about Hercules and Deianire;
She tricked him into setting himself on fire.

"He left out nothing of the miseries
Occasioned by his wives to Socrates.
Xantippe poured a piss-pot on his head.
The silly man sat still, as he were dead,
Wiping his head, but dared no more complain
Than say, 'Ere thunder stops, down comes the rain.'

"Next of Pasiphaë the Queen of Crete;
For wickedness he thought that story sweet;
Fie, say no more! It has a grisly sting,
Her horrible lust. How could she do the thing!

"And then he told of Clytemnestra's lechery
And how she made her husband die by treachery.
He read that story with a great devotion.

"He read me what occasioned the commotion
By which Amphiaraüs lost his life;
My husband had the legend of his wife
Eriphyle, who for a gaud in gold
Went to the Greeks in secret, and she told

Them where to find him, in what hiding-place.
At Thebes it was; he met with sorry grace.
 "Of Livia and Lucilia then he read,
And both of course had killed their husbands dead,
The one for love, the other out of hate.
Livia prepared some poison for him late
One evening and she killed him out of spite,
Lucilia out of lecherous delight.
For she, in order he might only think
Of her, prepared an aphrodisiac drink;
He drank it and was dead before the morning.
Such is the fate of husbands; it's a warning.
 "And then he told how one Latumius
Lamented to his comrade Arrius
That in his orchard-plot there grew a tree
On which his wives had hanged themselves, all three,
Or so he said, out of some spite or other;
To which this Arrius replied, 'Dear brother,
Give me a cutting from that blessed tree
And planted in my garden it shall be!'
 "Of wives of later date he also read,
How some had killed their husbands when in bed,
Then night-long with their lechers played the whore
While the poor corpse lay fresh upon the floor.
 "One drove a nail into her husband's brain
While he was sleeping and the man was slain;
Others put poison in their husbands' drink.
He spoke more harm of us than heart can think
And knew more proverbs too, for what they're worth,
Than there are blades of grass upon the earth.
 " 'Better,' says he, 'to share your habitation
With lion, dragon, or abomination
Than with a woman given to reproof.
Better,' says he, 'take refuge on the roof

Than with an angry wife, down in the house;
They are so wicked and cantankerous
They hate the things their husbands like,' he'd say.
'A woman always casts her shame away
When she casts off her smock, and that's in haste.
A pretty woman, if she isn't chaste,
Is like a golden ring in a sow's snout.'

   "Who could imagine, who could figure out
The torture in my heart? It reached the top.
And when I saw that he would never stop
Reading this cursed book, all night no doubt,
I suddenly grabbed and tore three pages out
Where he was reading, at the very place,
And fisted such a buffet in his face
That backwards down into the fire he fell.

   "Then like a maddened lion, with a yell
He started up and smote me on the head,
And down I fell upon the floor for dead.

   "And when he saw how motionless I lay
He was aghast and would have fled away,
But in the end I started to come to.
'O have you murdered me, you robber, you,
To get my land?' I said. 'Was that the game?
Before I'm dead I'll kiss you all the same.'

   "He came up close and kneeling gently down
He said, 'My love, my dearest Alison,
So help me God, I never again will hit
You, love; and if I did, you asked for it.
Forgive me!' But for all he was so meek
I up at once and smote him on the cheek
And said, 'Take that to level up the score!
Now let me die. I can't speak any more.'

   "We had a mort of trouble and heavy weather
But in the end we made it up together.

He gave the bridle over to my hand,
Gave me the government of house and land,
Of tongue and fist, indeed of all he'd got.
I made him burn that book upon the spot.
And when I'd mastered him, and out of deadlock
Secured myself the sovereignty in wedlock,
And when he said, 'My own and truest wife,
Do as you please for all the rest of life,
But guard your honor and my good estate,'
From that day forward there was no debate.
So help me God I was as kind to him
As any wife from Denmark to the rim
Of India, and as true. And he to me.
And I pray God that sits in majesty
To bless his soul and fill it with his glory.
Now, if you'll listen, I will tell my story."

*

Words Between the Summoner and the Friar

The Friar laughed when he had heard all this.
"Well, Ma'am," he said, "as God may send me bliss,
This is a long preamble to a tale!"
But when the Summoner heard the Friar rail,
"Just look at that!" he cried. "God's arms and skin!
These meddling friars are always butting in!
Don't we all know a friar and a fly
Go buzzing into every dish and pie!
What do you mean with your 'preambulation'?
Amble yourself, trot, do a meditation!
You're spoiling all our fun with your commotion."
The Friar smiled and said, "Is that your notion?
I promise on my word before I go
To find occasion for a tale or so

About a summoner that will make us laugh."
   "Well, damn your eyes, and on my own behalf,"
The Summoner answered, "mine be damned as well
If I can't think of several tales to tell
About the friars that will make you mourn
Before we get as far as Sittingbourne.
Have you no patience? Look, he's in a huff!"
   Our Host called out, "Be quiet, that's enough!
Shut up, and let the woman tell her tale.
You must be drunk, you've taken too much ale.
Now, Ma'am, you go ahead and no demur."
"All right," she said, "it's just as you prefer,
If I have license from this worthy friar."
"Nothing," said he, "that I should more desire."

*

The Wife of Bath's Tale

When good King Arthur ruled in ancient days,
A king that every Briton loves to praise,
This was a land brim-full of fairy folk.
The Elf-Queen and her courtiers joined and broke
Their elfin dance on many a green mead,
Or so was the opinion once, I read,
Hundreds of years ago, in days of yore.
But no one now sees fairies any more,
For now the saintly charity and prayer
Of holy friars seem to have purged the air;
They search the countryside through field and stream
As thick as motes that speckle a sun-beam,
Blessing the halls, the chambers, kitchens, bowers,
Cities and boroughs, castles, courts and towers,
Thorpes, barns and stables, outhouses and dairies,
And that's the reason why there are no fairies.

Wherever there was wont to walk an elf
To-day there walks the holy friar himself
As evening falls or when the daylight springs,
Saying his mattins and his holy things,
Walking his limit round from town to town.
Women can now go safely up and down,
By every bush or under every tree;
There is no other incubus but he,
So there is really no one else to hurt you
And he will do no more than take your virtue.

    Now it so happened, I began to say,
Long, long ago in good King Arthur's day,
There was a knight who was a lusty liver.
One day as he came riding from the river
He saw a maiden walking all forlorn
Ahead of him, alone as she was born.
And of that maiden, spite of all she said,
By very force he took her maidenhead.

    This act of violence made such a stir,
So much petitioning of the king for her,
That he condemned the knight to lose his head
By course of law. He was as good as dead
(It seems that then the statutes took that view)
But that the queen and other ladies too
Implored the king to exercise his grace
So ceaselessly, he gave the queen the case
And granted her his life, and she could choose
Whether to show him mercy or refuse.

    The queen returned him thanks with all her might,
And then she sent a summons to the knight
At her convenience, and expressed her will:
"Sir, your position is precarious still,"
She said, "you're on the edge of an abyss.
Yet you shall live if you can tell me this.

What is the thing that women most desire?
Beware the ax and say as I require.
    "If you can't answer on the moment, though,
I will concede you this: you are to go
A twelvemonth and a day to seek and learn
Sufficient answer, then you shall return.
I shall take gages from you to extort
Surrender of your body to the court."
    Sad was the knight and sorrowfully sighed,
But there! What option had he? He'd been tried.
And in the end he chose to go away
And to return after a year and day
Armed with such answer as there might be sent
To him by God. He took his leave and went.
    He knocked at every house, searched every place,
Yes, anywhere that offered hope of grace.
What could it be that women wanted most?
But all the same he never touched a coast,
Country or town in which there seemed to be
Any two people willing to agree.
    Some said that women wanted wealth and treasure,
Honor said some, some jollity and pleasure;
Some gorgeous clothes and others fun in bed
And "to be widowed and remarried," said
Yet others. Some said the thing that really mattered
Was that we should be gratified and flattered.
That's very near the truth, it seems to me;
A man can win us best with flattery.
Attentiveness and making a great fuss
About a woman, that's what fetches us.
    But others said a woman's real passion
Was liberty, behaving in what fashion
Might please her best, and not to be corrected
But told she's wise, encouraged and respected.

Truly there's not a woman in ten score
Who has a fault and someone rubs the sore
But she will kick if what he says is true;
You try it out and you will find so too.
However vicious we may be within
We like to be thought wise and void of sin.

Some people said that what we women treasure
Is to be thought dependable in pleasure,
Steadfast in keeping secrets from the jealous,
Not prone to blab the things a man may tell us.
But that opinion isn't worth a rush!
Good Lord, a woman keep a secret? Tush!
Remember Midas? Will you hear the tale?

Among some other little things now stale,
Ovid relates that Midas, it appears,
Had grown a great big pair of ass's ears
Under his flowing locks. As best he might
He kept this foul deformity from sight.
His wife—she was the only one that knew—
Was trusted by him, and he loved her too.
He begged her not to tell a living creature
That he possessed so horrible a feature.

She wouldn't tell for all the world, she swore,
It would be villainy, a sin what's more,
To earn her husband such a filthy name,
Besides it would redound to her own shame.
Nevertheless she thought she would have died
Keeping this secret bottled up inside;
It seemed to swell her heart and she, no doubt,
Thought it was on the point of bursting out.

Fearing to speak of it to woman or man,
Down to a reedy marsh she quickly ran
And reached the sedge. Her heart was all on fire
And, as a bittern bumbles in the mire,

She whispered to the water, near the ground,
"Betray me not, O water, with thy sound!
I have told no one yet, but it appears
My husband has a pair of ass's ears!
Ah! My heart's well again, the secret's out!
I couldn't have kept it longer, I don't doubt."
So, as you see, we women can't keep mum
For very long, but out the secrets come.
For what became of Midas, if you care
To turn up Ovid you will find it there.

This knight that I am telling you about
Perceived at last he never would find out
What it could be that women loved the best.
Faint was the soul within his sorrowful breast
As home he went, he dared no longer stay;
His year was up and now it was the day.

As he rode home in a dejected mood,
Suddenly, at the margin of a wood,
He saw a dance upon the leafy floor
Of four and twenty ladies, nay, and more.
Eagerly he approached, in hope to learn
Some words of wisdom ere he should return;
But lo! Before he came to where they were,
Dancers and dance all vanished into air!
There wasn't a living creature to be seen
Save one old woman crouched upon the green.
A fouler-looking creature I suppose
Could scarcely be imagined. She arose
And said, "Sir knight, there's no way on from here.
Tell me what you are looking for, my dear,
For peradventure that were best for you;
We old, old women know a thing or two."

"Dear Mother," said the knight, "alack the day!
I am as good as dead if I can't say

What thing it is that women most desire;
If you could tell me I would pay your hire."
"Give me your hand," she said, "and swear to do
Whatever I shall next require of you
—If so to do should lie within your might—
And you shall know the answer before night."
"Upon my honor," he answered, "I agree."
"Then," said the crone, "I dare to guarantee
Your life is safe; I shall make good my claim.
Upon my life the queen will say the same.
Show me the very proudest of them all
In costly coverchief or jeweled caul
That dare say no to what I have to teach.
Let us go forward without further speech."
And then she crooned her gospel in his ear
And told him to be glad and not to fear.

They came to court. This knight, in full array,
Stood forth and said, "O Queen, I've kept my day
And kept my word and have my answer ready."

There sat the noble matrons and the heady
Young girls, and widows too, that have the grace
Of wisdom, all assembled in that place,
And there the queen herself was throned to hear
And judge his answer. Then the knight drew near
And silence was commanded through the hall.

The queen then bade the knight to tell them all
What thing it was that women wanted most.
He stood not silent like a beast or post,
But gave his answer with the ringing word
Of a man's voice and the assembly heard:

"My liege and lady, in general," said he,
"Women desire the self-same sovereignty
On husbands as they have on those that love them,
And would be set in mastery above them;

That is your greatest wish. Now spare or kill
Me as you please; I stand here at your will."
   In all the court not one that shook her head
Or contradicted what the knight had said;
Maid, wife and widow cried, "He's saved his life!"
   And on the word up started the old wife,
The one the knight saw sitting on the green,
And cried, "Your mercy, sovereign lady queen!
Before the court disperses, do me right!
'Twas I who taught this answer to the knight,
For which he swore, and pledged his honor to it,
That the first thing I asked of him he'd do it,
So far as it should lie within his might.
Before this court I ask you then, sir knight,
To keep your word and take me for your wife;
For well you know that I have saved your life.
If this be false, deny it on your sword!"
   "Alas!" he said, "Old lady, by the Lord
I know indeed that such was my behest,
But for God's love think of a new request,
Take all my goods, but leave my body free."
"A curse on us," she said, "if I agree!
I may be foul, I may be poor and old,
Yet will not choose to be, for all the gold
That's bedded in the earth or lies above,
Less than your wife, nay, than your very love!"
   "My love?" said he. "By Heaven, my damnation!
Alas that any of my race and station
Should ever make so foul a misalliance!"
Yet in the end his pleading and defiance
All went for nothing, he was forced to wed.
He takes his ancient wife and goes to bed.
   Now peradventure some may well suspect
A lack of care in me since I neglect

To tell of the rejoicings and display
Made at the feast upon their wedding-day.
I have but a short answer to let fall;
I say there was no joy or feast at all,
Nothing but heaviness of heart and sorrow.
He married her in private on the morrow
And all day long stayed hidden like an owl,
It was such torture that his wife looked foul.

   Great was the anguish churning in his head
When he and she were piloted to bed;
He wallowed back and forth in desperate style.
His wife lay still and wore a quiet smile;
At last she said, "Dear husband, bless my soul!
Is this how knights treat wives upon the whole?
Are these the laws of good King Arthur's house?
Is all his knighthood so contemptuous?
I am your own beloved and your wife,
And I am she, indeed, that saved your life;
And certainly I never did you wrong.
Then why, this first of nights, so sad a song?
You're carrying on as if you were half-witted!
Say, for God's love, what sin have I committed?
I'll put things right if you will tell me how."

   "Put right?" he cried. "That never can be now!
Nothing can ever be put right again!
You're old, and so abominably plain,
So poor to start with, so low-bred to follow;
It's little wonder if I twist and wallow!
God, that my heart would burst within my breast!"

   "Is that," said she, "the cause of your unrest?"

   "Yes, certainly," he said, "and can you wonder?"

   "I could set right what you suppose a blunder,
That's if I cared to, in a day or two,
If I were shown more courtesy by you.

Just now," she said, "you spoke of gentle birth,
Such as descends from ancient wealth and worth.
If that's the claim you make for gentlemen
Such arrogance is hardly worth a hen.
Whoever loves to work for virtuous ends,
Public and private, and who most intends
To do what deeds of gentleness he can,
Take him to be the greatest gentleman.
Christ wills we take our gentleness from Him,
Not from a wealth of ancestry long dim,
Though they bequeath their whole establishment
By which we claim to be of high descent.
Our fathers cannot make us a bequest
Of all those virtues that became them best
And earned for them the name of gentleman,
But bade us follow them as best we can.

"Thus the wise poet of the Florentines,
Dante by name, has written in these lines,
For such is the opinion Dante launches:
'Seldom arises by these slender branches
Prowess of men, for it is God, no less,
Wills us to claim of Him our gentleness.'
For of our parents nothing can we claim
Save temporal things, and these may hurt and maim.

"But everyone knows this as well as I;
For if gentility were implanted by
The natural course of lineage down the line,
Public or not, it could not cease to shine
In doing the fair work of gentle deed.
No vice or villainy could then bear seed.

"Take fire and carry it to the darkest house
Between this kingdom and the Caucasus,
And shut the doors on it and leave it there.
It will burn on, and it will burn as fair

As if ten thousand men were there to see,
For fire will keep its nature and degree,
I can assure you, sir, until it dies.
  "But gentleness, as you will recognize,
Is not annexed in nature to possessions,
Men fail in living up to their professions;
But fire never ceases to be fire.
God knows you'll often find, if you inquire,
Some lording full of villainy and shame.
If you would be esteemed for the mere name
Of having been by birth a gentleman
And stemming from some virtuous, noble clan,
And do not live yourself by gentle deed
Or take your fathers' noble code and creed,
You are no gentleman, though duke or earl.
Vice and bad manners are what make a churl.
  "Gentility is only the renown
For bounty that your fathers handed down,
Quite foreign to your person, not your own;
Gentility must come from God alone.
That we are gentle comes to us by grace
And by no means is it bequeathed with place.
  "Reflect how noble (says Valerius)
Was Tullius surnamed Hostilius,
Who rose from poverty to nobleness,
and read Boethius, Seneca no less.
Thus they express themselves and are agreed:
'Gentle he is that does a gentle deed.'
And therefore, my dear husband, I conclude
That even if my ancestors were rude,
Yet God on high—and so I hope He will—
Can grant me grace to live in virtue still,
A gentlewoman only when beginning
To live in virtue and to shrink from sinning.

"As for my poverty which you reprove,
Almighty God Himself in whom we move,
Believe and have our being, chose a life
Of poverty, and every man or wife
And every child can see our Heavenly King
Would never stoop to choose a shameful thing.
No shame in poverty if the heart is gay,
As Seneca and all the learned say.
He who accepts his poverty unhurt
I'd say is rich although he lacked a shirt.
But truly poor are they who whine and fret
And covet what they cannot hope to get.
And he that having nothing covets not
Is rich, though you may think he is a sot.

"True poverty can find a song to sing.
Juvenal says a pleasant little thing:
'The poor can dance and sing in the relief
Of having nothing that will tempt a thief.'
Though it be hateful, poverty is good,
A great incentive to a livelihood,
And a great help to our capacity
For wisdom, if accepted patiently.
Poverty is, though wanting in estate,
A kind of wealth that none calumniate.
Poverty often, when the heart is lowly,
Brings one to God and teaches what is holy,
Gives knowledge of oneself and even lends
A glass by which to see one's truest friends.
And since it's no offense, let me be plain;
Do not rebuke my poverty again.

"Lastly you taxed me, sir, with being old.
Yet even if you never had been told
By ancient books, you gentlemen engage
Yourselves in honor to respect old age.

To call an old man 'father' shows good breeding,
And this could be supported from my reading.
   "You say I'm old and fouler than a fen.
You need not fear to be a cuckold, then.
Filth and old age, I'm sure you will agree,
Are powerful wardens upon chastity.
Nevertheless, well knowing your delights,
I shall fulfill your worldly appetites.
   "You have two choices; which one will you try?
To have me old and ugly till I die,
But still a loyal, true and humble wife
That never will displease you all her life,
Or would you rather I were young and pretty
And take your chance what happens in a city
Where friends will visit you because of me,
Yes, and in other places too, maybe.
Which would you have? The choice is all your own."
   The knight thought long, and with a piteous groan
At last he said with all the care in life,
"My lady and my love, my dearest wife,
I leave the matter to your wise decision.
You make the choice yourself, for the provision
Of what may be agreeable and rich
In honor to us both, I don't care which;
Whatever pleases you suffices me."
   "And have I won the mastery?" said she,
"Since I'm to choose and rule as I think fit?"
"Certainly, wife," he answered her, "that's it."
"Kiss me," she cried. "No quarrels! On my oath
And word of honor you shall find me both,
That is, both fair and faithful as a wife;
May I go howling mad and take my life
Unless I prove to be as good and true
As ever wife was since the world was new!

And if to-morrow when the sun's above
I seem less fair than any lady-love,
Than any queen or empress east or west,
Do with my life and death as you think best.
Cast up the curtain, husband. Look at me!"
    And when indeed the knight had looked to see,
Lo, she was young and lovely, rich in charms.
In ecstasy he caught her in his arms,
His heart went bathing in a bath of blisses
And melted in a hundred thousand kisses,
And she responded in the fullest measure
With all that could delight or give him pleasure.
    So they lived ever after to the end
In perfect bliss; and may Christ Jesus send
Us husbands meek and young and fresh in bed,
And grace to overbid them when we wed.
And—Jesu hear my prayer!—cut short the lives
Of those who won't be governed by their wives;
And all old, angry niggards of their pence,
God send them soon a very pestilence!

THE CLERK'S TALE

*

The Clerk's Prologue

"You, sir, from Oxford!" said the Host. "God's life!
As coy and quiet as a virgin-wife
Newly espoused and sitting mum at table!
You haven't said a word since we left the stable.
Studying, I suppose? On wisdom's wing?
Says Solomon, 'There's a time for everything.'
    "For goodness' sake cheer up, show animation!
This is no time for abstruse meditation.

Tell us a lively tale in Heaven's name;
For when a man has entered on a game
He's bound to keep the rules, it's by consent.
But don't you preach as friars do in Lent,
Dragging up all our sins to make us weep,
Nor tell a tale to send us all to sleep.

"Let it be brisk adventure, stuff that nourishes,
And not too much of your rhetorical flourishes.
Keep the 'high style' until occasion brings
A use for it, like when they write to kings,
And for the present put things plainly, pray,
So we can follow all you have to say."

This worthy cleric left the land of nod
And said benignly, "Sir, I kiss the rod!
Our company is under your control
And I am all obedience heart and soul,
That is, as far as reason will allow.

"I heard the story I shall tell you now
In Padua, from a learned man now dead,
Of proven worth in all he did and said.
Yes, he is dead and nailed up in his chest,
And I pray God his spirit may have rest.

"Francis Petrarch, the poet laureate,
They called him, whose sweet rhetoric of late
Illumined Italy with poesy,
As Lynian did with his philosophy
And law, and other special kinds of learning.
Death that allows no lingering or returning
In, as it were, the twinkling of an eye
Has slain them both; and we must also die.

"But, to return to this distinguished man
From whom I learnt the tale, as I began,
Let me say first he starts it by inditing
A preface in the highest style of writing,

Ere coming to the body of his tale,
Describing Piedmont, the Saluzzo vale,
And the high Apennines that one may see
Bounding the lands of western Lombardy;
And he is most particular to tell
Of Monte Viso, where, from a little well,
The river Po springs from its tiny source.
Eastwards it runs, increasing on its course,
Towards the Aemilian Way; Ferrara past,
It reaches Venice and the sea at last,
Which is not only far too long to tell
But, as I think, irrelevant as well,
Except to set the tale and engineer it
A frame-work. This is it, if you will hear it."

*

The Clerk's Tale

PART I

Upon the western shores of Italy
Where Monte Viso lifts into the cold,
There lies a plain of rich fertility
With many a town and tower to behold,
Built by their forefathers in days of old,
And other lovely things to see in legion.
Saluzzo it is called, this splendid region.

There was a marquis once who ruled that land,
As had his ancestors in days gone by.
His vassals were obedient at his hand
Ready to serve, the lowly and the high.
Honored and dreaded, under fortune's eye
He long had lived and found the living pleasant,
Beloved alike by nobleman and peasant.

He was, moreover, speaking of descent,
The noblest-born of all in Lombardy,
Handsome and young and strong; in him were blent
High honor and a gentle courtesy.
He was discreet in his authority,
Though in some things he was indeed to blame,
As you shall hear, and Walter was his name.

I blame his failure in consideration
Of what the distant future might provide.
He always fed his present inclination,
Hawking and hunting round the countryside.
As to more serious cares, he let them slide,
And worst of all, whatever might miscarry,
He could not be prevailed upon to marry.

This was the only point that really stung them,
And so one day a deputation went
To wait on him. The wisest man among them,
Or else the least unwilling to consent
To give the marquis their admonishment,
The ablest there to touch on such a head,
Boldly addressed the marquis thus and said:

"My noble lord, your great humanity
Gives us assurance; we are therefore bold
To speak on any point of urgency
Or heavy care of which you should be told.
Then, sir, let not your clemency withhold
A hearing to our pitiful petition;
Do not disdain my voice or our position.

"Though what I ask concerns me no more nearly
Than any of your subjects in this place,

Yet forasmuch as you have loved me dearly
And ever shown the favors of your grace,
I dare the better beg in such a case
For gentle audience; here is our request,
And you, my lord, must do as you think best.

"We love you well, sir, are indeed rejoiced
In all you do or ever did, and we
Scarce can imagine thoughts that could be voiced
To lap us round in more felicity
Save one thing only, would that it might be!
Did you but choose, my lord, to take a wife,
What sovereign comfort to your country's life!

"O bow your neck under that blessed yoke!
It is a kingdom, not a slavery;
Espousal, wedlock, it is called. Invoke
Your wisdom, ponder carefully and see
How variously days pass; the seasons flee
Away in sleeping, waking, roaming, riding.
Time passes on and there is no abiding.

"Still in the flower of your youth's delights
Age creeps upon you, silent as a stone.
Death menaces all ages and he smites
The high and low, the known and the unknown;
We see for certain, are obliged to own
That we must die, but we are ignorant all
Of when the hour's to come, the blow to fall.

"Incline to our petition for protection,
Hear us that never crossed your least behest,
And we, with your consent, will make election
Immediately and choose a wife possessed

Of gentlest quality and birth, the best
In all the land, beseeming to her place,
An honor both to God and to your Grace.

"Deliver us from anxious fears and rid
Our hearts of care, for blessed Jesu's sake;
For if it so befell—which God forbid!—
Your line should end, then might not fortune rake
Some strange successor in to come and take
Your heritage? Should we not all miscarry?
Therefore we beg you speedily to marry."

Their humble prayer and their imploring features
Made much impression on his clemency
And he replied, "My people, fellow-creatures,
Married's a thing I never thought to be.
I go rejoicing in my liberty,
And that and marriage seldom go together;
Where I was free, am I to take the tether?

"Yet, since your offer is sincerely meant,
And since I trust you now as in the past,
I freely will admit myself content
To humor you and take a wife at last.
But as for the suggestion you should cast
About to find me a bride, I must remit
That duty; kindly say no more of it.

"God knows it's true that children in the main
Are much unlike their elders gone before,
Natural goodness comes of God, no strain
Of blood can give it, no, nor ancestor;
I trust in God's good bounty; say no more.

My marriage, my condition, rank and ease
I lay on Him. Do He as He may please.

"Leave me alone to choose myself a wife,
That is my burden, my prerogative.
But I command you, charge you on your life,
Whoever I shall choose, you are to give
All honor to her, long as she may live,
In word and deed, here and elsewhere, no less
Than to an emperor's daughter or princess.

"And over this you furthermore shall swear
Never to grumble, never to check or strive
Against my choice, if I am to impair
My personal liberty that you may thrive.
Where I have set my heart I mean to wive;
If you withhold consent as to this latter
I beg you'll speak no more upon the matter."

With heart's goodwill they gave him their assent
To this demand, not one that made objection,
But begged the princely favor ere they went
That he would name a day for the election
Of his espoused, and quickly, for a section
Among his folk were yet uneasy, dreading
The marquis had no real thought of wedding.

He granted them a day of their own choosing
When he would wed in sober certainty;
He said he did so not to seem refusing
Their reasonable request, and reverently
In grave obedience then they bent the knee
Thanking him one and all, and were content,
Having achieved their aim, and home they went.

And thereupon he bade his ministers
To make such preparations as were fit
Against a feast, giving his officers
And squires such orders as he pleased for it,
And they obeyed him, setting all their wit
With diligence, the greatest and the least,
To make provision for a solemn feast.

PART II

Not far from where the noble palace stood
In which this marquis set about his wedding
There was a pretty village near a wood
Where the poor folk, each in his little steading,
Tended their animals with food and bedding
And took what sustenance they could from toil,
According to the bounty of the soil.

Among these poorer folk there dwelt a man
Who was esteemed the poorest of them all;
Yet there are times when God in Heaven can
Send grace into a little ox's stall.
Janicula the village used to call
This poor old man; his daughter was a pearl.
Griselda was the name of this young girl.

But in the virtuous beauty of her heart
She was among the loveliest man could ask,
For being poorly bred, no sensual part
Had learnt to use her beauty as a mask.
More often from the well than from the cask
She drank, and loving virtue, sought to please
By honest labor, not by idle ease.

And though as yet a girl of tender age,
Yet in the breast of her virginity
There was a ripeness, serious and sage.
With fostering love and reverent constancy
Her poor old father in his poverty
She tended, spun her wheel and watched his sheep
At pasture, never idle save asleep.

When she came homeward she would often bring
Roots, herbs and other grasses to the croft;
These she would shred and seethe for flavoring,
Then make her bed that was in nothing soft.
And thus she kept her father's heart aloft
With all the obedience, all the diligence
By which a child can show her reverence.

Griselda, though among his poorest creatures,
Walter had often seen, for riding by,
Hunting perhaps, a something in her features
Caught his regard, not that he sought to try
The frivolous glance of wantonness; his eye
Fell on her with a serious awareness
And he would often ponder on her fairness.

Her womanliness was what his heart commended,
Her goodness too, far passing the condition
Of one so young, was beautifully blended
In looks and deeds. A vulgar intuition
Lacks insight into virtue; his position
Taught him to recognize it and decide,
Were he to marry, she should be his bride.

The day appointed for his wedding came
But no one knew what woman it should be,

In wonder at which his people would exclaim,
Talking among themselves in privacy,
"When will the marquis quit his vanity
And take a wife? Alas to see him thus!
Why does he try to fool himself and us?"

Nevertheless the marquis bade prepare
Brooches and rings, all for Griselda, lit
With jewels, gold and lapis; he took care
Her wedding-garment should be made to fit,
But by another girl they measured it
Who was of equal stature; gems were sewn
On it to grace a wedding like his own.

And as the morning opened on the day
Appointed when the wedding was to be,
They decked the palace out in full array,
The hall, the chambers, each in its degree;
The store-rooms, bulging with a quantity
Of delicate viands, held in plenteous strength
Italy's best from all its breadth and length.

The royal marquis in his richest dress
With lords and ladies in a company
Invited to the banquet, and no less
His household officers and soldiery,
Rode off with many a sound of minstrelsy
Towards the little thorp I spoke about
And by the shortest road, in sumptuous rout.

How could the innocent Griselda tell
That all this pomp was leveled at her head?
She had gone off for water to the well
And having drawn it, home she quickly sped,

For she had heard the marquis was to wed;
She knew it was the day and hoped she might
Be present as he passed and see the sight.

She thought, "I'll stand among the other girls,
My own companions, by our door and see
The marchioness, the marquis and his earls.
I'll hurry home as quickly as can be
And finish off the work that's there for me
So that I can have leisure then to wait
And watch her riding to the castle gate."

She reached the threshold with her water-pot
And as she did the marquis called her name.
She, putting down her vessel on the spot
Beside the cattle-stall, returned and came
Before him, falling on her knees, the same
Serious-looking girl; she knelt quite still
And waited quietly to hear his will.

The thoughtful marquis, speaking with an air
Of sober gravity, said thus to her:
"Tell me, Griselda, is your father there?"
In all humility, without demur,
She answered, "He is here and ready, sir."
She rose at once and of her own accord
Fetched out her father to his overlord.

He took the poor old fellow by the hand,
Leading him off to speak with him apart.
"Janicula, I can no more withstand,
No, nor conceal, the pleasures of my heart.
If you consent, accepting from the start
Whatever follows, I will take to wife

Your daughter and will love her all my life.

"You love me as I know and would obey,
Being my liege-man born and faithful too;
Whatever pleases me I dare to say
May well succeed in also pleasing you.
Yet in this point I specially pursue
Tell me, I beg you, can my purpose draw
Consent to take me for your son-in-law?"

Wholly astounded at the news he heard
The old man turned deep red and stood there quaking,
So troubled he could hardly say a word,
Except, "My lord, my will is in your making;
What you desire in any undertaking
Let me not hinder; I am bound to do,
My dear, dear master, what best pleases you."

The marquis answered softly, "None the less
In your own cottage you and I and she
Must have a conference. Why? You cannot guess?
I have to ask her if her will may be
To marry and submit herself to me.
This must be done while you are by to hear,
I will not speak unless I have you near."

While they were in the chamber and about
The treaty, which you presently shall hear,
The throng pressed round their dwelling-place without
And wondered at its decency and cheer,
How well she tended on her father dear.
But she, Griseld, might wonder even more,
For such a sight she'd never seen before.

Nor is it strange Griselda was astounded
To see so great a guest in such a place,
She was not used to being so surrounded
By noble visitors. How pale her face . . .
But let me keep my story up to pace;
These are the words in which her lord conveyed
His will to this benign, true-hearted maid:

"Griselda, I would have you understand
As pleasing to your father and to me
That I should marry you, and here's my hand
If, as I may conjecture, you agree.
But I would rather ask you first," said he,
"Since all is done in such a hasty way,
Will you consent or pause before you say?"

"I warn you to be ready to obey
My lightest whim and pleasure; you must show
A willing heart, ungrudging night or day,
Whether I please to offer joy or woe.
When I say 'Yes' you never shall say 'No'
Either by word or frowning a defiance.
Swear this and I will swear to our alliance."

In wonder at these words, quaking for dread,
She answered, "Lord, unworthy though I be
Of so much honor, so unmerited,
If it seems good to you, it is to me.
And here I promise never willingly
To disobey in deed or thought or breath
Though I should die, and yet I fear my death."

"That is enough, Griselda mine!" said he.
He left the chamber then with sober tread

And reached the door; and after him came she.
And to the throng of people there he said:
"Here stands the wife it is my choice to wed.
Give her your reverence and love, I pray,
Whoever loves me. There's no more to say."

And that she might not take the smallest bit
Of her old gear into his house, he bade
His women strip her there, and I admit
Those ladies of the court were scarcely glad
To touch the rags in which the girl was clad.
Yet the bright beauty of her natural glow
Was clothed anew at last from top to toe.

They combed her hair that fell but rudely tressed
With slender hands as if preparatory
To coronation, and a crown was pressed
Upon her head with gems of changeful glory.
Why should I let her raiment stay my story?
She stood transfigured in her gorgeous dress
Scarce recognizable for loveliness.

The marquis then espoused her with a ring
Brought for the purpose; on a horse he set her,
It was a nobly-pacing snow-white thing.
And to the palace next with those that met her,
Leading the way with joyful heart he let her
Be brought in triumph, and the day had end
In revel till they saw the sun descend.

Shortly, to let my story quicken pace,
I say this young, new marchioness so stood
In favor with the Lord and Heaven's grace,
It could not seem by any likelihood

That she was born and bred in servitude,
As in a cottage or an oxen-stall,
But rather nourished in an emperor's hall.

To all that looked on her she grew so dear,
So much to be revered, where she was born
Those who had watched her childhood year by year
Could hardly credit it, and dared have sworn
That she had never labored in the corn
Nor was Janicula's child, for by her feature
Fancy would think she was some other creature.

Virtuous ever, as had long been known,
She had increased to such an excellence
Of grace she was as bounty on a throne,
Wise, and so lovely in her eloquence,
So grave and so benign, she charmed the sense
And gathered every heart in her embrace,
They loved her all that looked upon her face.

Nor only was Griselda thus renowned
Within Saluzzo, for her bounteous name
Was published forth in all the region round.
If one said well another said the same;
Indeed her goodness had so wide a fame,
Men, women too, the younger and the older,
Went to Saluzzo only to behold her.

And thus in humble, nay, in royal kind,
Walter espoused a love as fortunate
As it was fair. God's peace was in his mind
And he enjoyed the outward gifts of fate;
And in that he had seen in low estate
The hidden grace, men held him to have been

A prudent man, and that is seldom seen.

Nor was it only that by natural wit
She could accomplish all a woman should
In homely ways, for, were there call for it,
She also could advance the public good;
There was no rancor, no discordant mood
In all that country that she did not ease
Or use her grace and wisdom to appease.

She, in her husband's absence, did not cease
Her labors; if the nobles of the land
Fell into enmity she made their peace.
So wise and ripe the words at her command,
Her heart so equitable and her hand
So just, they thought that Heaven had sent her down
To right all wrongs and to protect the town.

And it was not long after, to her joy,
Griselda bore a daughter fine and fair,
And though she would have rather borne a boy,
Walter was glad and so his people were,
For though it was a girl, perchance an heir
Might yet be born to them and likely so,
Seeing she was not barren. Time would show.

PART III

It happened, as it often does in life,
While yet the child was sucking at her breast
The marquis, in obsession for his wife,
Longed to expose her constancy to the test.
He could not throw the thought away or rest,
Having a marvelous passion to assay her.
Needless, God knows, to frighten and dismay her.

He had assayed her faith enough before
And ever found her good; what was the need
Of heaping trial on her, more and more?
Though some may praise the subtlety, indeed
For my part I should say it could succeed
Only in evil; what could be the gain
In putting her to needless fear and pain?

But this was how he fed his prepossession;
He came alone one night to where she lay
With troubled features and a stern expression
And said, "Griseld, do you recall the day
I came and took you from your poor array
And raised you to the height of nobleness?
You've not forgotten that, or so I guess.

"I say, Griseld, this present dignity
To which I raised you cannot have, I know,
Made you forgetful of your debt to me
Who took you up from what was poor and low,
For all the little wealth that you could show.
Take heed of every word I say to you;
No one is there to hear it but us two.

"You may remember your arrival here
Into this house, it's not so long ago;
And though I love you much and hold you dear,
My noblemen are far from doing so.
They say it is a scandal and a show
That they should serve you, lifted from the tillage
As you have been, born in a little village.

"And now you've borne your daughter, all the more
No doubt they murmur phrases such as these.

But I desire, as I did before,
To live my life among them and in ease.
I cannot then ignore contingencies
And must dispose your daughter as is best,
Not as I wish to, but as they suggest.

"But still God knows it's painful to me too;
Yet without your full knowledge and consent
I will do nothing, but it is for you
To acquiesce and show no discontent.
Summon your patience, show that they were meant,
Those promises you gave me to obey,
Down in your village on our wedding-day."

Apparently unmoved as she received
What he had said, no change in her expression
Or tone of voice, Griselda unaggrieved
Replied, "My child and I are your possession
And at your pleasure; on my heart's profession
We are all yours and you may spare or kill
What is your own. Do therefore as you will.

"Nor is there anything, as God may save
My soul, that pleasing you displeases me,
Nor is there anything that I could crave
To have, or dread to lose, but you," said she.
"This is my heart's will and shall ever be;
This may no length of time, no death deface;
My heart will never turn or change its place."

If he were gladdened at her mild reply
There was no sign upon his face to show,
But gravely and with unrelenting eye
He gazed at her. At last he turned to go.

Soon after this, within a day or so,
He told a man in secret what he held
Was needful and he sent him to Griseld.

He was a sort of secret agent, one
That had been ever faithful in pursuing
Important tasks. When wickedness is done
Such men are very useful in the doing.
He loved and feared his master, and reviewing
What was commanded of him, made his way
With silent stalk to where Griselda lay.

"Madam," the fellow said, "I must be pardoned
For doing that to which I am constrained;
You are too wise to let your heart be hardened;
You know a lord's command must be sustained
And not refused, although it be complained
Against and wept for. Servants must obey,
And so will I. There is no more to say.

"It is commanded that I take this child."
He said no more but grabbed the innocent
Despitefully, his countenance as wild
As if he would have slain it ere he went.
Griselda had to suffer and consent,
And like a lamb she lay there, meek and still,
And let the cruel fellow do his will.

He was a man of ominous ill-fame,
In voice and feature ominous, as are such,
And ominous the hour at which he came.
Alas, her daughter that she loved so much
Would, as she thought, be murdered at his touch.
Nevertheless she wept not nor lamented;

It was her husband's will and she consented.

She found her voice at last and she began
Humbly imploring not to be denied
This mercy, as he was a gentleman,
To let her kiss the child before it died;
She took it to her breast with terrified
And stricken face, and lulled it in her loss;
She kissed it then and signed it with the cross,

Saying with love, "Farewell, O sacrificed
And blessed child that I shall never see;
Look, I have marked thee with the cross of Christ.
He is thy father, may He comfort thee,
Who died, for sake of us, upon a tree;
Thy little soul I offer in His sight
Since thou shalt die, for sake of me, to-night."

And had there been a nurse with her, God knows
She would have thought it pitiful to see;
Well might a mother then have wept her woes.
Yet she was grave, and gazing steadfastly
As one who suffers all adversity
In meek submission, turned with sorrow-laden
Spirit and said, "Take back your little maiden."

"Go now," she said, "and do as you are bidden.
But one thing let me beg you of your grace;
Bury the little body, be it hidden,
Unless my lord forbade it, in some place
That beasts and birds of prey can never trace."
Yet not a word in answer would he say;
He took the little child and went his way,

Reporting to the marquis once again
What she had said, how looked, if reconciled,
As briefly point by point he made all plain
And having done he gave him up the child.
And though some touch of tenderness beguiled
His master, yet he held his purpose still
As lords will do that mean to have their will.

He bade the fellow secretly to take
The child and wrap the softest winding round
Her little form and carefully to make
A chest to bear it in, and then he bound
The man on pain of death that not a sound
Of his intention should be uttered, dumb
On whither he was going or whence come.

But to Bologna, to the marquis' sister,
The Countess of Panaro, he must go,
Taking the child, and he must there enlist her
To help him in this matter and bestow
All fostering care, so that the child might grow
In gentle grace, but above all to hide
Whose child it was, whatever should betide.

The man went off and did as he was bidden.
Now let us watch the marquis as he ranged
In quick imagination for some hidden
Sign in his wife whether she were estranged;
Was there a chance word showing she had changed
Towards him? But he still could never find
Her anything but serious and kind,

As glad, as humble and as quick to serve,
And in her love as she was wont to be;

In everything the same, she did not swerve,
And of her daughter not a word said she.
There was no sign of that adversity
To see upon her; and her daughter's name
She never used in earnest or in game.

PART IV

Four years went by in this unaltered state
Before Griselda was with child once more,
And then she bore a boy as delicate
In grace and beauty as the child before.
The marquis being told set greatest store
On it, not only he but all the county,
And all gave thanks and honor to God's bounty.

When it was two years old, weaned from the breast
And taken from its nurse, there came a day
When Walter yet again was moved to test
The patience of his wife in the same way.
O needless, needless was the test, I say!
But married men too often use no measure
That have some patient creature at their pleasure.

"Wife," said the marquis, "as I said at first,
My people take it ill that we were married.
Now that my son is born they think the worst;
Never were things so bad, for I am harried
By murmurings and rumors that are carried
About my ears; I feel a deadly smart
That has indeed almost destroyed my heart.

"For now they say, 'When **Walter's reign** is done
Old Janicle's descendants will succeed
And be our masters, either that or none.'

Such is the common talk, it is indeed.
Murmurs like that a ruler has to heed,
And certainly I dread all such opinions,
Though secretly advanced, in my dominions.

"I mean to live in quiet if I may,
And so am utterly disposed in mind
To serve the brother in the self-same way
As I have served his sister. I designed
To give this warning lest you were inclined
To do some outrage in your violent grief;
I beg you to be patient then, in brief."

"I long have said," she answered, "Oh, believe me,
Nothing I will nor yet would have unwilled,
But as it pleases you. It does not grieve me
At all, though son and daughter both were killed
At your commandment; let it be fulfilled.
In my two children I have had no part
But sickness first, then pain and grief of heart.

"You are our sovereign, do with what is yours
Just as you please and do not bid me frame
Advice for you; for at my father's doors
I left my clothing. Was it not the same
To leave my will and freedom when I came?
I took your clothing and I therefore pray
Your pleasure may be done. I will obey.

"And surely had I had the prescience
To know your will before you told it me
I had performed it without negligence.
But knowing what your pleasure is to be,
I hold to it with firmest constancy.

For if I knew my death itself would ease you,
Then I would die, and gladly die, to please you.

"For death can never make comparison
Beside your love." And when the marquis saw
Her faithfulness he could not look upon
Her face and dropped his eyes in wondering awe,
Thinking, "What patience to endure the law
Of my caprices!" and he left the room
Happy at heart, but set his face in gloom.

The ugly officer as brutally
As he had snatched her daughter, or with more
Brutality if more in man could be,
Seized on her son, so beautiful, and tore
Him from her arms; she patient as before
Gave him no sign of suffering in her loss
But kissed her son and signed him with the cross.

But yet she begged the fellow, if he might,
To close the little body in a grave.
His tender limbs so delicate to sight
She sought in her extremity to save
From birds and beasts, but not a sign he gave
And snatched the child with careless cruelty,
But bore it to Bologna tenderly.

The marquis wondered ever more and more
At so much patience in her misery;
Had he not known for certain long before
How perfectly she loved her children, he
Would have supposed some cunning devilry
Of malice, some heart's cruelty or base
Indifference beneath her constant face.

But well the marquis knew it was no mask,
For she had ever loved her children best,
Next to himself. Now, I would like to ask
Of women, had he made sufficient test?
Could stubborn husband fancy or suggest
More that would prove a steadfast wifeliness
To one continuing stubborn to excess?

But there are folk in such a state of mind
That, if they finally resolve to take
Some certain course to which they feel inclined,
Cannot hold back, but fettered to their stake,
Hold to their purposes and cannot slake
Their fevered wills. So too this marquis nursed
His purposes, to test her as at first.

And so he waited for a word or glance
To show her change of heart, but there was none,
No variation in her countenance
Could he discover; face and heart were one.
And as she aged the love in her begun
Continued ever truer, made addition,
If that could be, in love and true submission.

Therefore there seemed to be between these two
One undivided will; if Walter pressed
For something, it became her joy to do;
And God be thanked all happened for the best.
And she gave proof that in whatever test
A wife, as of herself, in nothing should
Direct her will but as her husband would.

Walter's ill-fame began to mount and spread;
His cruel soul had led him to embark

For having wed a pauper, people said,
On murdering both his children in the dark.
Such was the common murmur and remark.
No wonder if it was; by what they heard
About it, murder was the only word.

And so the love his people felt of yore
Turned into hatred; scandal and ill-fame
Are things a man may well be hated for;
To be called murderer is a hateful name.
Yet he in game or earnest with the same
Cruel device drove on to what he sought;
To test her further was his only thought.

Now when his daughter was some twelve years old
He sent to Rome, long cunningly apprised
Of his intentions, and the court was told
That such and such a bull should be devised
That his fell purpose might be realized,
And that the Pope, to set all minds at rest,
Should bid him wed again as he thought best.

I say he ordered them to counterfeit
A papal bull declaring approbation
Of a divorce, for Walter then could meet
Objection with a papal dispensation
And calm the rancor and the indignation
Between his people and him. They framed the bull
And published the whole forgery in full.

The common people, and no wonder, held
Or else supposed that things were even so.
But when these tidings came to poor Griseld
I deem her heart was weighted down with woe.

But she, and now no less than long ago,
Was ready, humble creature, faithfully
To meet misfortune and adversity.

And still she waited on his will and pleasure
To whom she had been given, heart and soul,
As to her one unfailing worldly treasure.
Yet to be brief about it and control
My tale, the marquis now to reach his goal
Devised a letter that declared his aim,
And to Bologna secretly it came.

It was for Lord Panaro, for the earl
Who had espoused his sister, and requested
That he would send him home his boy and girl
In public state and openly invested
With every honor, but it still protested
That upon no account should he declare,
Even if questioned, whose the children were,

But say the maid was shortly to espouse
The Marquis of Saluzzo; and thereto
The earl agreed. As day began to rouse
He started on the journey and he drew
Towards Saluzzo with a retinue
Of many lords in rich array to guide
This maiden and the brother at her side.

All in her wedding-dress and fresh as heaven
She rode in pearl and gold without alloy,
Her brother too, a little lad of seven,
Looked freshly, in the tunic of a boy;
So with great splendor, every face in joy,

They shaped their journey, riding all the way;
And thus they neared Saluzzo day by day.

PART V

Meanwhile, according to his cruel bent
The marquis sought to test his wife yet more
And by the uttermost experiment
To prove her spirit to the very core,
Whether she still were steadfast as before;
And so in open audience one day
And in a blustering voice he chose to say:

"It was agreeable enough, forsooth,
To marry you, Griselda, in the flower
Of your obedient love and simple truth,
And not for lineage or worldly dower;
But now I know in very truth that power,
If one reflects, is nothing much to praise;
It is a servitude in many ways.

"I may not do as any plowman may;
My subjects are constraining me to take
Another wife, they clamor day by day.
Even the Pope has thought it fit to slake
Their rancor by consenting, you need make
No doubt of that; indeed I have to say
My second wife is now upon her way.

"Strengthen your heart to give her up your place.
As for the dowry that you brought of old,
Take it again, I grant it as a grace;
Go home, rejoin your father in his fold.
No one can count upon his luck to hold,
And I enjoin you to endure the smart

Of fortune's buffets with an even heart."

She answered patiently without pretense:
"My lord, I know as I have always done
That, set against your high magnificence,
My poverty makes no comparison.
It cannot be denied, and I for one
Was never worthy, never in my life,
To be your chambermaid, much less your wife.

"And in this house whose lady you have made me,
As God's my witness whom I love and fear,
And as His power may gladden me and aid me,
I never thought myself the mistress here,
Rather a servant, humble and sincere,
To your high honor; so I shall think forever
Of you, above all creatures whatsoever.

"That you so long, of your benignity,
Have held me high in honor and display,
Whereas I was not worthy so to be,
I thank my God and you; and now I pray
Revoke it, for there is no more to say.
Gladly I'll seek my father and will live
My life with him, whatever life may give.

"For I was fostered there when I was small,
Only a child, and there I'll live and die
A widow clean in body, heart and all;
I gave my maidenhead to you, and I
Am still your faithful wife, I do not lie.
And God forbid a wife to one so great
Should take another man to be her mate.

"Touching your second wife, may God in grace
Grant you both joy and long prosperity,
For I will gladly yield her up my place
That once was such a happiness to me.
But since it pleases you, my lord," said she,
"In whom was formerly my whole heart's rest,
Then I will go when you shall think it best.

"But as you proffer me what first I brought,
Such dowry as I had, it's in my mind
It was my wretched clothing and worth nought,
And would indeed be hard for me to find.
O blessed God, how noble and how kind
You seemed in speech, in countenance, in carriage,
That day, the day on which we made our marriage!

"It's truly said, at least I find it true
For the effect of it is proved in me,
'A love grown old is not the love once new.'
And yet whatever the adversity,
Though it were death, my lord, it cannot be
That ever I should repent, though I depart,
For having wholly given you my heart.

"My lord, you know that in my father's place
You stripped me of my rags and in their stead
Gave me rich garments, as an act of grace.
I brought you nothing else it may be said
But faith and nakedness and maidenhead.
Here I return your garments and restore
My wedding-ring as well, forevermore.

"And the remainder of the gems you lent
Are in your chamber I can safely say.

Naked out of my father's house I went
And naked I return again to-day;
Gladly I'll do your pleasure, if I may.
But yet I hope you will not make a mock
Of me or send me forth without a smock.

"So infamous a thing you could not do
As let the womb in which your children lay
Be seen in nakedness, bare to the view
Of all your people, let me not I pray
Go naked as a worm upon the way.
Bethink yourself, my own dear lord, because
I was your wife, unworthy though I was.

"Therefore in guerdon of my maidenhead
Which, hither brought, returns with me no more,
Vouchsafe a payment, give to me instead
Just such a simple smock as once I wore
To hide the womb of one that heretofore
Has been your wife; and here at last I leave you
And bid farewell, dear lord, lest I should grieve you."

"The smock," he said, "you have upon your back
You may retain; remove it to your stall."
Yet as he spoke his voice began to crack
For pity, and he turned and left the hall.
She stripped her garments in the sight of all
And in her smock, head bare and feet unshod,
Home to her father and his house she trod.

Folk followed weeping as she passed them by,
They railed on fate for all that had occurred.
Her eyes withheld their weeping and were dry
And at this time she did not speak a word.

The news soon reached her father; when he heard
He cursed the day and hour of his birth
That fashioned him a man to live on earth.

He, never doubt it, though so old and poor,
Had ever been suspicious of the match,
Had always thought it never could endure,
In that the marquis, having had the snatch
Of his desires, would feel disgrace attach
To his estate in such a low alliance,
And when he could would set it at defiance.

At her approach he hastened forth to meet her,
Led by the sound of many a beholder
That wept to see her pass, and he to greet her
Brought her old cloak and cast it on her shoulder
And wept. It fitted not, for it was older
By many a day than was her wedding-dress;
The cloth was coarsely woven, comfortless.

Thus with her father for a certain space
This flower of love and wifely patience stayed.
Never a word or look upon her face
In front of others or alone conveyed
A hint that she had suffered, or betrayed
Any remembrance of her former glory;
Her countenance told nothing of her story.

And that's no wonder; in her high estate
Her spirit had a full humility,
No tender mouth for food, no delicate
Heart's hungering after royal brilliancy
Or show of pomp; benignly, patiently,
She had lived wise in honor, void of pride,

Meek and unchanging at her husband's side.

They speak of Job and his humility,
For clerics when they wish to can endite
Its praises nobly, and especially,
In men—they praise few women when they write;
Yet none can reach a humbleness as white
As women can, nor can be half so true
As women are, or else it's something new.

PART VI

Now from Bologna he of whom I spoke,
The earl, arrived. The greater and the less
Got wind of it and all the common folk
Buzzed with the news a second marchioness
Was being brought in all the loftiness
Of pomp and splendor. Such a sight to see
Had never been known in all west Lombardy.

The marquis, who had planned and knew it all,
Before the earl had fully reached his place,
Sent down for poor Griselda in her stall;
And she with humble heart and happy face
Came at his bidding, all without a trace
Of swelling thought, and went upon her knees
And greeted him with reverence and at ease.

"Griseld," said he, "my will is firmly set.
This maiden hither brought to be my bride
To-morrow shall as royally be met
As possible with all I can provide
That's in my house. My servants, side by side
According to their rank, shall wait upon her
As may be best arranged in joy and honor.

"I have no women of sufficient skill
To decorate the chambers as I hold
They should be decorated. If you will
I should be glad to see it all controlled
By you who know me and my tastes of old.
And though your dress is not a thing of beauty
I hope at least that you will do your duty."

"Not only, lord, would I be glad," said she,
"To do your will; I long and shall endeavor
To serve and please you in my own degree
And not to faint in service, now or ever.
For neither grief or happiness can sever
My love from me. My heart can never rest
Save in the ceaseless will to love you best."

And she began upon the decorations;
There were the boards to set, the beds to make.
All she could do in many occupations
She did, and begged the maids for goodness' sake
To hurry and to sweep and dust and shake,
While she, most serviceable of them all,
Went garnishing the chambers and the hall.

The earl arrived, beginning to alight
With the two children early in the day,
And all the people ran to see the sight
Of so much opulence and rich array.
And soon among them there were those to say
That Walter was no fool, and though obsessed
To change his wife, it might be for the best.

"For she is lovelier," they all agreed,
"And younger than Griselda. Put the case

That fruit will fall to them; a fairer breed
Will issue from such lineage and grace."
Her brother had so beautiful a face
It caught them with delight, opinion changed
And now applauded with what their lord arranged.

"O stormy people, frivolous and fickle,
Void of true judgment, turning like a vane,
Whom every novelty and rumor tickle,
How like the moon you are to wax and wane.
Clapping your praises, shouting your disdain,
False judges, dear at a penny as a rule,
Who trusts to your opinion is a fool."

So said the serious people of the city
Who watched the throng go gazing up and down
Glad merely for the novelty, the pretty
New lady that had come to grace the town.
But let me leave the pleasure-seeking clown
And turn to my Griselda, in the press
Of all her labors, in her steadfastness.

Busy in all, she worked, disposed and settled,
Labored and strove to cater and adorn,
Nor did she seem at all abashed or nettled
Although her clothes were coarse and somewhat torn,
But with a face as cheerful as the morn
Went to the gate with all her retinue
To greet the marchioness, and then withdrew.

She met the guests so cheerfully and greeted them
With so much skill according to their rank
That none could find a fault in how she treated them
And all were wondering whom they had to thank,

For how could such a pauper, to be frank,
Know all the rules of honor and degree?
They praised her prudence as a rarity.

And in the meanwhile ceaselessly she still
Praised the young bride and praised her brother too
With so much heart, with such benign goodwill
That no one could have given them better due.
And in the end when all the retinue
Sat down to meat, Walter began to call
Griselda who was busy in the hall.

"Griseld," he said to her as if in jest.
"How do you like the beauty of my wife?"
"Indeed, my lord," she said, "I must protest
I never saw a lovelier in my life.
God give her joy and may there be no strife
Between you, and I pray that He may send
Your fill of happiness to your lives' end!"

"One thing I beg of you, and warn you too,
Never to goad her, never put on trial
This tender girl as I have known you do;
For she was fostered preciously, a vial
More delicate. I think the self-denial
Adversity might force on her would be
Harder for her to suffer than for me."

When Walter saw this patience in Griseld,
Her happy face, no malice there at all,
And thought of his offenses long upheld
To test her, ever constant as a wall,
Grave, innocent and ever at his call,
The stubborn marquis could no more repress

His pity for such wifely steadfastness.

"It is enough," he said, "Griselda mine!
Have no more fears, let not your heart be sore.
Your faith and gentleness as far outshine
All other faith as you were tested more
In wealth and want than any wife before.
Dear wife, I know your steadfastness by this."
He took her up into his arms to kiss.

She, lost in wonder, did not seem to grasp
Or even hear the words he uttered thus,
But as a sleeper breaking from the clasp
Of an amazement, woke incredulous.
"Griseld," said he, "by Him that died for us
You are my wife and I have none but you,
Nor ever had as God may judge me true!

"This is your daughter whom you so commended
As wife for me; the other on my oath
Shall be my heir as I have long intended,
They are the children of your body, both.
Bologna nourished them and fed their growth
In secret; take them back and never say
Your children have been lost or snatched away.

"Let those that otherwise have talked of me
Know that I did this, be it bad or good,
Neither in malice nor in cruelty
But for the trial of your womanhood.
What! Slay my children? God forbid I should!
Rather I kept them privately apart
Till I had proved the purpose of your heart."

On hearing this Griselda fell in swoon
In piteous joy, but made recovery
And called her children to her and they soon
Were folded in her arms. How tenderly
She kissed them as the salt tears falling free
Bathed them and glistened on their face and hair;
How like a mother stood Griselda there!

And Oh how pitiful it was to see
Her fainting and to hear her humble tone,
"All thanks to you, my dearest lord," said she,
"For you have saved my children, you alone!
Were I to die this moment I have known
Your love and have found favor in your sight,
And death were nothing, though I died to-night.

"O dear, O tender ones, so long away,
Your sorrowing mother steadfastly had thought
That some foul vermin, hound or beast of prey
Had eaten you. But God in mercy brought
You back to me and your kind father sought
In tender love to keep you safe and sound."
She suddenly swooned again and fell to the ground.

Though she had fainted, sadly, clingingly
She held her children in that first embrace,
And it was difficult for skill to free
Them from her arms, and touching to unlace.
O many a tear on many a pitying face
Ran down among those standing at her side,
Scarce able in her presence to abide.

Walter caressed her, loosed her from her grief,
And up she rose bewildered from her trance,

While all the rest in joy at her relief
Made much of her and cleared her countenance;
And Walter showed such loving vigilance
It was a dainty thing to see the air
Of new-found happiness between the pair.

The ladies round her, when the moment came,
Led her towards her chamber; there the old
Poor rags she wore, though never worn in shame,
They stripped and set on her a gown of gold;
A coronet of jewels manifold
They crowned her with and led her into hall
There to receive the homage of them all.

Thus to a piteous day a blissful close,
And every man and woman, as they might,
Gave themselves up to revelry; there rose
The stars, and all the welkin shone with light.
Greater the glad solemnities that night,
Greater the joy in feasting and defray
In treasure than upon their wedding-day.

For many a year in high prosperity
These two lived on in concord to the close;
Their daughter too they married worthily
And richly to a lord, best among those
In Italy. They also found repose
For old Janicula whom Walter kept
Safe at his court till soul from body crept.

Their son succeeded to the inheritance
After his father's day in peace and rest;
He married happily but did not chance
To put his wife to such a searching test.

This world of ours, it has to be confessed,
Is not so sturdy as it was of old.
Hear how my author ends the tale he told:

"This story does not mean it would be good
For wives to ape Griseld's humility,
It would be unendurable they should.
But everybody in their own degree
Should be as perfect in their constancy
As was Griselda." That is why Petrarch chose
To tell her story in his noble prose.

For since a woman showed such patience to
A mortal man, how much the more we ought
To take in patience all that God may do.
Reason He has to test what He has wrought,
Yet never tempts the souls that He has bought
Above what they are able, and St James
Tells us He tests us daily, and reclaims.

He will permit, to exercise our virtue,
The sharper scourges of adversity
To lash us often, not that they may hurt you,
Nor yet to test the will, for certainly
No one can know our frailty more than He
Who knew them ere our birth, and all is best;
Then let our virtues learn to suffer test.

But one word more, my lords, before I go.
It isn't very easy nowadays
To find Griseldas round the town, you know.
And if you try imposing these assays,
What gold they have is mixed with such allays
Of brass, that, though the coin looks right perhaps,

When you begin to bend the thing it snaps.

So, from affection for the Wife of Bath,
Whose life and all her sect may God maintain
In high authority upon their path
—And pity else—I sing you this refrain
With lusty heart, to gladden you again,
Dropping the note of earnest emphasis.
So listen to my song, it goes like this:

*

Chaucer's Envoy to the Clerk's Tale

Griselda and her patience both are dead
And buried in some far Italian vale.
So let it then in open court be said,
"Husbands, be not so hardy as to assail
The patience of your wives in hope to find
Griseldas, for you certainly will fail."

O noble wives, in highest prudence bred,
Allow no such humility to nail
Your tongues, or give a scholar cause to shed
Such light on you as this astounding tale
Sheds on Griselda, patient still and kind,
Lest Chichevache[1] engulf you like a whale.

Imitate Echo, she that never fled
In silence, but returns you hail for hail,

---

[1] [In an old French fable there were two cows called Chichevache and Bicorne.
Bicorne was fat because she made her diet on patient husbands who were
in plentiful supply. But the monster Chichevache was thin, for her diet was
only patient wives, poor cow.—TRANS.]

Never let innocence besot your head,
But take the helm yourselves and trim the sail,
And print this lesson firmly in your mind
For common profit; it can never stale.

Arch-wives, stand up, defend your board and bed!
Stronger than camels as you are, prevail!
Don't swallow insults, offer them instead.
And all you slender little wives and frail,
Be fierce as Indian tigers, since designed
To rattle like a windmill in a gale.

Never revere them, never be in dread,
For though your husband wears a coat of mail,
Your shafts of crabbed eloquence will thread
His armor through and drub him like a flail.
Voice your suspicions of him! Guilt will bind
Him down, he'll couch as quiet as a quail.

If you are beautiful, advance your tread,
Show yourself off to people, blaze the trail!
If you are ugly, spend and make a spread,
Get friends, they'll do the business of a male;
Dance like a linden-leaf if so inclined,
Leave him to weep and wring his hands and wail!

AESCHYLUS was born in about 525 B.C. in Eleusis, northwest of Athens, Greece. Euphorion, his father, is believed by some scholars to have been a tragic poet, and both parents were members of the nobility. The tragedies of Aeschylus have established him as an innovator who set early standards and conventions for the tragic form. Over the course of his life, Aeschylus wrote over seventy plays, many of which were honored with first prize in the Athenian tragic contests. Seven tragedies have survived: *The Persians, Prometheus Bound, Seven Against Thebes, Suppliants,* and the *Oresteia* trilogy (*Agamemnon, Choephori,* and *Eumenides*). As well as writing plays, Aeschylus probably served as producer, director, designer, choreographer, and composer of his works and acted in them. Apart from writing, Aeschylus was a soldier, fighting in the battle of Marathon in 490 and defending the Greeks against Persian invaders at Artemisium and Salamis. He also travelled to Sicily, where legend has it that he died in 456 B.C. when an eagle dropped a tortoise on his head.

From *The Oresteia,* translated by Robert Fagles. Publisher: Viking Penguin Inc., 1977. Pages 103–277.

Agamemnon

CHARACTERS

AGAMEMNON   WATCHMAN

CASSANDRA   CLYTAEMNESTRA

AEGISTHUS   HERALD

CHORUS, THE OLD MEN OF ARGOS
AND THEIR LEADER

*Attendants of Clytaemnestra and of Agamemnon,
bodyguard of Aegisthus*

*   *   *

TIME AND SCENE: *A night in the tenth and final autumn of the Trojan
war. The house of Atreus in Argos. Before it, an altar stands unlit; a*
WATCHMAN *on the high roofs fights to stay awake.*

WATCHMAN: Dear gods, set me free from all the pain,
   the long watch I keep, one whole year awake . . .
   propped on my arms, crouched on the roofs of Atreus
   like a dog.

   I know the stars by heart,
   the armies of the night, and there in the lead
   the ones that bring us snow or the crops of summer,

83

bring us all we have—
our great blazing kings of the sky,
I know them, when they rise and when they fall . . .
and now I watch for the light, the signal-fire
breaking out of Troy, shouting Troy is taken.
So she commands, full of her high hopes.
That woman—she manoeuvres like a man.

And when I keep to my bed, soaked in dew,
and the thoughts go groping through the night
and the good dreams that used to guard my sleep . . .
not here, it's the old comrade, terror, at my neck.
I mustn't sleep, no—

(Shaking himself awake.)

Look alive, sentry.
And I try to pick out tunes, I hum a little,
a good cure for sleep, and the tears start,
I cry for the hard times come to the house,
no longer run like the great place of old.

Oh for a blessed end to all our pain,
some godsend burning through the dark—

*(Light appears slowly in the east; he
struggles to his feet and scans it.)*

I salute you!
You dawn of the darkness, you turn night to day—
I see the light at last.
They'll be dancing in the streets of Argos
thanks to you, thanks to this new stroke of—

Aieeeeee!

There's your signal clear and true, my queen!
Rise up from bed—hurry, lift a cry of triumph
through the house, praise the gods for the beacon,
if they've taken Troy . . .

But there it burns,
fire all the way. I'm for the morning dances.
Master's luck is mine. A throw of the torch
has brought us triple-sixes—we have won!
My move now—

(*Beginning to dance, then breaking off,
lost in thought.*)

Just bring him home. My king,
I'll take your loving hand in mine and then . . .
the rest is silence. The ox is on my tongue.
Aye, but the house and these old stones,
give them a voice and what a tale they'd tell.
And so would I, gladly . . .
I speak to those who know; to those who don't
my mind's a blank. I never say a word.

(*He climbs down from the roof and
disappears into the palace through a
side entrance. A* CHORUS, *the old men
of Argos who have not learned the
news of victory, enters and marches
round the altar.*)

CHORUS: Ten years gone, ten to the day
our great avenger went for Priam—
Menelaus and lord Agamemnon,
two kings with the power of Zeus,
the twin throne, twin sceptre,
Atreus' sturdy yoke of sons
launched Greece in a thousand ships,
armadas cutting loose from the land,
armies massed for the cause, the rescue—

(*From within the palace* CLYTAEMNESTRA
raises a cry of triumph.)

the heart within them screamed for all-out war!
Like vultures robbed of their young,
the agony sends them frenzied,

soaring high from the nest, round and
round they wheel, they row their wings,
stroke upon churning thrashing stroke,
but all the labour, the bed of pain,
the young are lost forever.
Yet someone hears on high—Apollo,
Pan or Zeus—the piercing wail
these guests of heaven raise,
and drives at the outlaws, late
but true to revenge, a stabbing Fury!

(CLYTAEMNESTRA *appears at the
doors and pauses with her entourage.*)

So towering Zeus the god of guests
drives Atreus' sons at Paris,
all for a woman manned by many
the generations wrestle, knees
grinding the dust, the manhood drains,
the spear snaps in the first blood rites
that marry Greece and Troy.
And now it goes as it goes
and where it ends is Fate.
And neither by singeing flesh
nor tipping cups of wine
nor shedding burning tears can you
enchant away the rigid Fury.

(CLYTAEMNESTRA *lights the altar-fires.*)

We are the old, dishonoured ones,
the broken husks of men.
Even then they cast us off,
the rescue mission left us here
to prop a child's strength upon a stick.
What if the new sap rises in his chest?
He has no soldiery in him,
no more than we,

and we are aged past ageing,
gloss of the leaf shrivelled,
three legs at a time we falter on.
Old men are children once again,
a dream that sways and wavers
into the hard light of day.
                 But you,
daughter of Leda, queen Clytaemnestra,
what now, what news, what message
drives you through the citadel
burning victims? Look,
the city gods, the gods of Olympus,
gods of the earth and public markets—
all the altars blazing with your gifts!
Argos blazes! Torches
race the sunrise up her skies—
drugged by the lulling holy oils,
unadulterated,
run from the dark vaults of kings.
Tell us the news!
What you can, what is right—
Heal us, soothe our fears!
Now the darkness comes to the fore,
now the hope glows through your victims,
beating back this raw, relentless anguish
gnawing at the heart.

> (CLYTAEMNESTRA *ignores them and pursues her*
> *rituals; they assemble for the opening chorus.*)

O but I still have power to sound the god's command at the
    roads
that launched the kings. The gods breathe power through
    my song,
my fighting strength, Persuasion grows with the years—
I sing how the flight of fury hurled the twin command,
one will that hurled young Greece

and winged the spear of vengeance straight for Troy!
The kings of birds to kings of the beaking prows, one black,
one with a blaze of silver
skimmed the palace spearhand right
and swooping lower, all could see,
plunged their claws in a hare, a mother
bursting with unborn young—the babies spilling,
quick spurts of blood—cut off the race just dashing into life!
Cry, cry for death, but good win out in glory in the end.
But the loyal seer of the armies studied Atreus' sons,
two sons with warring hearts—he saw two eagle-kings
devour the hare and spoke the things to come,
"Years pass, and the long hunt nets the city of Priam,
the flocks beyond the walls,
a kingdom's life and soul—Fate stamps them out.
Just let no curse of the gods lour on us first,
shatter our giant armour
forged to strangle Troy. I see
pure Artemis bristle in pity—
yes, the flying hounds of the Father
slaughter for armies . . . their own victim . . . a woman
trembling young, all born to die—She loathes the eagles'
    feast!"
Cry, cry for death, but good win out in glory in the end.

"Artemis, lovely Artemis, so kind
to the ravening lion's tender, helpless cubs,
the suckling young of beasts that stalk the wilds—
bring this sign for all its fortune,
all its brutal torment home to birth!
I beg you, Healing Apollo, soothe her before
her crosswinds hold us down and moor the ships too long,
pressing us on to another victim . . .
nothing sacred, no
no feast to be eaten
the architect of vengeance

(Turning to the palace.)

growing strong in the house
with no fear of the husband
here she waits
the terror raging back and back in the future
the stealth, the law of the hearth, the mother—
Memory womb of Fury child-avenging Fury!"
So as the eagles wheeled at the crossroads,
Calchas clashed out the great good blessings mixed with doom
for the halls of kings, and singing with our fate
we cry, cry for death, but good win out in glory in the end.
Zeus, great nameless all in all,
if that name will gain his favour,
I will call him Zeus.
I have no words to do him justice,
weighing all in the balance,
all I have is Zeus, Zeus—
lift this weight, this torment from my spirit,
cast it once for all.

He who was so mighty once,
storming for the wars of heaven,
he has had his day.
And then his son who came to power
met his match in the third fall
and he is gone. Zeus, Zeus—
raise your cries and sing him Zeus the Victor!
You will reach the truth:

Zeus has led us on to know,
the Helmsman lays it down as law
that we must suffer, suffer into truth.
We cannot sleep, and drop by drop at the heart
the pain of pain remembered comes again,
and we resist, but ripeness comes as well.

From the gods enthroned on the awesome rowing-bench
there comes a violent love.

So it was that day the king,
the steersman at the helm of Greece,
would never blame a word the prophet said—
swept away by the wrenching winds of fortune
he conspired! Weatherbound we could not sail,
our stores exhausted, fighting strength hard-pressed,
and the squadrons rode in the shallows off Chalkis
where the riptide crashes, drags,
and winds from the north pinned down our hulls at Aulis,
port of anguish . . . head winds starving,
sheets and the cables snapped
and the men's minds strayed,
the pride, the bloom of Greece
was raked as time ground on,
ground down, and then the cure for the storm
and it was harsher—Calchas cried,
"My captains, Artemis must have blood!"—
so harsh the sons of Atreus
dashed their sceptres on the rocks,
could not hold back the tears,

and I still can hear the older warlord saying,
"Obey, obey, or a heavy doom will crush me!—
Oh but doom *will* crush me
once I rend my child,
the glory of my house—
a father's hands are stained,
blood of a young girl streaks the altar.
Pain both ways and what is worse?
Desert the fleets, fail the alliance?
No, but stop the winds with a virgin's blood,
feed their lust, their fury?—feed their fury!—

Law is law!—
> Let all go well."

And once he slipped his neck in the strap of Fate,
his spirit veering black, impure, unholy,
once he turned he stopped at nothing,
seized with the frenzy
blinding driving to outrage—
wretched frenzy, cause of all our grief!
Yes, he had the heart
to sacrifice his daughter,
to bless the war that avenged a woman's loss,
a bridal rite that sped the men-of-war.

"My father, father!"—she might pray to the winds;
no innocence moves her judges mad for war.
Her father called his henchmen on,
on with a prayer,
"Hoist her over the altar
like a yearling, give it all your strength!
She's fainting—lift her,
sweep her robes around her,
but slip this strap in her gentle curving lips . . .
here, gag her hard, a sound will curse the house"—

and the bridle chokes her voice . . . her saffron robes
pouring over the sand
> her glance like arrows showering
wounding every murderer through with pity
clear as a picture, live,
she strains to call their names . . .
I remember often the days with father's guests
when over the feast her voice unbroken,
pure as the hymn her loving father
bearing third libations, sang to Saving Zeus—
transfixed with joy, Atreus' offspring
throbbing out their love.

What comes next? I cannot see it, cannot say.
The strong techniques of Calchas do their work.
But Justice turns the balance scales,
sees that we suffer
and we suffer and we learn.
And we will know the future when it comes.
Greet it too early, weep too soon.
It all comes clear in the light of day.
Let all go well today, well as she could want,

(*Turning to* CLYTAEMNESTRA.)

our midnight watch, our lone defender,
single-minded queen.

LEADER: We've come,
Clytaemnestra. We respect your power.
Right it is to honour the warlord's woman
once he leave the throne.
                    But why these fires?
Good news, or more good hopes? We're loyal,
we want to hear, but never blame your silence.

CLYTAEMNESTRA: Let the new day shine—as the proverb
    says—
glorious from the womb of Mother Night.

(*Lost in prayer, then turning to the* CHORUS.)

You will hear a joy beyond your hopes.
Priam's citadel—the Greeks have taken Troy!

LEADER: No, what do you mean? I can't believe it.

CLYTAEMNESTRA: Troy is ours. Is that clear enough?

LEADER: The joy of it,
    stealing over me, calling up my tears—

CLYTAEMNESTRA: Yes, your eyes expose your loyal hearts.

LEADER: And you have proof?

CLYTAEMNESTRA: I do,
I must. Unless the god is lying.

LEADER: That,
or a phantom spirit sends you into raptures.

CLYTAEMNESTRA: No one takes me in with visions—senseless
dreams.

LEADER: Or giddy rumour, you haven't indulged yourself—

CLYTAEMNESTRA: You treat me like a child, you mock me?

LEADER: Then when did they storm the city?

CLYTAEMNESTRA: Last night, I say, the mother of this morning.

LEADER: And who on earth could run the news so fast?

CLYTAEMNESTRA: The god of fire—rushing fire from Ida!
And beacon to beacon rushed it on to me,
my couriers riding home the torch.

                              From Troy
to the bare rock of Lemnos, Hermes' Spur,
and the Escort winged the great light west
to the Saving Father's face, Mount Athos hurled it
third in the chain and leaping Ocean's back
the blaze went dancing on to ecstasy—pitch-pine
streaming gold like a new-born sun—and brought
the word in flame to Mount Makistos' brow.
No time to waste, straining, fighting sleep,
that lookout heaved a torch glowing over
the murderous straits of Euripos to reach
Messapion's watchmen craning for the signal.
Fire for word of fire! tense with the heather
withered gray, they stack it, set it ablaze—
the hot force of the beacon never flags,

it springs the Plain of Asôpos, rears
like a harvest moon to hit Kithairon's crest
and drives new men to drive the fire on.
That relay pants for the far-flung torch,
they swell its strength outstripping my commands
and the light inflames the marsh, the Gorgon's Eye,
it strikes the peak where the wild goats range—
my laws, my fire whips that camp!
They spare nothing, eager to build its heat,
and a huge beard of flame overcomes the headland
beetling down the Saronic Gulf, and flaring south
it brings the dawn to the Black Widow's face—
the watch that looms above your heads—and now
the true son of the burning flanks of Ida
crashes on the roofs of Atreus' sons!
And I ordained it all.
Torch to torch, running for their lives,
one long succession racing home my fire.
                                        One,
first in the laps and last, wins out in triumph.
There you have my proof, *my* burning sign, I tell you—
the power my lord passed on from Troy to me!

LEADER: We'll thank the gods, my lady—first this story,
let me lose myself in the wonder of it all!
Tell it start to finish, tell us all.

CLYTAEMNESTRA: The city's ours—in our hands this very day!
I can hear the cries in crossfire rock the walls.
Pour oil and wine in the same bowl,
what have you, friendship? A struggle to the end.
So with the victors and the victims—outcries,
you can hear them clashing like their fates.

They are kneeling by the bodies of the dead,
embracing men and brothers, infants over
the aged loins that gave them life, and sobbing,

as the yoke constricts their last free breath,
for every dear one lost.
                And the others,
there, plunging breakneck through the night—
the labour of battle sets them down, ravenous,
to breakfast on the last remains of Troy.
Not by rank but chance, by the lots they draw,
they lodge in the houses captured by the spear,
settling in so soon, released from the open sky,
the frost and dew. Lucky men, off guard at last,
they sleep away their first good night in years.
If only they are revering the city's gods,
the shrines of the gods who love the conquered land,
no plunderer will be plundered in return.
Just let no lust, no mad desire seize the armies
to ravish what they must not touch—
overwhelmed by all they've won!
                  The run for home
and safety waits, the swerve at the post,
the final lap of the grueling two-lap race.
And even if the men come back with no offence
to the gods, the avenging dead may never rest—
Oh let no new disaster strike! And here
you have it, what a woman has to say.
Let the best win out, clear to see.
A small desire but all that I could want.

LEADER: Spoken like a man, my lady, loyal,
    full of self-command. I've heard your sign
    and now your vision.

                (Reaching towards her as she turns and
                      re-enters the palace.)

           Now to praise the gods.
The joy is worth the labour.

CHORUS: O Zeus my king and Night, dear Night,
   queen of the house who covers us with glories,
   you slung your net on the towers of Troy,
   neither young nor strong could leap
   the giant dredge net of slavery,
   all-embracing ruin.
   I adore you, iron Zeus of the guests
   and your revenge—you drew your longbow
   year by year to a taut full draw
   till one bolt, not falling short
   or arching over the stars,
   could split the mark of Paris!

   The sky stroke of god!—it is all Troy's to tell,
   but even I can trace it to its cause:
   god does as god decrees.
   And still some say
   that heaven would never stoop to punish men
   who trample the lovely grace of things
   untouchable. How wrong they are!
   A curse burns bright on crime—
   full-blown, the father's crimes will blossom,
   burst into the son's.
   Let there be less suffering . . .
   give us the sense to live on what we need.

      Bastions of wealth
      are no defence for the man
      who treads the grand altar of Justice
      down and out of sight.

   Persuasion, maddening child of Ruin
   overpowers him—Ruin plans it all.
   And the wound will smoulder on,
   there is no cure,
   a terrible brilliance kindles on the night.

He is bad bronze scraped on a touchstone:
put to the test, the man goes black.
Like the boy who chases
a bird on the wing, brands his city,
brings it down and prays,
but the gods are deaf
to the one who turns to crime, they tear him down.

So Paris learned:
he came to Atreus' house
and shamed the tables spread for guests,
he stole away the queen.

And she left her land *chaos,* clanging shields,
companions tramping, bronze prows, men in bronze,
and she came to Troy with a dowry, death,
strode through the gates
defiant in every stride,
as prophets of the house looked on and wept,
"Oh the halls and the lords of war,
the bed and the fresh prints of love.
I *see* him, unavenging, unavenged,
the stun of his desolation is so clear—
he longs for the one who lies across the sea
until her phantom seems to sway the house.

Her curving images,
her beauty hurts her lord,
the eyes starve and the touch
of love is gone,

and radiant dreams are passing in the night,
the memories throb with sorrow, joy with pain . . .
it is pain to dream and see desires
slip through the arms,
a vision lost for ever

winging down the moving drifts of sleep."
So he grieves at the royal hearth
yet others' grief is worse, far worse.
All through Greece for those who flocked to war
they are holding back the anguish now,
you can feel it rising now in every house;
I tell you there is much to tear the heart.

    They knew the men they sent,
    but now in place of men
    ashes and urns come back
    to every hearth.

War, War, the great gold-broker of corpses
holds the balance of the battle on his spear!
Home from the pyres he sends them,
home from Troy to the loved ones,
heavy with tears, the urns brimmed full,
the heroes return in gold-dust,
dear, light ash for men; and they weep,
they praise them, "He had skill in the swordplay,"
"He went down so tall in the onslaught,"
"All for another's woman." So they mutter
in secret and the rancour steals
towards our staunch defenders, Atreus' sons.

    And there they ring the walls, the young,
    the lithe, the handsome hold the graves
    they won in Troy; the enemy earth
    rides over those who conquered.

The people's voice is heavy with hatred,
now the curses of the people must be paid,
and now I wait, I listen . . .
there—there is something breathing
under the night's shroud. God takes aim

at the ones who murder many;
the swarthy Furies stalk the man
gone rich beyond all rights—with a twist
of fortune grind him down, dissolve him
into the blurring dead—there is no help.
The reach for power can recoil,
the bolt of god can strike you at a glance.

Make me rich with no man's envy,
neither a raider of cities, no,
nor slave come face to face with life
overpowered by another.

(Speaking singly.)

—Fire comes and the news is good,
it races through the streets
but it is true? Who knows?
Or just another lie from heaven?

—Show us the man so childish, wonderstruck,
he's fired up with the first torch,
then when the message shifts
he's sick at heart.

—Just like a woman
to fill with thanks before the truth is clear.

—So gullible. Their stories spread like wildfire,
they fly fast and die faster;
rumours voiced by women come to nothing.

LEADER: Soon we'll know her fires for what they are,
her relay race of torches hand-to-hand—
know if they're real or just a dream,
the hope of a morning here to take our senses.
I see a herald running from the beach
and a victor's spray of olive shades his eyes

and the dust he kicks, twin to the mud of Troy,
shows he has a voice—no kindling timber
on the cliffs, no signal-fires for him.
He can shout the news and give us joy,
or else . . . please, not that.
                              Bring it on,
good fuel to build the first good fires.
And if anyone calls down the worst on Argos
let him reap the rotten harvest of his mind.

(*The* HERALD *rushes in and kneels on the ground.*)

HERALD: Good Greek earth, the soil of my fathers!
   Ten years out, and a morning brings me back.
   All hopes snapped but one—I'm home at last.
   Never dreamed I'd die in Greece, assigned
   the narrow plot I love the best.
                              And now
   I salute the land, the light of the sun,
   our high lord Zeus and the king of Pytho—
   no more arrows, master, raining on our heads!
   At Scamander's banks we took our share,
   your longbow brought us down like plague.
   Now come, deliver us, heal us—lord Apollo!
   Gods of the market, here, take my salute.
   And you, my Hermes, Escort,
   loving Herald, the herald's shield and prayer!—
   And the shining dead of the land who launched the armies,
   warm us home . . . we're all the spear has left.

   You halls of the kings, you roofs I cherish,
   sacred seats—you gods that catch the sun,
   if your glances ever shone on him in the old days,
   greet him well—so many years are lost.
   He comes, he brings us light in the darkness,
   free for every comrade, Agamemnon lord of men.

Give him the royal welcome he deserves!
He hoisted the pickaxe of Zeus who brings revenge,
he dug Troy down, he worked her soil down,
the shrines of her gods and the high altars, gone!—
and the seed of her wide earth he ground to bits.
That's the yoke he claps on Troy. The king,
the son of Atreus comes. The man is blest,
the one man alive to merit such rewards.

Neither Paris nor Troy, partners to the end,
can say their work outweighs their wages now.
Convicted of rapine, stripped of all his spoils,
and his father's house and the land that gave it life—
he's scythed them to the roots. The sons of Priam
pay the price twice over.

LEADER: Welcome home
from the wars, herald, long live your joy.

HERALD: *Our* joy—
now I could die gladly. Say the word, dear gods.

LEADER: Longing for your country left you raw?

HERALD: The tears fill my eyes, for joy.

LEADER: You too,
down the sweet disease that kills a man
with kindness . . .

HERALD: Go on, I don't see what you—

LEADER: Love
for the ones who love you—that's what took you.

HERALD: You mean
the land and the armies hungered for each other?

LEADER: There were times I thought I'd faint with longing.

HERALD: So anxious for the armies, why?

LEADER: For years now,
only my silence kept me free from harm.

HERALD: What,
with the kings gone did someone threaten you?

LEADER: So much . . .
now as you say, it would be good to die.

HERALD: True, we *have* done well.
Think back in the years and what have you?
A few runs of luck, a lot that's bad.
Who but a god can go through life unmarked?
A long, hard pull we had, if I would tell it all.
The iron rations, penned in the gangways
hock by jowl like sheep. Whatever miseries
break a man, our quota, every sun-starved day.

Then on the beaches it was worse. Dug in
under the enemy ramparts—deadly going.
Out of the sky, out of the marshy flats
the dews soaked us, turned the ruts we fought from
into gullies, made our gear, our scalps
crawl with lice.
                    And talk of the cold,
the sleet to freeze the gulls, and the big snows
come avalanching down from Ida. Oh but the heat,
the sea and the windless noons, the swells asleep,
dropped to a dead calm . . .

But why weep now?
It's over for us, over for them.
The dead can rest and never rise again;
no need to call their muster. We're alive,
do we have to go on raking up old wounds?
Good-bye to all that. Glad I am to say it.

For us, the remains of the Greek contingents,
the good wins out, no pain can tip the scales,
not now. So shout this boast to the bright sun—
fitting it is—wing it over the seas and rolling earth:

"Once when an Argive expedition captured Troy
they hauled these spoils back to the gods of Greece,
they bolted them high across the temple doors,
the glory of the past!"
                    And hearing that,
men will applaud our city and our chiefs,
and Zeus will have the hero's share of fame—
he did the work.
                    That's all I have to say.

LEADER: I'm convinced, glad that I was wrong.
Never too old to learn; it keeps me young.

                    (CLYTAEMNESTRA *enters with her women.*)

First the house and the queen, it's their affair,
but I can taste the riches.

CLYTAEMNESTRA: I cried out long ago!—
for joy, when the first herald came burning
through the night and told the city's fall.
And there were some who smiled and said,
"A few fires persuade you Troy's in ashes.
Women, women, elated over nothing."

You made me seem deranged.
For all that I sacrificed—a woman's way,
you'll say—station to station on the walls
we lifted cries of triumph that resounded
in the temples of the gods. We lulled and blessed
the fires with myrrh and they consumed our victims.

(*Turning to the* HERALD.)

But enough. Why prolong the story?
From the king himself I'll gather all I need.
Now for the best way to welcome home
my lord, my good lord . . .
                    No time to lose!
What dawn can feast a woman's eyes like this?
I can see the light, the husband plucked from war
by the Saving God and open wide the gates.

Tell him that, and have him come with speed,
the peoples' darling—how they long for him.
And for his wife,
may he return and find her true at hall,
just as the day he left her, faithful to the last.
A watchdog gentle to him alone,

                    (*Glancing towards the palace.*)

                    savage
to those who cross his path. I have not changed.
The strains of time can never break our seal.
In love with a new lord, in ill repute I am
as practised as I am in dyeing bronze.

That is my boast, teeming with the truth.
I am proud, a woman of my nobility—
I'd hurl it from the roofs!

                    (*She turns sharply, enters the palace.*)

LEADER: She speaks well, but it takes no seer to know
she only says what's right.

                    (*The* HERALD *attempts to leave; the
                    leader takes him by the arm.*)

                    Wait, one thing.
Menelaus, is he home too, safe with the men?
The power of the land—dear king.

HERALD: I doubt that lies will help my friends,
in the lean months to come.

LEADER: Help us somehow, tell the truth as well.
But when the two conflict it's hard to hide—
out with it.

HERALD: He's lost, gone from the fleets!
He and his ship, it's true.

LEADER: After you watched him
pull away from Troy? Or did some storm
attack you all and tear him off the line?

HERALD: There,
like a marksman, the whole disaster cut to a word.

LEADER: How do the escorts give him out—dead or alive?

HERALD: No clear report. No one knows . . .
only the wheeling sun that heats the earth to life.

LEADER: But then the storm—how did it reach the ships?
How did it end? Were the angry gods on hand?

HERALD: This blessed day, ruin it with *them?*
Better to keep their trophies far apart.

When a runner comes, his face in tears,
saddled with what his city dreaded most,
the armies routed, two wounds in one,
one to the city, one to the hearth and home . . .
our best men, droves of them, victims
herded from every house by the two-barb whip
that Ares likes to crack,
                    that charioteer
who packs destructions shaft by shaft,
careering on with his brace of bloody mares—
When he comes in, I tell you, dragging that much pain,
wail your battle-hymn to the Furies, and high time!

But when he brings salvation home to a city
singing out her heart—
how can I mix the good with so much bad
and blurt out this?—
                    "Storms swept the Greeks,
and not without the anger of the gods!"

Those enemies for ages, fire and water,
sealed a pact and showed it to the world—
they crushed our wretched squadrons.
                              Night looming,
breakers lunging in for the kill
and the black gales come brawling out of the north—
ships ramming, prow into hooking prow, gored
by the rush-and-buck of hurricane pounding rain
by the cloudburst—
                    ships stampeding into the darkness,
lashed and spun by the savage shepherd's hand!

But when the sun comes up to light the skies
I see the Aegean heaving into a great bloom
of corpses . . . Greeks, the pick of a generation
scattered through the wrecks and broken spars.

But not us, not our ship, our hull untouched.
Someone stole us away or begged us off.
No mortal—a god, death grip on the tiller,
or lady luck herself, perched on the helm,
she pulled us through, she saved us. Aye,
we'll never battle the heavy surf at anchor,
never shipwreck up some rocky coast.

But once we cleared that sea-hell, not even
trusting luck in the cold light of day,
we battened on our troubles, they were fresh—
the armada punished, bludgeoned into nothing.

And now if one of them still has the breath
he's saying *we* are lost. Why not?
We say the same of him. Well,
here's to the best.
                              And Menelaus?
Look to it, he's come back, and yet . . .
if a shaft of the sun can track him down,
alive, and his eyes full of the old fire—
thanks to the strategies of Zeus, Zeus
would never tear the house out by the roots—
then there's hope our man will make it home.

You've heard it all. Now you have the truth.

                                        (*Rushing out.*)

CHORUS: Who—what power named the name that drove your
      fate?—
   what hidden brain could divine your future,
   steer that word to the mark,
   to the bride of spears,
   the whirlpool churning armies,
   Oh for all the world a Helen!
   Hell at the prows, hell at the gates
   hell on the men-of-war,
   from her lair's sheer veils she drifted
   launched by the giant western wind,
   and the long tall waves of men in armour,
   huntsmen trailing the oar-blades' dying spoor
   slipped into her moorings,
   Simois' mouth that chokes with foliage,
   bayed for bloody strife,
   for Troy's Blood Wedding Day—she drives her word,
   her burning will to the birth, the Fury
   late but true to the cause,
   to the tables shamed
   and Zeus who guards the hearth—

the Fury makes the Trojans pay!
Shouting their hymns, hymns for the bride
hymns for the kinsmen doomed
to the wedding march of Fate.
Troy changed her tune in her late age,
and I think I hear the dirges mourning
"Paris, born and groomed for the bed of Fate!"
They mourn with their life breath,
they sing their last, the sons of Priam
born for bloody slaughter.

So a man once reared
a lion cub at hall, snatched
from the breast, still craving milk
in the first flush of life.
A captivating pet for the young,
and the old men adored it, pampered it
in their arms, day in, day out,
like an infant just born.
Its eyes on fire, little beggar,
fawning for its belly, slave to food.

But it came of age
and the parent strain broke out
and it paid its breeders back.
Grateful it was, it went
through the flock to prepare a feast,
an illicit orgy—the house swam with blood,
none could resist that agony—
massacre vast and raw!
From god there came a priest of ruin,
adopted by the house to lend it warmth.
And the first sensation Helen brought to Troy . . .
call it a spirit
shimmer of winds dying
glory light as gold

shaft of the eyes dissolving, open bloom
that wounds the heart with love.
But veering wild in mid-flight
she whirled her wedding on to a stabbing end,
slashed at the sons of Priam—hearthmate, friend to the death,
sped by Zeus who speeds the guest,
a bride of tears, a Fury.

There's an ancient saying, old as man himself:
men's prosperity
never will die childless,
once full-grown it breeds.
Sprung from the great good fortune in the race
comes bloom on bloom of pain—
insatiable wealth! But not I,
I alone say this. Only the reckless act
can breed impiety, multiplying crime on crime,
while the house kept straight and just
is blessed with radiant children.

But ancient Violence longs to breed,
new Violence comes
when its fatal hour comes, the demon comes
to take her toll—no war, no force, no prayer
can hinder the midnight Fury stamped
with parent Fury moving through the house.

But Justice shines in sooty hovels,
loves the decent life.
From proud halls crusted with gilt by filthy hands
she turns her eyes to find the pure in spirit—
spurning the wealth stamped counterfeit with praise,
she steers all things towards their destined end.

> (AGAMEMNON *enters in his chariot, his*
> *plunder borne before him by his entourage;*
> *behind him, half hidden, stands* CASSANDRA.
> *The old men press towards him.*)

Come, my king, the scourge of Troy,
the true son of Atreus—
How to salute you, how to praise you
neither too high nor low, but hit
the note of praise that suits the hour?
So many prize some brave display,
they prefer some flaunt of honour
once they break the bounds.
When a man fails they share his grief,
but the pain can never cut them to the quick.
When a man succeeds they share his glory,
torturing their faces into smiles.
But the good shepherd knows his flock.
When the eyes seem to brim with love
and it is only unction,
he will know, better than we can know.
That day you marshalled the armies
all for Helen—no hiding it now—
I drew you in my mind in black;
you seemed a menace at the helm,
sending men to the grave
to bring her home, that hell on earth.
But now from the depths of trust and love
I say Well fought, well won—
the end is worth the labour!
Search, my king, and learn at last
who stayed at home and kept their faith
and who betrayed the city.

AGAMEMNON: First,
    with justice I salute my Argos and my gods,
    my accomplices who brought me home and won
    my rights from Priam's Troy—the just gods.
    No need to hear our pleas. Once for all
    they consigned their lots to the urn of blood,
    they pitched on death for men, annihilation

for the city. Hope's hand, hovering
over the urn of mercy, left it empty.
Look for the smoke—it is the city's seamark,
building even now.
                        The storms of ruin live!
Her last dying breath, rising up from the ashes
sends us gales of incense rich in gold.

For that we must thank the gods with a sacrifice
our sons will long remember. For their mad outrage
of a queen we raped their city—we were right.
The beast of Argos, foals of the wild mare,
thousands massed in armour rose on the night
the Pleiades went down, and crashing through
their walls our bloody lion lapped its fill,
gorging on the blood of kings.
                        Our thanks to the gods,
long drawn out, but it is just the prelude.

                        (CLYTAEMNESTRA *approaches with*
                        her women; they are carrying dark red
                        tapestries. AGAMEMNON *turns*
                        to the leader.)

And your concern, old man, is on my mind.
I hear you and agree, I will support you.
How rare, men with the character to praise
a friend's success without a trace of envy,
poison to the heart—it deals a double blow.
Your own losses weigh you down but then,
look at your neighbour's fortune and you weep.
Well I know. I understand society,
the fawning mirror of the proud.
                        My comrades . . .
they're shadows, I tell you, ghosts of men
who swore they'd die for me. Only Odysseus:
I dragged that man to the wars but once in harness

he was a trace-horse, he gave his all for me.
Dead or alive, no matter, I can praise him.

And now this cause involving men and gods.
We must summon the city for a trial,
found a national tribunal. Whatever's healthy,
shore it up with law and help it flourish.
Wherever something calls for drastic cures
we make our noblest effort: amputate or wield
the healing iron, burn the cancer at the roots.

Now I go to my father's house—
I give the gods my right hand, my first salute.
The ones who sent me forth have brought me home.

> (*He starts down from the chariot,
> looks at* CLYTAEMNESTRA,
> *stops, and offers up a prayer.*)

Victory, you have sped my way before,
now speed me to the last.

> (CLYTAEMNESTRA *turns from the
> king to the* CHORUS.)

CLYTAEMNESTRA: Old nobility of Argos
gathered here, I am not ashamed to tell you
how I love the man. I am older,
and the fear dies away . . . I am human.
Nothing I say was learned from others.
This is my life, my ordeal, long as the siege
he laid at Troy and more demanding.
                                        First,
when a woman sits at home and the man is gone,
the loneliness is terrible,
unconscionable . . .
and the rumours spread and fester,

a runner comes with something dreadful,
close on his heels the next and his news worse,
and they shout it out and the whole house can hear;
and wounds—if he took one wound for each report
to penetrate these walls, he's gashed like a dragnet,
more, if he had only died . . .
for each death that swelled his record, he could boast
like a triple-bodied Geryon risen from the grave,
"Three shrouds I dug from the earth, one for every body
that went down!"
                    The rumours broke like fever,
broke and then rose higher. There were times
they cut me down and eased my throat from the noose.
I wavered between the living and the dead.

                              (*Turning to* AGAMEMNON.)

                                             And so
our child is gone, not standing by our side,
the bond of our dearest pledges, mine and yours;
by all rights our child should be here . . .
Orestes. You seem startled.
You needn't be. Our loyal brother-in-arms
will take good care of him, Strophios the Phocian.
He warned from the start we court two griefs in one.
You risk all on the wars—and what if the people
rise up howling for the king, and anarchy
should dash our plans?
                    Men, it is their nature,
trampling on the fighter once he's down.
Our child is gone. That is my self-defence
and it is true.
                    For me, the tears that welled
like springs are dry. I have no tears to spare.
I'd watch till late at night, my eyes still burn,
I sobbed by the torch I lit for you alone.

(*Glancing towards the palace.*)

I never let it die . . . but in my dreams
the high thin wail of a gnat would rouse me,
piercing like a trumpet—I could see you
suffer more than all
the hours that slept with me could ever bear.

I endured it all. And now, free of grief,
I would salute that man the watchdog of the fold,
the mainroyal, saving stay of the vessel,
rooted oak that thrusts the roof sky-high,
the father's one true heir.
Land at dawn to the shipwrecked past all hope,
light of the morning burning off the night of storm,
the cold clear spring to the parched horseman—
O the ecstasy, to flee the yoke of Fate!
It is right to use the titles he deserves.
Let envy keep her distance. We have suffered
long enough.

(*Reaching towards* AGAMEMNON.)

Come to me now, my dearest,
down from the car of war, but never set the foot
that stamped out Troy on earth again, my great one.

Women, why delay? You have your orders.
Pave his way with tapestries.

(*They begin to spread the crimson
tapestries between the king and
the palace doors.*)

Quickly.
Let the red stream flow and bear him home
to the home he never hoped to see—Justice,
lead him in!
Leave all the rest to me.

The spirit within me never yields to sleep.
We will set things right, with the god's help.
We will do whatever Fate requires.

AGAMEMNON: There
is Leda's daughter, the keeper of my house.
And the speech to suit my absence, much too long.
But the praise that does us justice,
let it come from others, then we prize it.
                                    This—
you treat me like a woman. Grovelling, gaping up at me—

what am I, some barbarian peacocking out of Asia?
Never cross my path with robes and draw the lightning.
Never—only the gods deserve the pomps of honour
and the stiff brocades of fame. To walk on them . . .
I am human, and it makes my pulses stir
with dread.
                    Give me the tributes of a man
and not a god, a little earth to walk on,
not this gorgeous work.
There is no need to sound my reputation.
I have a sense of right and wrong, what's more—
heaven's proudest gift. Call no man blest
until he ends his life in peace, fulfilled.
If I can live by what I say, I have no fear.

CLYTAEMNESTRA: One thing more. Be true to your ideals and
     tell me—

AGAMEMNON: True to my ideals? Once I violate them I am
     lost.

CLYTAEMNESTRA: Would you have sworn this act to god in a
     time of terror?

AGAMEMNON: Yes, if a prophet called for a last, drastic rite.

CLYTAEMNESTRA: But Priam—can you see him if he had your success?

AGAMEMNON: Striding on the tapestries of god, I see him now.

CLYTAEMNESTRA: And *you* fear the reproach of common men?

AGAMEMNON: The voice of the people—aye, they have enormous power.

CLYTAEMNESTRA: Perhaps, but where's the glory without a little gall?

AGAMEMNON: And where's the woman in all this lust for glory?

CLYTAEMNESTRA: But the great victor—it becomes him to give way.

AGAMEMNON: Victory in this . . . war of ours, it means so much to you?

CLYTAEMNESTRA: O give way! The power is yours if you surrender
all of your own free will to me.

AGAMEMNON: Enough.
If you are so determined—

(Turning to the women, pointing to his boots.)

Let someone help me off with these at least.
Old slaves, they've stood me well.
                          Hurry,
and while I tread his splendours dyed red in the sea,
may no god watch and strike me down with envy
from on high. I feel such shame—
to tread the life of the house, a kingdom's worth
of silver in the weaving.

(*He steps down from the chariot to the
tapestries and reveals* CASSANDRA,
*dressed in the sacred regalia, the fillets,
robes, and sceptre of Apollo.*)

Done is done.
Escort this stranger in, be gentle.
Conquer with compassion. Then the gods
shine down upon you, gently. No one chooses
the yoke of slavery, not of one's free will—
and she least of all. The gift of the armies,
flower and pride of all the wealth we won,
she follows me from Troy.
And now,
since you have brought me down with your insistence,
just this once I enter my father's house,
trampling royal crimson as I go.

(*He takes his first steps and pauses.*)

CLYTAEMNESTRA: There is the sea
and who will drain it dry? Precious as silver,
inexhaustible, ever-new, it breeds the more we reap it—
tides on tides of crimson dye our robes blood-red.
Our lives are based on wealth, my king,
the gods have seen to that.
Destitution, our house has never heard the word.
I would have sworn to tread on legacies of robes,
at one command from an oracle, deplete the house—
suffer the worst to bring that dear life back!

(*Encouraged,* AGAMEMNON *strides to the entrance.*)

When the root lives on, the new leaves come back,
spreading a dense shroud of shade across the house
to thwart the Dog Star's fury. So you return
to the father's hearth, you bring us warmth in winter
like the sun—

And you are Zeus when Zeus
tramples the bitter virgin grape for new wine
and the welcome chill steals through the halls, at last
the master moves among the shadows of his house, fulfilled.

> (AGAMEMNON *goes over the threshold;*
> *the women gather up the tapestries*
> *while* CLYTAEMNESTRA *prays.*)

Zeus, Zeus, master of all fulfilment, now fulfil our prayers —
speed our rites to their fulfilment once for all!

> (*She enters the palace, the doors close,*
> *the old men huddle in terror.*)

CHORUS: Why, why does it rock me, never stops,
   this terror beating down my heart,
   this seer that sees it all —
   it beats its wings, uncalled unpaid
   thrust on the lungs
   the mercenary song beats on and on
   singing a prophet's strain —
   and I can't throw it off
   like dreams that make no sense,
   and the strength drains
   that filled the mind with trust,
   and the years drift by and the driven sand
   has buried the mooring lines
   that churned when the armoured squadrons cut for Troy . . .
   and now I believe it, I can prove he's home,
   my own clear eyes for witness —
                     Agamemnon!
   Still it's chanting, beating deep so deep in the heart
   this dirge of the Furies, oh dear god,
   not fit for the lyre, its own master
   it kills our spirit
   kills our hopes

and it's real, true, no fantasy—
stark terror whirls the brain
and the end is coming
Justice comes to birth—
I pray my fears prove false and fall
and die and never come to birth!
Even exultant health, well we know,
exceeds its limits, comes so near disease
it can breach the wall between them.

Even a man's fate, held true on course,
in a blinding flash rams some hidden reef;
but if caution only casts the pick of the cargo—
one well-balanced cast—
the house will not go down, not outright;
labouring under its wealth of grief
the ship of state rides on.

Yes, and the great green bounty of god,
sown in the furrows year by year and reaped each fall
can end the plague of famine.

But a man's life-blood
is dark and mortal.
Once it wets the earth
what song can sing it back?
Not even the master-healer
who brought the dead to life—
Zeus stopped the man before he did more harm.

Oh, if only the gods had never forged
the chain that curbs our excess,
one man's fate curbing the next man's fate,
my heart would outrace my song, I'd pour out all I feel—
but no, I choke with anguish,
mutter through the nights.

Never to ravel out a hope in time
and the brain is swarming, burning—

> (CLYTAEMNESTRA *emerges from the*
> *palace and goes to* CASSANDRA,
> *impassive in the chariot.*)

CLYTAEMNESTRA: Won't you come inside? I mean you,
    Cassandra.
Zeus in all his mercy wants you to share
some victory libations with the house.
The slaves are flocking. Come, lead them
up to the altar of the god who guards
our dearest treasures.
                    Down from the chariot,
this is no time for pride. Why even Heracles,
they say, was sold into bondage long ago,
he had to endure the bitter bread of slaves.
But if the yoke descends on you, be grateful
for a master born and reared in ancient wealth.
Those who reap a harvest past their hopes
are merciless to their slaves.
                    From us
you will receive what custom says is right.

> (CASSANDRA *remains impassive.*)

LEADER: It's *you* she is speaking to, it's all too clear.
    You're caught in the nets of doom—obey
    if you can obey, unless you cannot bear to.

CLYTAEMNESTRA: Unless she's like a swallow, possessed
    of her own barbaric song, strange, dark.
    I speak directly as I can—she must obey.

LEADER: Go with her. Make the best of it, she's right.
    Step down from the seat, obey her.

CLYTAEMNESTRA: Do it *now*—
I have no time to spend outside. Already
the victims crowd the hearth, the Navelstone,
to bless this day of joy I never hoped to see!—
our victims waiting for the fire and the knife,
and you,
if you want to taste our mystic rites, come now.
If my words can't reach you—

(*Turning to the* LEADER.)

Give her a sign,
one of her exotic handsigns.

LEADER: I think
the stranger needs an interpreter, someone clear.
She's like a wild creature, fresh caught.

CLYTAEMNESTRA: She's mad,
her evil genius murmuring in her ears.
She comes from a *city* fresh caught.
She must learn to take the cutting bridle
before she foams her spirit off in blood—
and that's the last I waste on her contempt!

(*Wheeling, re-entering the palace. The*
LEADER *turns to* CASSANDRA,
who remains transfixed.)

LEADER: Not I, I pity her. I will be gentle.
Come, poor thing. Leave the empty chariot—
Of your own free will try on the yoke of Fate.

CASSANDRA: Aieeeeee! Earth—Mother—
Curse of the Earth—Apollo Apollo!

LEADER: Why cry to Apollo?
He's not the god to call with sounds of mourning.

CASSANDRA: Aieeeeee! Earth—Mother—
Rape of the Earth—Apollo Apollo!

LEADER: Again, it's a bad omen.
She cries for the god who wants no part of grief.

> (CASSANDRA *steps from the chariot, looks slowly*
> *towards the rooftops of the palace.*)

CASSANDRA: God of the long road,
Apollo *Apollo* my destroyer—
you destroy me once, destroy me twice—

LEADER: She's about to sense her own ordeal, I think.
Slave that she is, the god lives on inside her.

CASSANDRA: God of the iron marches,
Apollo *Apollo* my destroyer—
where, where have you led me now? what house—

LEADER: The house of Atreus and his sons. Really—
don't you know? It's true, see for yourself.

CASSANDRA: No . . . the house that hates god,
an echoing womb of guilt, kinsmen
torturing kinsmen, severed heads,
slaughterhouse of heroes, soil streaming blood—

LEADER: A keen hound, this stranger.
Trailing murder, and murder she will find.

CASSANDRA: See, my witnesses—
I trust to them, to the babies
wailing, skewered on the sword,
their flesh charred, the father gorging on their parts—

LEADER: We'd heard your fame as a seer,
but no one looks for seers in Argos.

CASSANDRA: Oh no, what horror, what new plot,
new agony this?—

it's growing, massing, deep in the house,
a plot, a monstrous—*thing*
to crush the loved ones, no,
there is no cure, and rescue's far away and—

LEADER: I can't read these signs; I knew the first,
the city rings with them.

CASSANDRA: You, you godforsaken—you'd do *this?*
The lord of your bed,
you bathe him . . . his body glistens, then—
how to tell the climax?—
comes so quickly, see,
hand over hand shoots out, hauling ropes—

then lunge!

LEADER: Still lost. Her riddles, her dark words of god—
I'm groping, helpless.

CASSANDRA: No no, look *there!*—
what's that? some net flung out of hell—
No, *she* is the snare,
the bedmate, deathmate, murder's strong right arm!
Let the insatiate discord in the race
rear up and shriek "Avenge the victim—stone them dead!"

LEADER: What Fury is this? Why rouse it, lift its wailing
through the house? I hear you and lose hope.

CHORUS: Drop by drop at the heart, the gold of life ebbs out.
We are the old soldiers . . . wounds will come
with the crushing sunset of our lives.
Death is close, and quick.

CASSANDRA: Look out! *look out!*—
Ai, drag the great bull from the mate!—
a thrash of robes, she traps him—
writhing—

black horn glints, twists—

she gores him through!
And now he buckles, look, the bath swirls red—
There's stealth and murder in the cauldron, do you hear?

LEADER: I'm no judge, I've little skill with the oracles,
but even I know danger when I hear it.

CHORUS: What good are the oracles to men? Words, more words,
and the hurt comes on us, endless words
and a seer's techniques have brought us
terror and the truth.

CASSANDRA: The agony—O I am breaking!—Fate's so hard,
and the pain that floods my voice is mine alone.
Why have you brought me here, tormented as I am?
Why, unless to die with him, why else?

LEADER AND CHORUS: Mad with the rapture—god speeds you on
to the song, the deathsong,
like the nightingale that broods on sorrow,
mourns her son, her son,
her life inspired with grief for him,
she lilts and shrills, dark bird that lives for night.

CASSANDRA: The nightingale—O for a song, a fate like hers!
The gods gave her a life of ease, swathed her in wings,
no tears, no wailing. The knife waits for me.
They'll splay me on the iron's double edge.

LEADER AND CHORUS: Why?—what god hurls you on, stroke on stroke
to the long dying fall?
Why the horror clashing through your music,
terror struck to song?—
why the anguish, the wild dance?
Where do your words of god and grief begin?

CASSANDRA: Ai, the wedding, wedding of Paris,
   death to the loved ones. Oh Scamander,
   you nursed my father . . . once at your banks
   I nursed and grew, and now at the banks
   of Acheron, the stream that carries sorrow,
   it seems I'll chant my prophecies too soon.

LEADER AND CHORUS: What are you saying? Wait, it's clear,
   a child could see the truth, it wounds within,
   like a bloody fang it tears —
   I hear your destiny — breaking sobs,
   cries that stab the ears.

CASSANDRA: Oh the grief, the grief of the city
   ripped to oblivion. Oh the victims,
   the flocks my father burned at the wall,
   rich herds in flames . . . no cure for the doom
   that took the city after all, and I,
   her last ember, I go down with her.

LEADER AND CHORUS: You cannot stop, your song goes on —
   some spirit drops from the heights and treads you down
   and the brutal strain grows —
   your death-throes come and come and
   I cannot see the end!

CASSANDRA: Then off with the veils that hid the fresh young
      bride —
   we will see the truth.
   Flare up once more, my oracle! Clear and sharp
   as the wind that blows towards the rising sun,
   I can feel a deeper swell now, gathering head
   to break at last and bring the dawn of grief.
   No more riddles. I will teach you.
   Come, bear witness, run and hunt with me.
   We trail the old barbaric works of slaughter.

These roofs—look up—there is a dancing troupe
that never leaves. And they have their harmony
but it is harsh, their words are harsh, they drink
beyond the limit. Flushed on the blood of men
their spirit grows and none can turn away
their revel breeding in the veins—the Furies!
They cling to the house for life. They sing,
sing of the frenzy that began it all,
strain rising on strain, showering curses
on the man who tramples on his brother's bed.

There. Have I hit the mark or not? Am I a fraud,
a fortune-teller babbling lies from door to door?
Swear how well I know the ancient crimes
that live within this house.

LEADER: And if I did?
Would an oath bind the wounds and heal us?
But you amaze me. Bred across the sea,
your language strange, and still you sense the truth
as if you had been here.

CASSANDRA: Apollo the Prophet
introduced me to his gift.

LEADER: A *god*—and moved with love?

CASSANDRA: I was ashamed to tell this once,
but now . . .

LEADER: We spoil ourselves with scruples,
long as things go well.

CASSANDRA: He came like a wrestler,
magnificent, took me down and breathed his fire
through me and—

LEADER: You bore him a child?

CASSANDRA: I yielded,
then at the climax I recoiled—I deceived Apollo!

LEADER: But the god's skills—they seized you even then?

CASSANDRA: Even then I told my people all the grief to come.

LEADER: And Apollo's anger never touched you?—is it possible?

CASSANDRA: Once I betrayed him I could never be believed.

LEADER: We believe you. Your visions seem so true.

CASSANDRA: Aieeeeee!
—the pain, the terror! the birth-pang of the seer
who tells the truth—
                    it whirls me, oh,
the storm comes again, the crashing chords!
Look, you see them nestling at the threshold?
Young, young in the darkness like a dream,
like children really, yes, and their loved ones
brought them down . . .
                        their hands, they fill their hands
with their own flesh, they are serving it like food,
holding out their entrails . . . now it's clear,
I can see the armfuls of compassion, see the father
reach to taste and—
                    For so much suffering,
I tell you, someone plots revenge.
A lion who lacks a lion's heart,
he sprawled at home in the royal lair
and set a trap for the lord on his return.
My lord . . . I must wear his yoke, I am his slave.
The lord of the men-of-war, he obliterated Troy—
he is so blind, so lost to that detestable hellhound
who pricks her ears and fawns and her tongue draws out
her glittering words of welcome—
                                No, he cannot see
the stroke that Fury's hiding, stealth, and murder.

What outrage—the woman kills the man!

        What to call
that . . . monster of Greece, and bring my quarry down?
Viper coiling back and forth?

       Some sea-witch?—
Scylla crouched in her rocky nest—nightmare of sailors?
Raging mother of death, storming deathless war against
the ones she loves!

      And how she howled in triumph,
boundless outrage. Just as the tide of battle
broke her way, she seems to rejoice that he
is safe at home from war, saved for her.
Believe me if you will. What will it matter
if you won't? It comes when it comes,
and soon you'll see it face to face
and say the seer was all too true.
You will be moved with pity.

LEADER: Thyestes' feast,
 the children's flesh—that I know,
 and the fear shudders through me. It's true,
 real, no dark signs about it. I hear the rest
 but it throws me off the scent.

CASSANDRA: Agamemnon.
 You will see him dead.

LEADER: Peace, poor girl!
 Put those words to sleep.

CASSANDRA: No use,
 the Healer has no hand in this affair.

LEADER: Not if it's true—but god forbid it is!

CASSANDRA: You pray, and they close in to kill!

LEADER: What man prepares this, this dreadful—

CASSANDRA: Man?
  You *are* lost, to every word I've said.

LEADER: Yes—
  I don't see who can bring the evil off.

CASSANDRA: And yet I know my Greek, too well.

LEADER: So does the Delphic oracle,
  but he's hard to understand.

CASSANDRA: His *fire!*—
  sears me, sweeps me again—the torture!
  Apollo Lord of the Light, you burn,
  you blind me—
                  Agony!
              She is the lioness,
  she rears on her hind legs, she beds with the wolf
  when her lion king goes ranging—
                              she will kill me—
  Ai, the torture!
              She is mixing her drugs,
  adding a measure more of hate for me.
  She gloats as she whets the sword for him.
  He brought me home and we will pay in carnage.

  Why mock yourself with these—trappings, the rod,
  the god's wreath, his yoke around my throat?
  Before I die I'll tread you—

                    (*Ripping off her regalia, stamping it
                                into the ground.*)

                  Down, out,
  die die die!
  Now you're down. I've paid you back.
  Look for another victim—I am free at last—
  make her rich in all your curse and doom.

*(Staggering backwards as if wrestling
with a spirit tearing at her robes.)*

                                    See,
Apollo himself, his fiery hands—I feel him again,
he's stripping off my robes, the Seer's robes!
And after he looked down and saw me mocked,
even in these, his glories, mortified by friends
I loved, and they hated me, they were so blind
to their own demise—
                        I went from door to door,
I was wild with the god, I heard them call me
"Beggar! Wretch! Starve for bread in hell!"

And I endured it all, and now he will
extort me as his due. A seer for the Seer.
He bring me here to die like this,
not to serve at my father's altar. No,
the block is waiting. The cleaver steams
with my life blood, the first blood drawn
for the king's last rites.

*(Regaining her composure and
moving to the altar.)*

                        We will die,
but not without some honour from the gods.
There will come another to avenge us,
born to kill his mother, born
his father's champion. A wanderer, a fugitive
driven off his native land, he will come home
to cope the stones of hate that menace all he loves.
The gods have sworn a monumental oath: as his father lies
upon the ground he draws him home with power like a
    prayer.

Then why so pitiful, why so many tears?

I have seen my city faring as she fared,
and those who took her, judged by the gods,
faring as they fare. I must be brave.
It is my turn to die.

(Approaching the doors.)

I address you as the Gates of Death.
I pray it comes with one clear stroke,
no convulsions, the pulses ebbing out
in gentle death. I'll close my eyes and sleep.

LEADER: So much pain, poor girl, and so much truth,
you've told so much. But if you *see* it coming,
clearly—how can you go to your own death,
like a beast to the altar driven on by god,
and hold your head so high?

CASSANDRA: No escape, my friends,
not now.

LEADER: But the last hour should be savoured.

CASSANDRA: My time has come. Little to gain from flight.

LEADER: You're brave, believe me, full of gallant heart.

CASSANDRA: Only the wretched go with praise like that.

LEADER: But to go nobly lends a man some grace.

CASSANDRA: My noble father—you and your noble children.

*(She nears the threshold and recoils,
groaning in revulsion.)*

LEADER: What now? what terror flings you back?
Why? Unless some horror in the brain—

CASSANDRA: Murder.
The house breathes with murder—bloody shambles!

LEADER: No, no, only the victims at the hearth.

CASSANDRA: I know that odour. I smell the open grave.

LEADER: But the Syrian myrrh, it fills the hall with splendour, can't you sense it?

CASSANDRA: Well, I must go in now,
mourning Agamemnon's death and mine.
Enough of life!

> (*Approaching the doors again
> and crying out.*)

          Friends—I cried out,
not from fear like a bird fresh caught,
but that you will testify to *how* I died.
When the queen, woman for woman, dies for me,
and a man falls for the man who married grief.
That's all I ask, my friends. A stranger's gift
for one about to die.

LEADER: Poor creature, you
and the end you see so clearly. I pity you.

CASSANDRA: I'd like a few words more, a kind of dirge,
it is my own. I pray to the sun,
the last light I'll see,
that when the avengers cut the assassins down
they will avenge me too, a slave who died,
an easy conquest.
          Oh men, your destiny.
When all is well a shadow can overturn it.
When trouble comes a stroke of the wet sponge,
and the picture's blotted out. And that,
I think that breaks the heart.

> (*She goes through the doors.*)

CHORUS: But the lust for power never dies—
men cannot have enough.
No one will lift a hand to send it

from his door, to give it warning,
"Power, never come again!"
Take this man: the gods in glory
gave him Priam's city to plunder,
brought him home in splendour like a god.
But now if he must pay for the blood
his fathers shed, and die for the deaths
he brought to pass, and bring more death
to avenge his dying, show us one
who boasts himself born free
of the raging angel, once he hears—

(*Cries break out within the palace.*)

AGAMEMNON: Aagh!
Struck deep—the death-blow, deep—

LEADER: Quiet. Cries,
but who? Someone's stabbed—

AGAMEMNON: Aaagh, again . . .
second blow—struck home.

LEADER: The work is done,
you can feel it. The king, and the great cries—
Close ranks now, find the right way out.

(*But the old men scatter, each speaks singly.*)

CHORUS: —I say send out heralds, muster the guard,
they'll save the house.

—And I say rush in now,
catch them red-handed—butchery running on their blades.

—Right with you, do something—now or never!

—Look at them, beating the drum for insurrection.

—Yes,

we're wasting time. They rape the name of caution,
their hands will never sleep.

                        — Not a plan in sight.
Let men of action do the planning, too.

— I'm helpless. Who can raise the dead with words?

— What, drag out our lives? bow down to the tyrants,
the ruin of the house?

                        — Never, better to die
on your feet than live on your knees.

                              — Wait,
do we take the cries for signs, prophesy like seers
and give him up for dead?

                        — No more suspicions,
not another word till we have proof.

                              — Confusion
on all sides — one thing to do. See how it stands
with Agamemnon, once and for all we'll see —

> (*He rushes at the doors. They open and
> reveal a silver cauldron that holds
> the body of* AGAMEMNON *shrouded in
> bloody robes, with the body of*
> CASSANDRA *to his left and*
> CLYTAEMNESTRA *standing to his
> right, sword in hand. She strides
> towards the* CHORUS.)

CLYTAEMNESTRA: Words, endless words I've said to serve the
     moment —
now it makes me proud to tell the truth.

How else to prepare a death for deadly men
who seem to love you? How to rig the nets
of pain so high no man can overleap them?

I brooded on this trial, this ancient blood feud
year by year. At last my hour came.
Here I stand and here I struck
and here my work is done.
I did it all. I don't deny it, no.
He had no way to flee or fight his destiny—

> (*Unwinding the robes from*
> AGAMEMNON's *body, spreading them*
> *before the altar where the old men*
> *cluster around them, unified as a*
> *chorus once again.*)

our never-ending, all embracing net, I cast it
wide for the royal haul, I coil round and round
in the wealth, the robes of doom, and then I strike him
once, twice, and at each stroke he cries in agony—
he buckles at the knees and crashes here!
And when he's down I add the third, last blow,
to the Zeus who saves the dead beneath the ground
I send that third blow home in homage like a prayer.

So he goes down, and the life is bursting out of him—
great sprays of blood, and the murderous shower
wounds me, dyes me black and I, I revel
like the Earth when the spring rains come down,
the blessed gifts of god, and the new green spear
splits the sheath and rips to birth in glory!

So it stands, elders of Argos gathered here.
Rejoice if you can rejoice—I glory.
And if I'd pour upon his body the libation
it deserves, what wine could match my words?

It is right and more than right. He flooded
the vessel of our proud house with misery,
with the vintage of the curse and now
he drains the dregs. My lord is home at last.

LEADER: You appal me, you, your brazen words—
exulting over your fallen king.

CLYTAEMNESTRA: And you,
you try me like some desperate woman.
My heart is steel, well you know. Praise me,
blame me as you choose. It's all one.
Here is Agamemnon, my husband made a corpse
by this right hand—a masterpiece of Justice.
Done is done.

CHORUS: Woman!—what poison cropped from the soil
or strained from the heaving sea, what nursed you,
drove you insane? You brave the curse of Greece.
You have cut away and flung away and now
the people cast you off to exile,
broken with our hate.

CLYTAEMNESTRA: And now you sentence me?—
you banish *me* from the city, curses breathing
down my neck? But *he*—
name one charge you brought against him then.
He thought no more of it than killing a beast,
and his flocks were rich, teeming in their fleece,
but he sacrificed his own child, our daughter,
the agony I laboured into love
to charm away the savage winds of Thrace.

Didn't the law demand you banish him?—
hunt him from the land for all his guilt?
But now you witness what I've done
and you are ruthless judges.
                    Threaten away!

I'll meet you blow for blow. And if I fall
the throne is yours. If god decrees the reverse,
late as it is, old men, you'll learn your place.

CHORUS: Mad with ambition,
shrilling pride!—some Fury
crazed with the carnage rages through your brain—
I can see the flecks of blood inflame your eyes!
But vengeance comes—you'll lose your loved ones,
stroke for painful stroke.

CLYTAEMNESTRA: Then learn this, too, the power of my oaths.
By the child's Rights I brought to birth,
by Ruin, by Fury—the three gods to whom
I sacrificed this man—I swear my hopes
will never walk the halls of fear so long
as Aegisthus lights the fire on my hearth.
Loyal to me as always, no small shield
to buttress my defiance.
                    Here he lies.
He brutalized me. The darling of all
the golden girls who spread the gates of Troy.
And here his spear-prize . . . what wonders she beheld!—
the seer of Apollo shared my husband's bed,
his faithful mate who knelt at the rowing-benches,
worked by every hand.
                    They have their rewards.
He as you know. And she, the swan of the gods
who lived to sing her latest, dying song—
his lover lies beside him.
She brings a fresh, voluptuous relish to my bed!

CHORUS: Oh quickly, let me die—
no bed of labour, no, no wasting illness . . .
bear me off in the sleep that never ends,
now that he has fallen,
now that our dearest shield lies battered—

Woman made him suffer,
woman struck him down.

Helen the wild, maddening Helen,
one for the many, the thousand lives
you murdered under Troy. Now you are crowned
with this consummate wreath, the blood
that lives in memory, glistens age to age.
Once in the halls she walked and she was war,
angel of war, angel of agony, lighting men to death.

CLYTAEMNESTRA: Pray no more for death, broken
as you are. And never turn
your wrath on her, call her
the scourge of men, the one alone
who destroyed a myriad Greek lives—
Helen the grief that never heals.

CHORUS: The *spirit!*—you who tread
the house and the twinborn sons of Tantalus—
you empower the sisters, Fury's twins
whose power tears the heart!
Perched on the corpse your carrion raven
glories in her hymn,
her screaming hymn of pride.

CLYTAEMNESTRA: Now you set your judgement straight,
you summon *him!* Three generations
feed the spirit in the race.
Deep in the veins he feeds our bloodlust—
aye, before the old wound dies
it ripens in another flow of blood.

CHORUS: The great curse of the house, the spirit,
dead weight wrath—and you can praise it!
Praise the insatiate doom that feeds
relentless on our future and our sons.
Oh all through the will of Zeus,

the cause of all, the one who works it all.
What comes to birth that is not Zeus?
Our lives are pain, what part not come from god?

Oh my king, my captain,
how to salute you, how to mourn you?
What can I say with all my warmth and love?
Here in the black widow's web you lie,
gasping out your life
in a sacrilegious death, dear god,
reduced to a slave's bed,
my king of men, yoked by stealth and Fate,
by the wife's hand that thrust the two-edged sword.

CLYTAEMNESTRA: You claim the work is mine, call me
　　Agamemnon's wife—you are so wrong.
　　Fleshed in the wife of this dead man,
　　the spirit lives within me,
　　our savage ancient spirit of revenge.
　　In return for Atreus' brutal feast
　　he kills his perfect son—for every
　　murdered child, a crowning sacrifice.

CHORUS: And *you*, innocent of his murder?
　　And who could swear to that? and how? . . .
　　and still an avenger could arise,
　　bred by the fathers' crimes, and lend a hand.
　　He wades in the blood of brothers,
　　stream on mounting stream—black war erupts
　　and where he strides revenge will stride,
　　clots will mass for the young who were devoured.

Oh my king, my captain,
how to salute you, how to mourn you?
What can I say with all my warmth and love?
Here in the black widow's web you lie,
gasping out your life

in a sacrilegious death, dear god,
reduced to a slave's bed,
my king of men, yoked by stealth and Fate,
by the wife's hand that thrust the two-edged sword.

CLYTAEMNESTRA: No slave's death, I think—
no stealthier than the death he dealt
our house and the offspring of our loins,
Iphigeneia, girl of tears.
Act for act, wound for wound!
Never exult in Hades, swordsman,
here you are repaid. By the sword
you did your work and by the sword you die.

CHORUS: The mind reels—where to turn?
All plans dashed, all hope! I cannot think . . .
the roofs are toppling, I dread the drumbeat thunder
the heavy rains of blood will crush the house
the first light rains are over—
Justice bring new acts of agony, yes,
on new grindstones Fate is grinding sharp the sword of Justice.
Earth, dear Earth,
if only you'd drawn me under
long before I saw him huddled
in the beaten silver bath.
Who will bury him, lift his dirge?

                                        (*Turning to* CLYTAEMNESTRA.)
You, can you dare *this?*
To kill your lord with your own hand
then mourn his soul with tributes, terrible tributes—
do his enormous works a great dishonour.
This god-like man, this hero. Who at the grave
will sing his praises, pour the wine of tears?
Who will labour there with truth of heart?

CLYTAEMNESTRA: This is no concern of yours.
The hand that bore and cut him down

will hand him down to Mother Earth.
This house will never mourn for him.
Only our daughter Iphigeneia,
by all rights, will rush to meet him
first at the churning straits,
the ferry over tears—
she'll fling her arms around her father,
pierce him with her love.

CHORUS: Each charge meets counter-charge.
None can judge between them. Justice.
The plunderer plundered, the killer pays the price.
The truth still holds while Zeus still holds the throne:
the one who acts must suffer—
that is law. Who can tear from the veins
the bad seed, the curse? The race is welded to its ruin.

CLYTAEMNESTRA: At last you see the future and the truth!
But I will swear a pact with the spirit
born within us. I embrace his works,
cruel as they are but done at last,
if he will leave our house
in the future, bleed another line
with kinsmen murdering kinsmen.
Whatever he may ask. A few things
are all I need, once I have purged
our fury to destroy each other—
purged it from our halls.

> (AEGISTHUS *has emerged from the*
> *palace with his bodyguard and stands*
> *triumphant over the body of*
> AGAMEMNON.)

AEGISTHUS: O what a brilliant day
it is for vengeance! Now I can say once more
there are gods in heaven avenging men,
blazing down on all the crimes of earth.

Now at last I see this man brought down
in the Furies' tangling robes. It feasts my eyes—
he pays for the plot his father's hand contrived.

Atreus, this man's father, was king of Argos.
My father, Thyestes—let me make this clear—
Atreus' brother challenged him for the crown,
and Atreus drove him out of house and home
then lured him back, and home Thyestes came,
poor man, a suppliant to his own hearth,
to pray that Fate might save him.
                                   So it did.
There was no dying, no staining our native ground
with *his* blood. Thyestes was the guest,
and this man's godless father—

                    (*Pointing to* AGAMEMNON.)

the zeal of the host outstripping a brother's love,
made my father a feast that seemed a feast for gods,
a love feast of his children's flesh.
                                   He cuts
the extremities, feet and delicate hands,
into small pieces, scatters them over the dish
and serves it to Thyestes throned on high.
He picks at the flesh he cannot recognize,
the soul of innocence eating the food of ruin—
look,
                    (*Pointing to the bodies at his feet.*)

       that feeds upon the house! And then,
when he sees the monstrous thing he's done, he shrieks,
he reels back head first and vomits up that butchery,
tramples the feast—brings down the curse of Justice:
"Crash to ruin, all the race of Pleisthenes, crash down!"

So you see him, down. And I, the weaver of Justice,

plotted out the kill. Atreus drove us into exile,
my struggling father and I, a babe-in-arms,
his last son, but I became a man
and Justice brought me home. I was abroad
but I reached out and seized my man,
link by link I clamped the fatal scheme
together. Now I could die gladly, even I—
now I see this monster in the nets of Justice.

LEADER: Aegisthus, you revel in pain—you sicken me.
You say you killed the king in cold blood,
single-handed planned his pitiful death?
I say there's no escape. In the hour of judgement,
trust to this, your head will meet the people's
rocks and curses.

AEGISTHUS: You say! you slaves at the oars—
while the master on the benches cracks the whip?
You'll learn, in your late age, how much it hurts
to teach old bones their places. We have techniques—
chains and the pangs of hunger,
two effective teachers, excellent healers.
They can even cure old men of pride and gall.
Look—can't you see? The more you kick
against the pricks, the more you suffer.

LEADER: You, pathetic—
the king had just returned from battle.
You waited out the war and fouled his lair,
you planned my great commander's fall.

AEGISTHUS: Talk on—
you'll scream for every word, my little Orpheus.
We'll see if the world comes dancing to your song,
your absurd barking—snarl your breath away!
I'll make you dance, I'll bring you all to heel.

LEADER: *You* rule Argos? You who schemed his death
but cringed to cut him down with your own hand?

AEGISTHUS: The treachery was the woman's work, clearly.
I was a marked man, his enemy for ages.
But I will use his riches, stop at nothing
to civilize his people. All but the rebel:
him I'll yoke and break—
no cornfed colt, running free in the traces.
Hunger, ruthless mate of the dark torture-chamber,
trains her eyes upon him till he drops!

LEADER: Coward, why not kill the man yourself?
Why did the woman, the corruption of Greece
and the gods of Greece, have to bring him down?
Orestes—
                If he still sees the light of day,
bring him home, good Fates, home to kill
this pair at last. Our champion in slaughter!

AEGISTHUS: Bent on insolence? Well, you'll learn, quickly.
At them, men—you have your work at hand!

> (*His men draw swords; the old men*
> *take up their sticks.*)

LEADER: At them, fist at the hilt, to the last man—

AEGISTHUS: Fist at the hilt, I'm not afraid to die.

LEADER: It's death you want and death you'll have—
we'll make that word your last.

> (CLYTAEMNESTRA *moves between*
> *them, restraining* AEGISTHUS.)

CLYTAEMNESTRA: No more, my dearest,
no more grief. We have too much to reap
right here, our mighty harvest of despair.
Our lives are based on pain. No bloodshed now.

Father of Argos, turn for home before you act
and suffer for it. What we did was destiny.
If we could end the suffering, how we would rejoice.
The spirit's brutal hoof has struck our heart.
And that is what a woman has to say.
Can you accept the truth?

(CLYTAEMNESTRA *turns to leave.*)

AEGISTHUS: But these . . . mouths
that bloom in filth—spitting insults in my teeth.
You tempt your fates, you insubordinate dogs—
to hurl abuse at me, your master!

LEADER: No Greek
worth his salt would grovel at your feet.

AEGISTHUS: I—I'll stalk you all your days!

LEADER: Not if the spirit brings Orestes home.

AEGISTHUS: Exiles feed on hope—well I know.

LEADER: More,
gorge yourself to bursting—soil justice, while you can.

AEGISTHUS: I promise you, you'll pay, old fools—in good time,
too!

LEADER: Strut on your own dunghill, you cock beside your
mate.

CLYTAEMNESTRA: Let them howl—they're impotent. You and
I have power now.
We will set the house in order once for all.

(*They enter the palace; the great doors
close behind them; the old men
disband and wander off.*)

HENRY JAMES was born in New York City in 1843.
His grandfather, an Irish trader, had immigrated to
New York state in 1793 and made his fortune there.
(Grandfather James, Jacob Astor, and Stephen Van
Rensselaer were the wealthiest residents of the state in
their day.) The family fortune freed James' father to
devote himself to the study of theology and philosophy.
As an infant and a child, James was taken by his
family for extended visits to Europe. He was educated
abroad, for the most part. "I saw my parents home-
sick . . . for the ancient order," he remarked of the
family's frequent continental travels. "It's a complex
fate being an American." James studied painting and
law briefly, but gave them up to write fiction. His first
published short story appeared in the *Atlantic Monthly*
in 1865. Numerous novels, stories, plays (produced
but not successful), and volumes of criticism and travel
writing followed. After many years of residence in
England, James became a British subject in 1915, giving
up his country "without a sovereign," "without a
court," and "without a literature." He insisted, "It
takes an old civilization to set a novelist in motion," yet
wrote perceptively about Americans. James, "infinitely
curious and incorrigibly patient," died in London in
1916.

From *The Turn of the Screw and Other Short Novels.*
Publisher: New American Library, Inc., 1962.

The Beast in the Jungle

1

What determined the speech that startled him in the course of
their encounter scarcely matters, being probably but some words
spoken by himself quite without intention—spoken as they lingered and slowly moved together after their renewal of acquaintance. He had been conveyed by friends, an hour or two
before, to the house at which she was staying; the party of
visitors at the other house, of whom he was one, and thanks to
whom it was his theory, as always, that he was lost in the crowd,
had been invited over to luncheon. There had been after luncheon much dispersal, all in the interest of the original motive, a
view of Weatherend itself and the fine things, intrinsic features,
pictures, heirlooms, treasures of all the arts, that made the place
almost famous; and the great rooms were so numerous that
guests could wander at their will, hang back from the principal
group, and, in cases where they took such matters with the last
seriousness, give themselves up to mysterious appreciations and
measurements. There were persons to be observed, singly or in
couples, bending toward objects in out-of-the-way corners with
their hands on their knees and their heads nodding quite as
with the emphasis of an excited sense of smell. When they were
two they either mingled their sounds of ecstasy or melted into
silences of even deeper import, so that there were aspects of the
occasion that gave it for Marcher much the air of the "look
round," previous to a sale highly advertised, that excites or
quenches, as may be, the dream of acquisition. The dream of

147

acquisition at Weatherend would have had to be wild indeed, and John Marcher found himself, among such suggestions, disconcerted almost equally by the presence of those who knew too much and by that of those who knew nothing. The great rooms caused so much poetry and history to press upon him that he needed to wander apart to feel in a proper relation with them, though his doing so was not, as happened, like the gloating of some of his companions, to be compared to the movements of a dog sniffing a cupboard. It had an issue promptly enough in a direction that was not to have been calculated.

It led, in short, in the course of the October afternoon, to his closer meeting with May Bartram, whose face, a reminder, yet not quite a remembrance, as they sat, much separated, at a very long table, had begun merely by troubling him rather pleasantly. It affected him as the sequel of something of which he had lost the beginning. He knew it, and for the time quite welcomed it, as a continuation, but didn't know what it continued, which was an interest, or an amusement, the greater as he was also somehow aware—yet without a direct sign from her—that the young woman herself had not lost the thread. She had not lost it, but she wouldn't give it back to him, he saw, without some putting forth of his hand for it; and he not only saw that, but saw several things more, things odd enough in the light of the fact that at the moment some accident of grouping brought them face to face he was still merely fumbling with the idea that any contact between them in the past would have had no importance. If it had had no importance he scarcely knew why his actual impression of her should so seem to have so much; the answer to which, however, was that in such a life as they all appeared to be leading for the moment one could but take things as they came. He was satisfied, without in the least being able to say why, that this young lady might roughly have ranked in the house as a poor relation; satisfied also that she was not there on a brief visit, but was more or less a part of the establishment—almost a working, a remunerated part. Didn't she enjoy at periods a protection that she paid for by helping, among other services, to show the place and explain it, deal with the tiresome people, answer questions about the dates of the buildings, the styles of the furniture, the authorship of the pictures, the favorite haunts of the ghost? It wasn't that she looked as if you could have given her shillings—it was impossible to look less so. Yet when she finally drifted toward him, distinctly handsome, though ever so much older—older than when he had seen her before—it might have been as an effect of her guessing that he had, within the couple of hours, devoted more imagination to her than to all the others put together, and had thereby penetrated to a kind of truth that the others were too stupid for. She *was* there on harder terms than anyone; she was there as a consequence of things suffered, in one way and another, in the interval of years; and she remembered him very much as she was remembered—only a good deal better.

By the time they at last thus came to speech they were alone in one of the rooms—remarkable for a fine portrait over the chimney-place—out of which their friends had passed, and the charm of it was that even before they had spoken they had practically arranged with each other to stay behind for talk. The charm, happily, was in other things, too; it was partly in there being scarce a spot at Weatherend without something to stay behind for. It was in the way the autumn day looked into the high windows as it waned; in the way the red light, breaking at the close from under a low, somber sky, reached out in a long shaft and played over old wainscots, old tapestry, old gold, old color. It was most of all perhaps in the way she came to him as if, since she had been turned on to deal with the simpler sort, he might, should he choose to keep the whole thing down, just take her mild attention for a part of her general business. As soon as he heard her voice, however, the gap was filled up and the missing link supplied; the slight irony he divined in her attitude lost its advantage. He almost jumped at it to get there before her. "I met you years and years ago in Rome. I remember all about it." She confessed to disappointment—she had been so sure he didn't; and to prove how well he did he began to pour forth the particular recollections that popped up as he called for them. Her face and her voice, all at his service now, worked the miracle—the impression operating like the torch of a lamplighter who touches into flame, one by one, a long row of gas jets. Marcher flattered himself that the illumination was brilliant, yet he was really still more pleased on her showing him, with amusement, that in his haste to make everything right he had got most things rather wrong. It hadn't been at Rome—it had been at Naples; and it hadn't been seven years before—it had been more nearly ten. She hadn't been either with her uncle and aunt, but with her mother and her brother; in addition to which it was not with the Pembles that *he* had been, but with the Boyers, coming down in their company from Rome—a point on which she insisted, a little to his confusion, and as to which she had her evidence in hand. The Boyers she had known, but she didn't know the Pembles, though she had heard of them, and it was the people he was with who had made them acquainted. The incident of the thunderstorm that had raged round them with such violence as to drive them for refuge into an excavation—this incident had not occurred at the Palace of the Caesars, but at Pompeii, on an occasion when they had been present there at an important find.

He accepted her amendments, he enjoyed her corrections, though the moral of them was, she pointed out, that he *really* didn't remember the least thing about her; and he only felt it as a drawback that when all was made comfortable to the truth there didn't appear much of anything left. They lingered together still, she neglecting her office—for from the moment he was so clever she had no proper right to him—and both ne-

glecting the house, just waiting as to see if a memory or two
more wouldn't again breathe upon them. It had not taken them
many minutes, after all, to put down on the table, like the cards
of a pack, those that constituted their respective hands; only
what came out was that the pack was unfortunately not
perfect—that the past, invoked, invited, encouraged, could give
them, naturally, no more than it had. It had made them
meet—her at twenty, him at twenty-five; but nothing was so
strange, they seemed to say to each other, as that, while so
occupied, it hadn't done a little more for them. They looked at
each other as with the feeling of an occasion missed; the present
one would have been so much better if the other, in the far
distance, in the foreign land, hadn't been so stupidly meager.
There weren't, apparently, all counted, more than a dozen little
old things that had succeeded in coming to pass between them;
trivialities of youth, simplicities of freshness, stupidities of ignorance, small possible germs, but too deeply buried—too deeply
(didn't it seem?) to sprout after so many years. Marcher said to
himself that he ought to have rendered her some service—saved
her from a capsized boat in the bay, or at least recovered her
dressing bag, filched from her cab, in the streets of Naples, by
a lazzarone with a stiletto. Or it would have been nice if he
could have been taken with fever, alone, at his hotel, and she
could have come to look after him, to write to his people, to
drive him out in convalescence. *Then* they would be in possession
of the something or other that their actual show seemed to lack.
It yet somehow presented itself, this show, as too good to be
spoiled; so that they were reduced for a few minutes more to
wondering a little helplessly why—since they seemed to know
a certain number of the same people—their reunion had been
so long averted. They didn't use that name for it, but their
delay from minute to minute to join the others was a kind of
confession that they didn't quite want it to be a failure. Their
attempted supposition of reasons for their not having met but

showed how little they knew of each other. There came in fact a moment when Marcher felt a positive pang. It was vain to pretend she was an old friend, for all the communities were wanting, in spite of which it was as an old friend that he saw she would have suited him. He had new ones enough—was surrounded with them, for instance, at that hour at the other house; as a new one he probably wouldn't have so much as noticed her. He would have liked to invent something, get her to make believe with him that some passage of a romantic or critical kind *had* originally occurred. He was really almost reaching out in imagination—as against time—for something that would do, and saying to himself that if it didn't come this new incident would simply and rather awkwardly close. They would separate, and now for no second or for no third chance. They would have tried and not succeeded. Then it was, just at the turn, as he afterward made it out to himself, that, everything else failing, she herself decided to take up the case and, as it were, save the situation. He felt as soon as she spoke that she had been consciously keeping back what she said and hoping to get on without it; a scruple in her that immensely touched him when, by the end of three or four minutes more, he was able to measure it. What she brought out, at any rate, quite cleared the air and supplied the link—the link it was such a mystery he should frivolously have managed to lose.

"You know you told me something that I've never forgotten and that again and again has made me think of you since; it was that tremendously hot day when we went to Sorrento, across the bay, for the breeze. What I allude to was what you said to me, on the way back as we sat, under the awning of the boat, enjoying the cool. Have you forgotten?"

He had forgotten, and he was even more surprised than ashamed. But the great thing was that he saw it was no vulgar reminder of any "sweet" speech. The vanity of women had long memories, but she was making no claim on him of a compliment or a mistake. With another woman, a totally different one, he might have feared the recall possibly even of some imbecile "offer." So, in having to say that he had indeed forgotten, he was conscious rather of a loss than of a gain; he already saw an interest in the matter of her reference. "I try to think—but I give it up. Yet I remember the Sorrento day."

"I'm not very sure you do," May Bartram after a moment said; "and I'm not very sure I ought to want you to. It's dreadful to bring a person back, at any time, to what he was ten years before. If you've lived away from it," she smiled, "so much the better."

"Ah, if *you* haven't why should I?" he asked.

"Lived away, you mean, from what I myself was?"

"From what *I* was. I was of course an ass," Marcher went on; "but I would rather know from you just the sort of ass I was than—from the moment you have something in your mind—not know anything."

Still, however, she hesitated. "But if you've completely ceased to be that sort—?"

"Why, I can then just so all the more bear to know. Besides, perhaps I haven't."

"Perhaps. Yet if you haven't," she added, "I should suppose you would remember. Not indeed that *I* in the least connect with my impression the invidious name you use. If I had only thought you foolish," she explained, "the thing I speak of wouldn't so have remained with me. It was about yourself." She waited, as if it might come to him; but as, only meeting her eyes in wonder, he gave no sign, she burned her ships. "Has it ever happened?"

Then it was that, while he continued to stare, a light broke for him and the blood slowly came to his face, which began to burn with recognition. "Do you mean I told you—?" But he faltered, lest what came to him shouldn't be right, lest he should only give himself away.

"It was something about yourself that it was natural one shouldn't forget—that is if one remembered you at all. That's why I ask you," she smiled, "if the thing you then spoke of has ever come to pass?"

Oh, then he saw, but he was lost in wonder and found himself embarrassed. This, he also saw, made her sorry for him, as if her allusion had been a mistake. It took him but a moment, however, to feel that it had not been, much as it had been a surprise. After the first little shock of it her knowledge on the contrary began, even if rather strangely, to taste sweet to him. She was the only other person in the world then who would have it, and she had had it all these years, while the fact of his having so breathed his secret had unaccountably faded from him. No wonder they couldn't have met as if nothing had happened. "I judge," he finally said, "that I know what you mean. Only I had strangely enough lost the consciousness of having taken you so far into my confidence."

"Is it because you've taken so many others as well?"

"I've taken nobody. Not a creature since then."

"So that I'm the only person who knows?"

"The only person in the world."

"Well," she quickly replied, "I myself have never spoken. I've never, never repeated of you what you told me." She looked at him so that he perfectly believed her. Their eyes met over it in such a way that he was without a doubt. "And I never will."

She spoke with an earnestness that, as if almost excessive, put him at ease about her possible derision. Somehow the whole question was a new luxury to him—that is, from the moment she was in possession. If she didn't take the ironic view she clearly took the sympathetic, and that was what he had had, in all the long time, from no one whomsoever. What he felt was that he couldn't at present have begun to tell her and yet could profit perhaps exquisitely by the accident of having done so of old. "Please don't then. We're just right as it is."

"Oh, I am," she laughed, "if you are!" To which she added: "Then you do still feel in the same way?"

It was impossible to him not to take to himself that she was really interested, and it all kept coming as a sort of revelation. He had thought of himself so long as abominably alone, and, lo, he wasn't alone a bit. He hadn't been, it appeared, for an hour—since those moments on the Sorrento boat. It was *she* who had been, he seemed to see as he looked at her—she who had been made so by the graceless fact of his lapse of fidelity. To tell her what he had told her—what had it been but to ask something of her? something that she had given, in her charity, without his having, by a remembrance, by a return of the spirit, failing another encounter, so much as thanked her. What he had asked of her had been simply at first not to laugh at him. She had beautifully not done so for ten years, and she was not doing so now. So he had endless gratitude to make up. Only for that he must see just how he had figured to her. "What, exactly, was the account I gave—?"

"Of the way you did feel? Well, it was very simple. You said you had had from your earliest time, as the deepest thing within you, the sense of being kept for something rare and strange, possibly prodigious and terrible, that was sooner or later to happen to you, that you had in your bones the foreboding and the conviction of, and that would perhaps overwhelm you."

"Do you call that very simple?" John Marcher asked.

She thought a moment. "It was perhaps because I seemed, as you spoke, to understand it."

"You do understand it?" he eagerly asked.

Again she kept her kind eyes on him. "You still have the belief?"

"Oh!" he exclaimed helplessly. There was too much to say.

"Whatever it is to be," she clearly made out, "it hasn't yet come."

He shook his head in complete surrender now. "It hasn't yet come. Only, you know, it isn't anything I'm to *do*, to achieve in the world, to be distinguished or admired for. I'm not such an ass as *that*. It would be much better, no doubt, if I were."

"It's to be something you're merely to suffer?"

"Well, say to wait for—to have to meet, to face, to see suddenly break out in my life; possibly destroying all further consciousness, possibly annihilating me; possibly, on the other hand, only altering everything, striking at the root of my world and leaving me to the consequences, however they shape themselves."

She took this in, but the light in her eyes continued for him not to be that of mockery. "Isn't what you describe perhaps but the expectation—or, at any rate, the sense of danger, familiar to so many people—of falling in love?"

John Marcher thought. "Did you ask me that before?"

"No—I wasn't so free and easy then. But it's what strikes me now."

"Of course," he said after a moment, "it strikes you. Of course it strikes *me*. Of course what's in store for me may be no more than that. The only thing is," he went on, "that I think that if it had been that, I should by this time know."

"Do you mean because you've *been* in love?" And then as he but looked at her in silence: "You've been in love, and it hasn't meant such a cataclysm, hasn't proved the great affair?"

"Here I am, you see. It hasn't been overwhelming."

"Then it hasn't been love," said May Bartram.

"Well, I at least thought it was. I took it for that—I've taken it till now. It was agreeable, it was delightful, it was miserable," he explained. "But it wasn't strange. It wasn't what *my* affair's to be."

"You want something all to yourself—something that nobody else knows or *has* known?"

"It isn't a question of what I 'want'—God knows I don't want anything. It's only a question of the apprehension that haunts me—that I live with day by day."

He said this so lucidly and consistently that, visibly, it further imposed itself. If she had not been interested before, she would have been interested now. "Is it a sense of coming violence?"

Evidently now, too, again, he liked to talk of it. "I don't know of it as—when it does come—necessarily violent. I only think of it as natural and as of course, above all, unmistakable. I think of it simply as *the* thing. *The* thing will of itself appear natural."

"Then how will it appear strange?"

Marcher bethought himself. "It won't—to *me*."

"To whom then?"

"Well," he replied, smiling at last, "say to you."

"Oh, then, I'm to be present?"

"Why, you *are* present—since you know."

"I see." She turned it over. "But I mean at the catastrophe."

At this, for a minute, their lightness gave way to their gravity; it was as if the long look they exchanged held them together. "It will only depend on yourself—if you'll watch with me."

"Are you afraid?" she asked.

"Don't leave me *now*," he went on.

"Are you afraid?" she repeated.

"Do you think me simply out of my mind?" he pursued instead of answering. "Do I merely strike you as a harmless lunatic?"

"No," said May Bartram. "I understand you. I believe you."

"You mean you feel how my obsession—poor old thing!—may correspond to some possible reality?"

"To some possible reality."

"Then you *will* watch with me?"

She hesitated, then for the third time put her question. "Are you afraid?"

"Did I tell you I was—at Naples?"

"No, you said nothing about it."

"Then I don't know. And I should *like* to know," said John Marcher. "You'll tell me yourself whether you think so. If you'll watch with me, you'll see."

"Very good then." They had been moving by this time across the room, and at the door, before passing out, they paused as if for the full windup of their understanding. "I'll watch with you," said May Bartram.

2

The fact that she "knew"—knew and yet neither chaffed him nor betrayed him—had in a short time begun to constitute between them a sensible bond, which became more marked when, within the year that followed their afternoon at Weatherend, the opportunities for meeting multiplied. The event that thus promoted these occasions was the death of the ancient lady, her great-aunt, under whose wing, since losing her mother, she had to such an extent found shelter, and who, though but the widowed mother of the new successor to the property, had succeeded—thanks to a high tone and a high temper—in not forfeiting the supreme position at the great house. The deposition of this personage arrived but with her death, which, followed by many changes, made in particular a difference for the young woman in whom Marcher's expert attention had recognized from the first a dependent with a pride that might ache though it didn't bristle. Nothing for a long time had made him easier than the thought that the aching must have been much soothed by Miss Bartram's now finding herself able to set up a small home in London. She had acquired property, to an amount that made that luxury just possible, under her aunt's extremely complicated will, and when the whole matter began to be straightened out, which indeed took time, she let him know that the happy issue was at last in view. He had seen her again before that day, both because she had more than once accompanied the ancient lady to town and because he had paid another visit to the friends who so conveniently made of Weatherend one of the charms of their own hospitality. These friends had taken him back there; he had achieved there again with Miss Bartram some quiet detachment; and he had in London succeeded in persuading her to more than one brief absence from her aunt. They went together, on these latter occasions, to the National Gallery and the South Kensington Museum, where, among vivid reminders, they talked of Italy at large—not now attempting to recover, as at first, the taste of their youth and their ignorance. That recovery, the first day at Weatherend, had served its purpose well, had given them quite enough; so that they were, to Marcher's sense, no longer hovering about the headwaters of their stream, but had felt their boat pushed sharply off and down the current.

They were literally afloat together; for our gentleman this was marked, quite as marked as that the fortunate cause of it was just the buried treasure of her knowledge. He had with his own hands dug up this little hoard, brought to light—that is to within reach of the dim day constituted by their discretions and privacies—the object of value the hiding place of which he had, after putting it into the ground himself, so strangely, so long forgotten. The exquisite luck of having again just stumbled on the spot made him indifferent to any other question; he would doubtless have devoted more time to the odd accident of his lapse of memory if he had not been moved to devote so much to the sweetness, the comfort, as he felt, for the future, that this accident itself had helped to keep fresh. It had never entered into his plan that anyone should "know," and mainly for the reason that it was not in him to tell anyone. That would have been impossible, since nothing but the amusement of a cold world would have waited on it. Since, however, a mysterious fate had opened his mouth in youth, in spite of him, he would count that a compensation and profit by it to the utmost. That the right person *should* know tempered the asperity of his secret

more even than his shyness had permitted him to imagine; and
May Bartram was clearly right, because—well, because there she
was. Her knowledge simply settled it; he would have been sure
enough by this time had she been wrong. There was that in his
situation, no doubt, that disposed him too much to see her as
a mere confidante, taking all her light for him from the fact—
the fact only—of her interest in his predicament, from her mercy,
sympathy, seriousness, her consent not to regard him as the
funniest of the funny. Aware, in fine, that her price for him
was just in her giving him this constant sense of his being
admirably spared, he was careful to remember that she had,
after all, also a life of her own, with things that might happen
to *her*, things that in friendship one should likewise take account
of. Something fairly remarkable came to pass with him, for that
matter, in this connection—something represented by a certain
passage of his consciousness, in the suddenest way, from one
extreme to the other.

He had thought himself, so long as nobody knew, the most
disinterested person in the world, carrying his concentrated burden, his perpetual suspense, ever so quietly, holding his tongue
about it, giving others no glimpse of it nor of its effect upon
his life, asking of them no allowance and only making on his
side all those that were asked. He had disturbed nobody with
the queerness of having to know a haunted man, though he
had had moments of rather special temptation on hearing people
say that they were "unsettled." If they were as unsettled as he
was—he who had never been settled for an hour in his life—
they would know what it meant. Yet it wasn't, all the same,
for him to make them, and he listened to them civilly enough.
This was why he had such good—though possibly such rather
colorless—manners; this was why, above all, he could regard
himself, in a greedy world, as decently—as, in fact, perhaps even
a little sublimely—unselfish. Our point is accordingly that he
valued this character quite sufficiently to measure his present

danger of letting it lapse, against which he promised himself to be much on his guard. He was quite ready, nonetheless, to be selfish just a little, since, surely, no more charming occasion for it had come to him. "Just a little," in a word, was just as much as Miss Bartram, taking one day with another, would let him. He never would be in the least coercive, and he would keep well before him the lines on which consideration for her—the very highest—ought to proceed. He would thoroughly establish the heads under which her affairs, her requirements, her peculiarities—he went so far as to give them the latitude of that name—would come into their intercourse. All this naturally was a sign of how much he took the intercourse itself for granted. There was nothing more to be done about *that*. It simply existed; had sprung into being with her first penetrating question to him in the autumn light there at Weatherend. The real form it should have taken on the basis that stood out large was the form of their marrying. But the devil in this was that the very basis itself put marrying out of the question. His conviction, his apprehension, his obsession, in short, was not a condition he could invite a woman to share; and that consequence of it was precisely what was the matter with him. Something or other lay in wait for him, amid the twists and turns of the months and the years, like a crouching Beast in the Jungle. It signified little whether the crouching Beast were destined to slay him or to be slain. The definite point was the inevitable spring of the creature; and the definite lesson from that was that a man of feeling didn't cause himself to be accompanied by a lady on a tiger hunt. Such was the image under which he had ended by figuring his life.

They had at first, nonetheless, in the scattered hours spent together, made no allusion to that view of it; which was a sign he was handsomely ready to give that he didn't expect, that he in fact didn't care always to be talking about it. Such a feature in one's outlook was really like a hump on one's back. The difference it made every minute of the day existed quite independently of discussion. One discussed, of course, *like* a hunchback, for there was always, if nothing else, the hunchback face. That remained, and she was watching him; but people watched best, as a general thing, in silence, so that such would be predominantly the manner of their vigil. Yet he didn't want, at the same time, to be solemn; solemn was what he imagined he too much tended to be with other people. The thing to be, with the one person who knew, was easy and natural—to make the reference rather than be seeming to avoid it, to avoid it rather than be seeming to make it, and to keep it, in any case, familiar, facetious even, rather than pedantic and portentous. Some such consideration as the latter was doubtless in his mind, for instance, when he wrote pleasantly to Miss Bartram that perhaps the great thing he had so long felt as in the lap of the gods was no more than this circumstance, which touched him so nearly, of her acquiring a house in London. It was the first allusion they had yet again made, needing any other hitherto so little; but when she replied, after having given him the news, that she was by no means satisfied with such a trifle, as the climax to so special a suspense, she almost set him wondering if she hadn't even a larger conception of singularity for him than he had for himself. He was at all events destined to become aware little by little, as time went by, that she was all the while looking at his life, judging it, measuring it, in the light of the thing she knew, which grew to be at last, with the consecration of the years, never mentioned between them save as "the real truth" about him. That had always been his own form of reference to it, but she adopted the form so quietly that, looking back at the end of a period, he knew there was no moment at which it was traceable that she had, as he might say, got inside his condition, or exchanged the attitude of beautifully indulging for that of still more beautifully believing him.

It was always open to him to accuse her of seeing him but as the most harmless of maniacs, and this, in the long run—

since it covered so much ground—was his easiest description of their friendship. He had a screw loose for her, but she liked him in spite of it, and was practically, against the rest of the world, his kind, wise keeper, unremunerated, but fairly amused and, in the absence of other near ties, not disreputably occupied. The rest of the world of course thought him queer, but she, she only, knew how, and above all why, queer; which was precisely what enabled her to dispose the concealing veil in the right folds. She took his gaiety from him—since it had to pass with them for gaiety—as she took everything else; but she certainly so far justified by her unerring touch his finer sense of the degree to which he had ended by convincing her. *She* at least never spoke of the secret of his life except as "the real truth about you," and she had in fact a wonderful way of making it seem, as such, the secret of her own life too. That was in fine how he so constantly felt her as allowing for him; he couldn't on the whole call it anything else. He allowed for himself, but she, exactly, allowed still more; partly because, better placed for a sight of the matter, she traced his unhappy perversion through portions of its course into which he could scarce follow it. He knew how he felt, but, besides knowing that, she knew how he *looked* as well; he knew each of the things of importance he was insidiously kept from doing, but she could add up the amount they made, understand how much, with a lighter weight on his spirit, he might have done, and thereby establish how, clever as he was, he fell short. Above all she was in the secret of the difference between the forms he went through—those of his little office under government, those of caring for his modest patrimony, for his library, for his garden in the country, for the people in London whose invitations he accepted and repaid— and the detachment that reigned beneath them and that made of all behavior, all that could in the least be called behavior, a long act of dissimulation. What it had come to was that he wore a mask painted with the social simper, out of the eyeholes of which there looked eyes of an expression not in the least matching the other features. This the stupid world, even after years, had never more than half discovered. It was only May Bartram who had, and she achieved, by an art indescribable, the feat of at once—or perhaps it was only alternately—meeting the eyes from in front and mingling her own vision, as from over his shoulder, with their peep through the apertures.

So, while they grew older together, she did watch with him, and so she let this association give shape and color to her own existence. Beneath *her* forms as well detachment had learned to sit, and behavior had become for her, in the social sense, a false account of herself. There was but one account of her that would have been true all the while, and that she could give, directly, to nobody, least of all to John Marcher. Her whole attitude was a virtual statement, but the perception of that only seemed destined to take its place for him as one of the many things necessarily crowded out of his consciousness. If she had, more-over, like himself, to make sacrifices to their real truth, it was to be granted that her compensation might have affected her as more prompt and more natural. They had long periods, in this London time, during which, when they were together, a stranger might have listened to them without in the least pricking up his ears; on the other hand, the real truth was equally liable at any moment to rise to the surface, and the auditor would then have wondered indeed what they were talking about. They had from an early time made up their mind that society was, luckily, unintelligent, and the margin that this gave them had fairly become one of their commonplaces. Yet there were still moments when the situation turned almost fresh—usually under the effect of some expression drawn from herself. Her expressions doubtless repeated themselves, but her intervals were generous. "What saves us, you know, is that we answer so completely to so usual an appearance: that of the man and woman whose friendship has become such a daily habit, or almost, as to be at last indispensable.'' That, for instance, was a remark she had frequently enough had occasion to make, though she had given it at different times different developments. What we are especially concerned with is the turn it happened to take from her one afternoon when he had come to see her in honor of her birthday. This anniversary had fallen on a Sunday, at a season of thick fog and general outward gloom; but he had brought her his customary offering, having known her now long enough to have established a hundred little customs. It was one of his proofs to himself, the present he made her on her birthday, that he had not sunk into real selfishness. It was mostly nothing more than a small trinket, but it was always fine of its kind, and he was regularly careful to pay for it more than he thought he could afford. "Our habit saves you, at least, don't you see? because it makes you, after all, for the vulgar, indistinguishable from other men. What's the most inveterate mark of men in general? Why, the capacity to spend endless time with dull women—to spend it, I won't say without being bored, but without minding that they are, without being driven off at a tangent by it; which comes to the same thing. I'm your dull woman, a part of the daily bread for which you pray at church. That covers your tracks more than anything."

"And what covers yours?" asked Marcher, whom his dull woman could mostly to this extent amuse. "I see of course what you mean by your saving me, in one way and another, so far as other people are concerned—I've seen it all along. Only, what is it that saves *you*? I often think, you know, of that."

She looked as if she sometimes thought of that, too, but in rather a different way. "Where other people, you mean, are concerned?"

"Well, you're really so in with me, you know—as a sort of result of my being so in with yourself. I mean of my having such an immense regard for you, being so tremendously grateful for all you've done for me. I sometimes ask myself if it's quite fair. Fair I mean to have so involved and—since one may say it—interested you. I almost feel as if you hadn't really had time to do anything else."

"Anything else but be interested?" she asked. "Ah, what else does one ever want to be? If I've been 'watching' with you, as we long ago agreed that I was to do, watching is always in itself an absorption."

"Oh, certainly," John Marcher said, "if you hadn't had your curiosity—! Only, doesn't it sometimes come to you, as time goes on, that your curiosity is not being particularly repaid?"

May Bartram had a pause. "Do you ask that, by any chance, because you feel at all that yours isn't? I mean because you have to wait so long."

Oh, he understood what she meant. "For the thing to happen that never does happen? For the beast to jump out? No, I'm just where I was about it. It isn't a matter as to which I can *choose,* I can decide for a change. It isn't one as to which there *can* be a change. It's in the lap of the gods. One's in the hands of one's law—there one is. As to the form the law will take, the way it will operate, that's its own affair."

"Yes," Miss Bartram replied; "of course one's fate is coming, of course it *has* come, in its own form and its own way, all the while. Only, you know, the form and the way in your case were to have been—well, something so exceptional and, as one may say, so particularly *your* own."

Something in this made him look at her with suspicion. "You say 'were to *have* been,' as if in your heart you had begun to doubt."

"Oh!" she vaguely protested.

"As if you believed," he went on, "that nothing will now take place."

She shook her head slowly, but rather inscrutably. "You're far from my thought."

He continued to look at her. "What then is the matter with you?"

"Well," she said after another wait, "the matter with me is simply that I'm more sure than ever my curiosity, as you call it, will be but too well repaid."

They were frankly grave now; he had got up from his seat, had turned once more about the little drawing room to which, year after year, he brought his inevitable topic; in which he had, as he might have said, tasted their intimate community with every sauce, where every object was as familiar to him as the things of his own house and the very carpets were worn with his fitful walk very much as the desks in old countinghouses are worn by the elbows of generations of clerks. The generations of his nervous moods had been at work there, and the place was the written history of his whole middle life. Under the impression of what his friend had just said he knew himself, for some reason, more aware of these things, which made him, after a moment, stop again before her. "Is it, possibly, that you've grown afraid?"

"Afraid?" He thought, as she repeated the word, that his question had made her, a little, change color; so that, lest he should have touched on a truth, he explained very kindly. "You remember that that was what you asked *me* long ago—that first day at Weatherend."

"Oh, yes, and you told me you didn't know—that I was to see for myself. We've said little about it since, even in so long a time."

"Precisely," Marcher interposed—"quite as if it were too delicate a matter for us to make free with. Quite as if we might find, on pressure, that I *am* afraid. For then," he said, "we shouldn't, should we? quite know what to do."

She had for the time no answer to this question. "There have been days when I thought you were. Only, of course," she added, "there have been days when we have thought almost anything."

"Everything. Oh!" Marcher softly groaned as with a gasp, half-spent, at the face, more uncovered just then than it had been for a long while, of the imagination always with them. It had always had its incalculable moments of glaring out, quite as with the very eyes of the very Beast, and, used as he was to them, they could still draw from him the tribute of a sigh that rose from the depths of his being. All that they had thought, first and last, rolled over him; the past seemed to have been reduced to mere barren speculation. This in fact was what the place had just struck him as so full of—the simplification of everything but the state of suspense. That remained only by seeming to hang in the void surrounding it. Even his original fear, if fear it had been, had lost itself in the desert. "I judge, however," he continued, "that you see I'm not afraid now."

"What I see is, as I make it out, that you've achieved something almost unprecedented in the way of getting used to danger. Living with it so long and so closely, you've lost your sense of it; you know it's there, but you're indifferent, and you cease even, as of old, to have to whistle in the dark. Considering what the danger is," May Bartram wound up, "I'm bound to say that I don't think your attitude could well be surpassed."

John Marcher faintly smiled. "It's heroic?"

"Certainly—call it that."

He considered. "I *am,* then, a man of courage?"

"That's what you were to show me."

He still, however, wondered. "But doesn't the man of courage know what he's afraid of—or *not* afraid of? I don't know *that,* you see. I don't focus it. I can't name it. I only know I'm exposed."

"Yes, but exposed—how shall I say?—so directly. So intimately. That's surely enough."

"Enough to make you feel, then—as what we may call the end of our watch—that I'm not afraid?"

"You're not afraid. But it isn't," she said, "the end of our watch. That is it isn't the end of yours. You've everything still to see."

"Then why haven't *you?*" he asked. He had had, all along, today, the sense of her keeping something back, and he still had it. As this was his first impression of that, it made a kind of date. The case was the more marked as she didn't at first answer; which in turn made him go on. "You know something I don't." Then his voice, for that of a man of courage, trembled a little. "You know what's to happen." Her silence, with the face she showed, was almost a confession—it made him sure. "You know, and you're afraid to tell me. It's so bad that you're afraid I'll find out."

All this might be true, for she did look as if, unexpectedly to her, he had crossed some mystic line that she had secretly drawn round her. Yet she might, after all, not have worried; and the real upshot was that he himself, at all events, needn't. "You'll never find out."

<h1 style="text-align:center">3</h1>

It was all to have made, nonetheless, as I have said, a date; as came out in the fact that again and again, even after long intervals, other things that passed between them wore, in relation to this hour, but the character of recalls and results. Its immediate effect had been indeed rather to lighten insistence—almost to provoke a reaction; as if their topic had dropped by its own weight and as if moreover, for that matter, Marcher had been visited by one of his occasional warnings against egotism. He had kept up, he felt, and very decently on the whole, his consciousness of the importance of not being selfish, and it was true that he had never sinned in that direction without promptly enough trying to press the scales the other way. He often repaired his fault, the season permitting, by inviting his friend to accompany him to the opera; and it not infrequently thus happened that, to show he didn't wish her to have but one sort of food for her mind, he was the cause of her appearing there with him a dozen nights in the month. It even happened

that, seeing her home at such times, he occasionally went in
with her to finish, as he called it, the evening, and, the better
to make his point, sat down to the frugal but always careful
little supper that awaited his pleasure. His point was made, he
thought, by his not eternally insisting with her on himself; made
for instance, at such hours, when it befell that, her piano at
hand and each of them familiar with it, they went over passages
of the opera together. It chanced to be on one of these occasions,
however, that he reminded her of her not having answered a
certain question he had put to her during the talk that had
taken place between them on her last birthday. "What is it that
saves *you?*"—saved her, he meant, from that appearance of
variation from the usual human type. If he had practically escaped remark, as she pretended, by doing, in the most important
particular, what most men do—find the answer to life in patch-
ing up an alliance of a sort with a woman no better than
himself—how had she escaped it, and how could the alliance,
such as it was, since they must suppose it had been more or
less noticed, have failed to make her rather positively talked
about?

"I never said," May Bartram replied, "that it hadn't made
me talked about."

"Ah, well, then, you're not 'saved.' "

"It has not been a question for me. If you've had your woman,
I've had," she said, "my man."

"And you mean that makes you all right?"

She hesitated. "I don't know why it shouldn't make me—
humanly, which is what we're speaking of—as right as it makes
you."

"I see," Marcher returned. " 'Humanly,' no doubt, as showing that you're living for something. Not, that is, just for me
and my secret."

May Bartram smiled. "I don't pretend it exactly shows that
I'm not living for you. It's my intimacy with you that's in
question."

He laughed as he saw what she meant. "Yes, but since, as you say, I'm only, so far as people make out, ordinary, you're —aren't you?—no more than ordinary either. You help me to pass for a man like another. So if I *am,* as I understand you, you're not compromised. Is that it?"

She had another hesitation, but she spoke clearly enough. "That's it. It's all that concerns me—to help you to pass for a man like another."

He was careful to acknowledge the remark handsomely. "How kind, how beautiful, you are to me! How shall I ever repay you?"

She had her last grave pause, as if there might be a choice of ways. But she chose. "By going on as you are."

It was into this going on as he was that they relapsed, and really for so long a time that the day inevitably came for a further sounding of their depths. It was as if these depths, constantly bridged over by a structure that was firm enough in spite of its lightness and of its occasional oscillation in the somewhat vertiginous air, invited on occasion, in the interest of their nerves, a dropping of the plummet and a measurement of the abyss. A difference had been made moreover, once for all, by the fact that she had, all the while, not appeared to feel the need of rebutting his charge of an idea within her that she didn't dare to express, uttered just before one of the fullest of their later discussions ended. It had come up for him then that she "knew" something and that what she knew was bad—too bad to tell him. When he had spoken of it as visibly so bad that she was afraid he might find it out, her reply had left the matter too equivocal to be let alone and yet, for Marcher's special sensibility, almost too formidable again to touch. He circled about it at a distance that alternately narrowed and widened and that yet was not much affected by the consciousness in him that there was nothing she could "know," after all, any better than he did. She had no source of knowledge that he hadn't equally—except of course that she might have finer nerves. That was what women had where they were interested; they made out things, where people were concerned, that the people often couldn't have made out for themselves. Their nerves, their sensibility, their imagination, were conductors and revealers, and the beauty of May Bartram was in particular that she had given herself so to his case. He felt in these days what, oddly enough, he had never felt before, the growth of a dread of losing her by some catastrophe—some catastrophe that yet wouldn't at all be *the* catastrophe: partly because she had, almost of a sudden, begun to strike him as useful to him as never yet, and partly by reason of an appearance of uncertainty in her health, coincident and equally new. It was characteristic of the inner detachment he had hitherto so successfully cultivated and to which our whole account of him is a reference, it was characteristic that his complications, such as they were, had never yet seemed so as at this crisis to thicken about him, even to the point of making him ask himself if he were, by any chance, of a truth, within sight or sound, within touch or reach, within the immediate jurisdiction of the thing that waited.

When the day came, as come it had to, that his friend confessed to him her fear of a deep disorder in her blood, he felt somehow the shadow of a change and the chill of a shock. He immediately began to imagine aggravations and disasters, and above all to think of her peril as the direct menace for himself of personal privation. This indeed gave him one of those partial recoveries of equanimity that were agreeable to him—it showed him that what was still first in his mind was the loss she herself might suffer. "What if she should have to die before knowing, before seeing—?" It would have been brutal, in the early stages of her trouble, to put that question to her; but it had immediately sounded for him to his own concern, and the possibility was what most made him sorry for her. If she did "know," moreover, in the sense of her having had some—what should he think?—mystical, irresistible light, this would make the matter not better, but worse, inasmuch as her original adoption of his own curiosity had quite become the basis of her life. She had been living to see what would *be* to be seen, and it would be cruel to her to have to give up before the accomplishment of the vision. These reflections, as I say, refreshed his generosity; yet, make them as he might, he saw himself, with the lapse of the period, more and more disconcerted. It lapsed for him with a strange, steady sweep, and the oddest oddity was that it gave him, independently of the threat of much inconvenience, almost the only positive surprise his career, if career it could be called, had yet offered him. She kept to the house as she had never done; he had to go to her to see her—she could meet him nowhere now, though there was scarce a corner of their loved old London in which she had not in the past, at one time or another, done so; and he found her always seated by her fire in the deep, old-fashioned chair she was less and less able to leave. He had been struck one day, after an absence exceeding his usual measure, with her suddenly looking much older to him than he had ever thought of her being; then he recognized that the suddenness was all on his side—he had just been suddenly struck. She looked older because inevitably, after so many years, she *was* old, or almost; which was of course true in still greater measure of her companion. If she was old, or almost, John Marcher assuredly was, and yet it was her showing of the lesson, not his own, that brought the truth home to him. His surprises began here; when once they had begun they multiplied; they came rather with a rush: it was as if, in the oddest way in the world, they had all been kept back, sown in a thick cluster, for the late afternoon of life, the time at which, for people in general, the unexpected has died out.

One of them was that he should have caught himself—for he *had* so done—*really* wondering if the great accident would take form now as nothing more than his being condemned to see this charming woman, this admirable friend, pass away from him. He had never so unreservedly qualified her as while confronted in thought with such a possibility; in spite of which there was small doubt for him that as an answer to his long riddle the mere effacement of even so fine a feature of his situation would be an abject anticlimax. It would represent, as connected with his past attitude, a drop of dignity under the shadow of which his existence could only become the most grotesque of failures. He had been far from holding it a failure—long as he had waited for the appearance that was to make it a success. He had waited for a quite other thing, not for such a one as that. The breath of his good faith came short, however, as he recognized how long he had waited, or how long, at least, his companion had. That she, at all events, might be recorded as having waited in vain—this affected him sharply, and all the more because of his at first having done little more than amuse himself with the idea. It grew more grave as the gravity of her condition grew, and the state of mind it produced in him, which he ended by watching, himself, as if it had been some definite disfigurement of his outer person, may pass for another of his surprises. This conjoined itself still with another, the really stupefying consciousness of a question that he would have allowed to shape itself had he dared. What did everything mean—what, that is, did *she* mean, she and her vain waiting and her probable death and the soundless admonition of it all —unless that, at this time of day, it was simply, it was overwhelmingly too late? He had never, at any stage of his queer consciousness, admitted the whisper of such a correction; he had never, till within these last few months, been so false to his conviction as not to hold that what was to come to him had time, whether *he* struck himself as having it or not. That at last, at last, he certainly hadn't it, to speak of, or had it but in the scantiest measure—such, soon enough, as things went with him, became the inference with which his old obsession had to reckon: and this it was not helped to do by the more and more confirmed appearance that the great vagueness casting the long shadow in which he had lived had, to attest itself, almost no margin left. Since it was in Time that he was to have met his fate, so it was in Time that his fate was to have acted; and as he waked up to the sense of no longer being young, which was exactly the sense of being stale, just as that, in turn, was the sense of being weak, he waked up to another matter beside. It all hung together; they were subject, he and the great vagueness, to an equal and indivisible law. When the possibilities themselves had, accordingly, turned stale, when the secret of the gods had grown faint, had perhaps even quite evaporated, that, and that only, was failure. It wouldn't have been failure to be bankrupt, dishonored, pilloried, hanged; it was failure not to be anything. And so, in the dark valley into which his path had taken its unlooked-for twist, he wondered not a little as he groped. He didn't care what awful crash might overtake him, with what ignominy or what monstrosity he might yet be associated — since he wasn't, after all, too utterly old to suffer — if it would only be decently proportionate to the posture he had kept, all his life, in the promised presence of it. He had but one desire left — that he shouldn't have been "sold."

4

Then it was that one afternoon, while the spring of the year was young and new, she met, all in her own way, his frankest betrayal of these alarms. He had gone in late to see her, but evening had not settled, and she was presented to him in that long, fresh light of waning April days which affects us often with a sadness sharper than the grayest hours of autumn. The week had been warm, the spring was supposed to have begun early, and May Bartram sat, for the first time in the year, without a fire, a fact that, to Marcher's sense, gave the scene of which she formed part a smooth and ultimate look, an air of knowing, in its immaculate order and its cold, meaningless cheer, that it would never see a fire again. Her own aspect—he could scarce have said why—intensified this note. Almost as white as wax, with the marks and signs in her face as numerous and as fine as if they had been etched by a needle, with soft white draperies relieved by a faded green scarf, the delicate tone of which had been consecrated by the years, she was the picture of a serene, exquisite, but impenetrable sphinx, whose head, or indeed all whose person, might have been powdered with silver. She was a sphinx, yet with her white petals and green fronds she might have been a lily, too—only an artificial lily, wonderfully imitated and constantly kept, without dust or stain, though not exempt from a slight droop and a complexity of faint creases, under some clear glass bell. The perfection of household care, of high polish and finish, always reigned in her rooms, but they especially looked to Marcher at present as if everything had been wound up, tucked in, put away, so that she might sit with folded hands and with nothing more to do. She was "out of it," to his vision; her work was over; she communicated with him as across some gulf, or from some island of rest that she had already reached, and it made him feel strangely abandoned. Was it—or, rather wasn't it—that if for so long she had been watching with him the answer to their question had swum into her ken and taken on its name, so that her occupation was verily gone? He had as much as charged her with this in saying to her, many months before, that she even then knew something she was keeping from him. It was a point he had never since ventured to press, vaguely fearing, as he did, that it might become a difference, perhaps a disagreement, between them. He had in short, in this later time, turned nervous, which was what, in all the other years, he had never been; and the oddity was that his nervousness should have waited till he had begun to doubt, should have held off so long as he was sure. There was something, it seemed to him, that the wrong word would bring down on his head, something that would so at least put an end to his suspense. But he wanted not to speak the wrong word; that would make everything ugly. He wanted the knowledge he lacked to drop on him, if drop it could, by its own august weight. If she was to forsake him it was surely for her to take leave. This was why he didn't ask her again, directly, what she knew; but it was also why, approaching the matter from another side, he said to her in the course of his visit: "What do you regard as the very worst that, at this time of day, *can* happen to me?"

He had asked her that in the past often enough; they had, with the odd irregular rhythm of their intensities and avoidances, exchanged ideas about it and then had seen the ideas washed away by cool intervals, washed like figures traced in sea sand. It had ever been the mark of their talk that the oldest allusions in it required but a little dismissal and reaction to come out again, sounding for the hour as new. She could thus at present meet his inquiry quite freshly and patiently. "Oh, yes, I've repeatedly thought, only it always seemed to me of old that I couldn't quite make up my mind. I thought of dreadful things, between which it was difficult to choose; and so must you have done."

"Rather! I feel now as if I had scarce done anything else. I appear to myself to have spent my life in thinking of nothing *but* dreadful things. A great many of them I've at different times named to you, but there were others I couldn't name."

"They were too, too dreadful?"

"Too, too dreadful—some of them."

She looked at him a minute, and there came to him as he met it an inconsequent sense that her eyes, when one got their full clearness, were still as beautiful as they had been in youth, only beautiful with a strange, cold light—a light that somehow was a part of the effect, if it wasn't rather a part of the cause, of the pale, hard sweetness of the season and the hour. "And yet," she said at last, "there are horrors we have mentioned."

It deepened the strangeness to see her, as such a figure in such a picture, talk of "horrors," but she was to do, in a few minutes, something stranger yet—though even of this he was to take the full measure but afterward—and the note of it was already in the air. It was, for the matter of that, one of the signs that her eyes were having again such a high flicker of their prime. He had to admit, however, what she said. "Oh, yes, there were times when we did go far." He caught himself in the act, speaking as if it all were over. Well, he wished it were; and the consummation depended, for him, clearly, more and more on his companion.

But she had now a soft smile. "Oh, far—!"

It was oddly ironic. "Do you mean you're prepared to go further?"

She was frail and ancient and charming as she continued to look at him, yet it was rather as if she had lost the thread. "Do you consider that we went so far?"

"Why, I thought it the point you were just making—that we *had* looked most things in the face."

"Including each other?" She still smiled. "But you're quite right. We've had together great imaginations, often great fears; but some of them have been unspoken."

"Then the worst—we haven't faced that. I *could* face it, I believe, if I knew what you think it. I feel," he explained, "as if I had lost my power to conceive such things." And he wondered if he looked as blank as he sounded. "It's spent."

"Then why do you assume," she asked, "that mine isn't?"

"Because you've given me signs to the contrary. It isn't a question for you of conceiving, imagining, comparing. It isn't a question now of choosing." At last he came out with it. "You know something that I don't. You've showed me that before."

These last words affected her, he could see in a moment, remarkably, and she spoke with firmness. "I've shown you, my dear, nothing."

He shook his head. "You can't hide it."

"Oh, oh!" May Bartram murmured over what she couldn't hide. It was almost a smothered groan.

"You admitted it months ago, when I spoke of it to you as of something you were afraid I would find out. Your answer was that I couldn't, that I wouldn't, and I don't pretend I have. But you had something therefore in mind, and I see now that it must have been, that it still is, the possibility that, of all possibilities, has settled itself for you as the worst. This," he went on, "is why I appeal to you. I'm only afraid of ignorance now—I'm not afraid of knowledge." And then as for a while she said nothing: "What makes me sure is that I see in your face and feel here, in this air and amid these appearances, that you're out of it. You've done. You've had your experience. You leave me to my fate."

Well, she listened, motionless and white in her chair, as if she had in fact a decision to make, so that her whole manner was a virtual confession, though still with a small, fine, inner stiffness, an imperfect surrender. "It *would* be the worst," she finally let herself say. "I mean the thing that I've never said."

It hushed him a moment. "More monstrous than all the monstrosities we've named?"

"More monstrous. Isn't that what you sufficiently express," she asked, "in calling it the worst?"

Marcher thought. "Assuredly—if you mean, as I do, something that includes all the loss and all the shame that are thinkable."

"It would if it *should* happen," said May Bartram. "What we're speaking of, remember, is only my idea."

"It's your belief," Marcher returned. "That's enough for me. I feel your beliefs are right. Therefore if, having this one, you give me no more light on it, you abandon me."

"No, no!" she repeated. "I'm with you—don't you see?—still." And as if to make it more vivid to him she rose from her chair—a movement she seldom made in these days—and showed herself, all draped and all soft, in her fairness and slimness. "I haven't forsaken you."

It was really, in its effort against weakness, a generous assurance, and had the success of the impulse not, happily, been great, it would have touched him to pain more than to pleasure. But the cold charm in her eyes had spread, as she hovered before him, to all the rest of her person, so that it was, for the minute, almost like a recovery of youth. He couldn't pity her for that; he could only take her as she showed—as capable still of helping him. It was as if, at the same time, her light might at any instant go out; wherefore he must make the most of it. There passed before him with intensity the three or four things he wanted most to know; but the question that came of itself to his lips really covered the others. "Then tell me if I shall consciously suffer."

She promptly shook her head. "Never!"

It confirmed the authority he imputed to her, and it produced on him an extraordinary effect. "Well, what's better than that? Do you call that the worst?"

"You think nothing is better?" she asked.

She seemed to mean something so special that he again sharply wondered, though still with the dawn of a prospect of relief. "Why not, if one doesn't *know?*" After which, as their eyes, over his question, met in a silence, the dawn deepened and something to his purpose came, prodigiously, out of her very face. His own, as he took it in, suddenly flushed to the forehead, and he gasped with the force of a perception to which, on the instant, everything fitted. The sound of his gasp filled the air; then he became articulate. "I see—if I don't suffer!"

In her own look, however, was doubt. "You see what?"

"Why, what you mean—what you've always meant."

She again shook her head. "What I mean isn't what I've always meant. It's different."

"It's something new?"

She hesitated. "Something new. It's not what you think. I see what you think."

His divination drew breath then; only her correction might be wrong. "It isn't that I *am* a donkey?" he asked between faintness and grimness. "It isn't that it's all a mistake?"

"A mistake?" she pityingly echoed. *That* possibility, for her, he saw, would be monstrous; and if she guaranteed him the immunity from pain it would accordingly not be what she had in mind. "Oh, no," she declared; "it's nothing of that sort. You've been right."

Yet he couldn't help asking himself if she weren't, thus pressed, speaking but to save him. It seemed to him he should be most lost if his history should prove all a platitude. "Are you telling me the truth, so that I shan't have been a bigger idiot than I can bear to know? I *haven't* lived with a vain imagination, in the most besotted illusion? I haven't waited but to see the door shut in my face?"

She shook her head again. "However the case stands, *that* isn't the truth. Whatever the reality, it *is* a reality. The door isn't shut. The door's open," said May Bartram.

"Then something's to come?"

She waited once again, always with her cold, sweet eyes on him. "It's never too late." She had, with her gliding step, diminished the distance between them, and she stood nearer to him, close to him, a minute, as if still full of the unspoken. Her movement might have been for some finer emphasis of what she was at once hesitating and deciding to say. He had been standing by the chimney piece, fireless and sparely adorned, a small, perfect old French clock and two morsels of rosy Dresden constituting all its furniture; and her hand grasped the shelf while she kept him waiting, grasped it a little as for support and encouragement. She only kept him waiting, however; that is, he only waited. It had become suddenly, from her movement

and attitude, beautiful and vivid to him that she had something
more to give him; her wasted face delicately shone with it, and
it glittered, almost as with the white lustre of silver, in her
expression. She was right, incontestably, for what he saw in her
face was the truth, and strangely, without consequence, while
their talk of it as dreadful was still in the air, she appeared to
present it as inordinately soft. This, prompting bewilderment,
made him but gape the more gratefully for her revelation, so
that they continued for some minutes silent, her face shining at
him, her contact imponderably pressing, and his stare all kind,
but all expectant. The end, nonetheless, was that what he had
expected failed to sound. Something else took place instead,
which seemed to consist at first in the mere closing of her eyes.
She gave way at the same instant to a slow, fine shudder, and
though he remained staring—though he stared, in fact, but the
harder—she turned off and regained her chair. It was the end
of what she had been intending, but it left him thinking only
of that.

"Well, you don't say—?"

She had touched in her passage a bell near the chimney and
had sunk back, strangely pale. "I'm afraid I'm too ill."

"Too ill to tell me?" It sprang up sharp to him, and almost
to his lips, the fear that she would die without giving him light.
He checked himself in time from so expressing his question,
but she answered as if she had heard the words.

"Don't you know—now?"

" 'Now'—?" She had spoken as if something that had made
a difference had come up within the moment. But her maid,
quickly obedient to her bell, was already with them. "I know
nothing." And he was afterward to say to himself that he must
have spoken with odious impatience, such an impatience as to
show that, supremely disconcerted, he washed his hands of the
whole question.

"Oh!" said May Bartram.

"Are you in pain?" he asked as the woman went to her.

"No," said May Bartram.

Her maid, who had put an arm round her as if to take her to her room, fixed on him eyes that appealingly contradicted her; in spite of which, however, he showed once more his mystification. "What then has happened?"

She was once more, with her companion's help, on her feet, and, feeling withdrawal imposed on him, he had found, blankly, his hat and gloves and had reached the door. Yet he waited for her answer. "What *was* to," she said.

5

He came back the next day, but she was then unable to see him, and as it was literally the first time this had occurred in the long stretch of their acquaintance he turned away, defeated and sore, almost angry—or feeling at least that such a break in their custom was really the beginning of the end—and wandered alone with his thoughts, especially with one of them that he was unable to keep down. She was dying, and he would lose her; she was dying, and his life would end. He stopped in the park, into which he had passed, and stared before him at his recurrent doubt. Away from her the doubt pressed again; in her presence he had believed her, but as he felt his forlornness he threw himself into the explanation that, nearest at hand, had most of a miserable warmth for him and least of a cold torment. She had deceived him to save him—to put him off with something in which he should be able to rest. What could the thing that was to happen to him be, after all, but just this thing that had begun to happen? Her dying, her death, his consequent solitude—*that* was what he had figured as the Beast in the Jungle, that was what had been in the lap of the gods. He had had her word for it as he left her; for what else, on earth, could she have meant? It wasn't a thing of a monstrous order; not a fate rare and distinguished; not a stroke of fortune that overwhelmed and immortalized; it had only the stamp of the common doom. But poor Marcher, at this hour, judged the common doom sufficient. It would serve his turn, and even as the consummation of infinite waiting he would bend his pride to accept it. He sat down on a bench in the twilight. He hadn't been a fool. Something had *been*, as she had said, to come. Before he rose indeed it had quite struck him that the final fact really matched with the long avenue through which he had had to reach it. As sharing his suspense, and as giving herself all, giving her life, to bring it to an end, she had come with him every step of the way. He had lived by her aid, and to leave her behind would be cruelly, damnably to miss her. What could be more overwhelming than that?

Well, he was to know within the week, for though she kept him a while at bay, left him restless and wretched during a series of days on each of which he asked about her only again to have to turn away, she ended his trial by receiving him where she had always received him. Yet she had been brought out at some hazard into the presence of so many of the things that were, consciously, vainly, half their past, and there was scant service left in the gentleness of her mere desire, all too visible, to check his obsession and wind up his long trouble. That was clearly what she wanted; the one thing more, for her own peace, while she could still put out her hand. He was so affected by her state that, once seated by her chair, he was moved to let everything go; it was she herself therefore who brought him back, took up again, before she dismissed him, her last word of the other time. She showed how she wished to leave their affair in order. "I'm not sure you understood. You've nothing to wait for more. It *has* come."

Oh, how he looked at her! "Really?"

"Really."

"The thing that, as you said, *was* to?"

"The thing that we began in our youth to watch for."

Face to face with her once more he believed her; it was a claim to which he had so abjectly little to oppose. "You mean that it has come as a positive, definite occurrence, with a name and a date?"

"Positive. Definite. I don't know about the 'name,' but, oh, with a date!"

He found himself again too helplessly at sea. "But come in the night—come and pass me by?"

May Bartram had her strange, faint smile. "Oh, no, it hasn't passed you by!"

"But if I haven't been aware of it, and it hasn't touched me—?"

"Ah, your not being aware of it," and she seemed to hesitate an instant to deal with this—"your not being aware of it is the strangeness *in* the strangeness. It's the wonder *of* the wonder." She spoke as with the softness almost of a sick child, yet now at last, at the end of all, with the perfect straightness of a sybil. She visibly knew that she knew, and the effect on him was of something co-ordinate, in its high character, with the law that had ruled him. It was the true voice of the law; so on her lips would the law itself have sounded. "It *has* touched you," she went on. "It has done its office. It has made you all its own."

"So utterly without my knowing it?"

"So utterly without your knowing it." His hand, as he leaned to her, was on the arm of her chair, and, dimly smiling always now, she placed her own on it. "It's enough if *I* know it."

"Oh!" he confusedly sounded, as she herself of late so often had done.

"What I long ago said is true. You'll never know now, and I think you ought to be content. You've *had* it," said May Bartram.

"But had what?"

"Why, what was to have marked you out. The proof of your law. It has acted. I'm too glad," she then bravely added, "to have been able to see what it's *not*."

He continued to attach his eyes to her, and with the sense
that it was all beyond him, and that *she* was too, he would still
have sharply challenged her, had he not felt it an abuse of her
weakness to do more than take devoutly what she gave him,
take it as hushed as to a revelation. If he did speak, it was out
of the foreknowledge of his loneliness to come. "If you're glad
of what it's 'not,' it might then have been worse?"

She turned her eyes away, she looked straight before her with
which, after a moment: "Well, you know our fears."

He wondered. "It's something then we never feared?"

On this, slowly, she turned to him. "Did we ever dream,
with all our dreams, that we should sit and talk of it thus?"

He tried for a little to make out if they had; but it was as
if their dreams, numberless enough, were in solution in some
thick, cold mist, in which thought lost itself. "It might have
been that we couldn't talk?"

"Well"—she did her best for him—"not from this side. This,
you see," she said, "is the *other* side."

"I think," poor Marcher returned, "that all sides are the same
to me." Then, however, as she softly shook her head in correction: "We mightn't, as it were, have got across—?"

"To where we are—no. We're *here*"—she made her weak
emphasis.

"And much good does it do us!" was her friend's frank
comment.

"It does us the good it can. It does us the good that *it* isn't
here. It's past. It's behind," said May Bartram. "Before—" but
her voice dropped.

He had got up, not to tire her, but it was hard to combat
his yearning. She after all told him nothing but that his light
had failed—which he knew well enough without her. "Before—?" he blankly echoed.

"Before, you see, it was always to *come*. That kept it present."

"Oh, I don't care what comes now! Besides," Marcher added, "it seems to me I liked it better present, as you say, than I can like it absent with *your* absence."

"Oh, mine!"—and her pale hands made light of it.

"With the absence of everything." He had a dreadful sense of standing there before her for—so far as anything but this proved, this bottomless drop was concerned—the last time of their life. It rested on him with a weight he felt he could scarce bear, and this weight it apparently was that still pressed out what remained in him of speakable protest. "I believe you; but I can't begin to pretend I understand. *Nothing,* for me, is past; nothing *will* pass until I pass myself, which I pray my stars may be as soon as possible. Say, however," he added, "that I've eaten my cake, as you contend, to the last crumb—how can the thing I've never felt at all be the thing I was marked out to feel?"

She met him, perhaps, less directly, but she met him unperturbed. "You take your 'feelings' for granted. You were to suffer your fate. That was not necessarily to know it."

"How in the world—when what is such knowledge but suffering?"

She looked up at him a while, in silence. "No—you don't understand."

"I suffer," said John Marcher.

"Don't, don't!"

"How can I help at least *that?*"

"*Don't!*" May Bartram repeated.

She spoke it in a tone so special, in spite of her weakness, that he stared an instant—stared as if some light, hitherto hidden, had shimmered across his vision. Darkness again closed over it, but the gleam had already become for him an idea. "Because I haven't the right—?"

"Don't *know*—when you needn't," she mercifully urged. "You needn't—for we shouldn't."

"Shouldn't?" If he could but know what she meant!

"No—it's too much."

"Too much?" he still asked—but with a mystification that was the next moment, of a sudden, to give way. Her words, if they meant something, affected him in this light—the light also of her wasted face—as meaning *all,* and the sense of what knowledge had been for herself came over him with a rush which broke through into a question. "Is it of that, then, you're dying?"

She but watched him, gravely at first, as if to see, with this, where he was, and she might have seen something, or feared something, that moved her sympathy. "I would live for you still—if I could." Her eyes closed for a little, as if, withdrawn into herself, she were, for a last time, trying. "But I can't!" she said as she raised them again to take leave of him.

She couldn't indeed, as but too promptly and sharply appeared, and he had no vision of her after this that was anything but darkness and doom. They had parted forever in that strange talk; access to her chamber of pain, rigidly guarded, was almost wholly forbidden him; he was feeling now moreover, in the face of doctors, nurses, the two or three relatives attracted doubtless by the presumption of what she had to "leave," how few were the rights, as they were called in such cases, that he had to put forward, and how odd it might even seem that their intimacy shouldn't have given him more of them. The stupidest fourth cousin had more, even though she had been nothing in such a person's life. She had been a feature of features in *his,* for what else was it to have been so indispensable? Strange beyond saying were the ways of existence, baffling for him the anomaly of his lack, as he felt it to be, of producible claim. A woman might have been, as it were, everything to him, and it might yet present him in no connection that anyone appeared obliged to recognize. If this was the case in these closing weeks it was the case more sharply on the occasion of the last offices rendered, in the great gray London cemetery, to what had been mortal, to what had been precious, in his friend. The concourse at her grave was not numerous, but he saw himself treated as scarce more nearly concerned with it than if there had been a thousand others. He was in short from this moment face to face with the fact that he was to profit extraordinarily little by the interest May Bartram had taken in him. He couldn't quite have said what he expected, but he had somehow not expected this approach to a double privation. Not only had her interest failed him, but he seemed to feel himself unattended—and for a reason he couldn't sound—by the distinction, the dignity, the propriety, if nothing else, of the man markedly bereaved. It was as if, in the view of society, he had not *been* markedly bereaved, as if there still failed some sign or proof of it, and as if, nonetheless, his character could never be affirmed, nor the deficiency ever made up. There were moments, as the weeks went by, when he would have liked, by some almost aggressive act, to take his stand on the intimacy of his loss, in order that it *might* be questioned and his retort, to the relief of his spirit, so recorded; but the moments of an irritation more helpless followed fast on these, the moments during which, turning things over with a good conscience but with a bare horizon, he found himself wondering if he oughtn't to have begun, so to speak, further back.

He found himself wondering indeed at many things, and this last speculation had others to keep it company. What could he have done, after all, in her lifetime, without giving them both, as it were, away? He couldn't have made it known she was watching him, for that would have published the superstition of the Beast. This was what closed his mouth now—now that the Jungle had been threshed to vacancy and that the Beast had stolen away. It sounded too foolish and too flat; the difference for him in this particular, the extinction in his life of the element of suspense, was such in fact as to surprise him. He could scarce have said what the effect resembled; the abrupt cessation, the positive prohibition, of music perhaps, more than anything else, in some place all adjusted and all accustomed to sonority and to attention. If he could at any rate have conceived lifting the veil from his image at some moment of the past (what had he done, after all, if not lift it to *her?*) so to do this today, to talk to people at large of the jungle cleared and confide to them that he now felt it as safe, would have been not only to see them listen as to a goodwife's tale, but really to hear himself tell one. What it presently came to in truth was that poor Marcher waded through his beaten grass, where no life stirred, where no breath sounded, where no evil eye seemed to gleam from a possible lair, very much as if vaguely looking for the Beast, and still more as if missing it. He walked about in an existence that had grown strangely more spacious, and, stopping fitfully in places where the undergrowth of life struck him as closer, asked himself yearningly, wondered secretly and sorely, if it would have lurked here or there. It would have at all events *sprung;* what was at least complete was his belief in the truth itself of the assurance given him. The change from his old sense to his new was absolute and final: what was to happen *had* so absolutely and finally happened that he was as little able to know a fear for his future as to know a hope; so absent in short was any question of anything still to come. He was to live entirely with the other question, that of his unidentified past, that of his having to see his fortune impenetrably muffled and masked.

The torment of this vision became then his occupation; he couldn't perhaps have consented to live but for the possibility of guessing. She had told him, his friend, not to guess; she had forbidden him, so far as he might, to know, and she had even in a sort denied the power in him to learn: which were so many things, precisely, to deprive him of rest. It wasn't that he wanted, he argued for fairness, that anything that had happened to him should happen over again; it was only that he shouldn't, as an anticlimax, have been taken sleeping so sound as not to be able to win back by an effort of thought the lost stuff of consciousness. He declared to himself at moments that he would either win it back or have done with consciousness forever; he made this idea his one motive, in fine, made it so much his passion that none other, to compare with it, seemed ever to have touched him. The lost stuff of consciousness became thus for him as a strayed or stolen child to an unappeasable father; he hunted it up and down very much as if he were knocking at doors and inquiring of the police. This was the spirit in which, inevitably, he set himself to travel; he started on a journey that was to be as long as he could make it; it danced before him that, as the other side of the globe couldn't possibly have less to say to him, it might, by a possibility of suggestion, have more. Before he quitted London, however, he made a pilgrimage to May Bartram's grave, took his way to it through the endless avenues of the grim suburban necropolis, sought it out in the wilderness of tombs, and, though he had come but for the renewal of the act of farewell, found himself, when he had at last stood by it, beguiled into long intensities. He stood for an hour, powerless to turn away and yet powerless to penetrate the darkness of death; fixing with his eyes her inscribed name and date, beating his forehead against the fact of the secret they kept, drawing his breath, while he waited as if, in pity of him, some sense would rise from the stones. He kneeled on the stones, however, in vain; they kept what they concealed; and if the face of the tomb did become a face for him it was because her two names were like a pair of eyes that didn't know him. He gave them a last long look, but no palest light broke.

6

He stayed away, after this, for a year; he visited the depths of Asia, spending himself on scenes of romantic interest, of superlative sanctity; but what was present to him everywhere was that for a man who had known what *he* had known the world was vulgar and vain. The state of mind in which he had lived for so many years shone out to him, in reflection, as a light that colored and refined, a light beside which the glow of the East was garish, cheap, and thin. The terrible truth was that he had lost—with everything else—a distinction as well; the things he saw couldn't help being common when he had become common to look at them. He was simply now one of them himself—he was in the dust, without a peg for the sense of difference; and there were hours when, before the temples of gods and the sepulchers of kings, his spirit turned, for nobleness of association, to the barely discriminated slab in the London suburb. That had become for him, and more intensely with time and distance, his one witness of a past glory. It was all that was left to him for proof or pride, yet the past glories of pharaohs were nothing to him as he thought of it. Small wonder then that he came back to it on the morrow of his return. He was drawn there this time as irresistibly as the other, yet with a confidence, almost, that was doubtless the effect of the many months that had elapsed. He had lived, in spite of himself, into his change of feeling, and in wandering over the earth had wandered, as might be said, from the circumference to the center of his desert. He had settled to his safety and accepted perforce his extinction; figuring to himself, with some color, in the likeness of certain little old men he remembered to have seen, of whom, all meager and wizened as they might look, it was related that they had in their time fought twenty duels or been loved by ten princesses. They indeed had been wondrous for others, while he was but wondrous for himself; which, however, was exactly the cause of his haste to renew the wonder by getting back, as he might put it, into his own presence. That had quickened his steps and checked his delay. If his visit was prompt it was because he had been separated so long from the part of himself that alone he now valued.

It is accordingly not false to say that he reached his goal with a certain elation, and stood there again with a certain assurance.

The creature beneath the sod *knew* of his rare experience, so
that, strangely now, the place had lost for him its mere blankness
of expression. It met him in mildness—not, as before, in mockery; it wore for him the air of conscious greeting that we find,
after absence, in things that have closely belonged to us and
which seem to confess of themselves to the connection. The plot
of ground, the graven tablet, the tended flowers affected him
so as belonging to him that he quite felt for the hour like a
contented landlord reviewing a piece of property. Whatever had
happened—well, had happened. He had not come back this
time with the vanity of that question, his former worrying,
"What, *what?*" now practically so spent. Yet he would, nonetheless, never again so cut himself off from the spot; he would
come back to it every month, for if he did nothing else by its
aid he at least held up his head. It thus grew for him, in the
oddest way, a positive resource; he carried out his idea of pe-
riodical returns, which took their place at last among the most
inveterate of his habits. What it all amounted to, oddly enough,
was that, in his now so simplified world, this garden of death
gave him the few square feet of earth on which he could still
most live. It was as if, being nothing anywhere else for anyone,
nothing even for himself, he were just everything here, and if
not for a crowd of witnesses, or indeed for any witness but John
Marcher, then by clear right of the register that he could scan
like an open page. The open page was the tomb of his friend,
and *there* were the facts of the past, there the truth of his life,
there the backward reaches in which he could lose himself. He
did this, from time to time, with such effect that he seemed to
wander through the old years with his hand in the arm of a
companion who was, in the most extraordinary manner, his
other, his younger self; and to wander, which was more extraordinary yet, round and round a third presence—not wandering she, but stationary, still, whose eyes, turning with his
revolution, never ceased to follow him, and whose seat was his

point, so to speak, of orientation. Thus in short he settled to
live—feeding only on the sense that he once *had* lived, and
dependent on it not only for a support but for an identity.

It sufficed him, in its way, for months, and the year elapsed;
it would doubtless even have carried him further but for an
accident, superficially slight, which moved him, in a quite other
direction, with a force beyond any of his impressions of Egypt
or of India. It was a thing of the merest chance—the turn, as
he afterward felt, of a hair, though he was indeed to live to
believe that if light hadn't come to him in this particular fashion
it would still have come in another. He was to live to believe
this, I say, though he was not to live, I may not less definitely
mention, to do much else. We allow him at any rate the benefit
of the conviction, struggling up for him at the end, that, whatever might have happened or not happened, he would have
come round of himself to the light. The incident of an autumn
day had put the match to the train laid from of old by his
misery. With the light before him he knew that even of late
his ache had only been smothered. It was strangely drugged,
but it throbbed; at the touch it began to bleed. And the touch,
in the event, was the face of a fellow mortal. This face, one gray
afternoon when the leaves were thick in the alleys, looked into
Marcher's own, at the cemetery, with an expression like the cut
of a blade. He felt it, that is, so deep down that he winced at
the steady thrust. The person who so mutely assaulted him was
a figure he had noticed, on reaching his own goal, absorbed by
a grave a short distance away, a grave apparently fresh, so that
the emotion of the visitor would probably match it for frankness.
This fact alone forbade further attention, though during the
time he stayed he remained vaguely conscious of his neighbor,
a middle-aged man apparently, in mourning, whose bowed back,
among the clustered monuments and mortuary yews, was constantly presented. Marcher's theory that these were elements in
contact with which he himself revived, had suffered, on this

occasion, it may be granted, a sensible though inscrutable check. The autumn day was dire for him as none had recently been, and he rested with a heaviness he had not yet known on the low stone table that bore May Bartram's name. He rested without power to move, as if some spring in him, some spell vouchsafed, had suddenly been broken forever. If he could have done that moment as he wanted he would simply have stretched himself on the slab that was ready to take him, treating it as a place prepared to receive his last sleep. What in all the wide world had he now to keep awake for? He stared before him with the question, and it was then that, as one of the cemetery walks passed near him, he caught the shock of the face.

His neighbor at the other grave had withdrawn, as he himself, with force in him to move, would have done by now, and was advancing along the path on his way to one of the gates. This brought him near, and his pace was slow, so that—and all the more as there was a kind of hunger in his look—the two men were for a minute directly confronted. Marcher felt him on the spot as one of the deeply stricken—a perception so sharp that nothing else in the picture lived for it, neither his dress, his age, nor his presumable character and class; nothing lived but the deep ravage of the features that he showed. He *showed* them— that was the point; he was moved, as he passed, by some impulse that was either a signal for sympathy or, more possibly, a challenge to another sorrow. He might already have been aware of our friend, might, at some previous hour, have noticed in him the smooth habit of the scene, with which the state of his own senses so scantily consorted, and might thereby have been stirred as by a kind of overt discord. What Marcher was at all events conscious of was, in the first place, that the image of scarred passion presented to him was conscious, too—of something that profaned the air; and, in the second, that, roused, startled, shocked, he was yet the next moment looking after it, as it went, with envy. The most extraordinary thing that had happened to him—though he had given that name to other matters as well—took place, after his immediate vague stare, as a consequence of this impression. The stranger passed, but the raw glare of his grief remained, making our friend wonder in pity what wrong, what wound it expressed, what injury not to be healed. What had the man *had* to make him, by the loss of it, so bleed and yet live?

Something—and this reached him with a pang—that *he*, John Marcher, hadn't; the proof of which was precisely John Marcher's arid end. No passion had ever touched him, for this was what passion meant; he had survived and maundered and pined, but where had been *his* deep ravage? The extraordinary thing we speak of was the sudden rush of the result of this question. The sight that had just met his eyes named to him, as in letters of quick flame, something he had utterly, insanely missed, and what he had missed made these things a train of fire, made them mark themselves in an anguish of inward throbs. He had seen *outside* of his life, not learned it within, the way a woman was mourned when she had been loved for herself; such was the force of his conviction of the meaning of the stranger's face, which still flared for him like a smoky torch. It had not come to him, the knowledge, on the wings of experience; it had brushed him, jostled him, upset him, with the disrespect of chance, the insolence of an accident. Now that the illumination had begun, however, it blazed to the zenith, and what he presently stood there gazing at was the sounded void of his life. He gazed, he drew breath, in pain; he turned in his dismay, and, turning, he had before him in sharper incision than ever the open page of his story. The name on the table smote him as the passage of his neighbor had done, and what it said to him, full in the face, was that *she* was what he had missed. This was the awful thought, the answer to all the past, the vision at the dread clearness of which he turned as cold as the stone beneath him. Everything fell together, confessed, explained, overwhelmed; leaving him most of all stupefied at the blindness he had cherished. The fate he had been marked for he had met with a vengeance—he had emptied the cup to the lees; he had been the man of his time, *the* man, to whom nothing on earth was to have happened. That was the rare stroke—that was his visitation. So he saw it, as we say, in pale horror, while the pieces fitted and fitted. So *she* had seen it, while he didn't, and so she served at this hour to drive the truth home. It was the truth, vivid and monstrous, that all the while he had waited the wait was itself his portion. This the companion of his vigil had at a given moment perceived, and she had then offered him the chance to baffle his doom. One's doom, however, was never baffled, and on the day she had told him that his own had come down she had seen him but stupidly stare at the escape she offered him.

The escape would have been to love her; then, *then* he would have lived. *She* had lived—who could say now with what passion?—since she had loved him for himself; whereas he had never thought of her (ah, how it hugely glared at him!) but in the chill of his egotism and the light of her use. Her spoken words came back to him, and the chain stretched and stretched. The Beast had lurked indeed, and the Beast, at its hour, had sprung; it had sprung in the twilight of the cold April when, pale, ill, wasted, but all beautiful, and perhaps even then recoverable, she had risen from her chair to stand before him and let him imaginably guess. It had sprung as he didn't guess; it had sprung as she hopelessly turned from him, and the mark, by the time he left her, had fallen where it *was* to fall. He had justified his fear and achieved his fate; he had failed, with the last exactitude, of all he was to fail of; and a moan now rose to his lips as he remembered she had prayed he mightn't know. This horror of waking—*this* was knowledge, knowledge under the breath of which the very tears in his eyes seemed to freeze. Through them, nonetheless, he tried to fix it and hold it; he kept it there before him so that he might feel the pain. That at least, belated and bitter, had something of the taste of life. But the bitterness suddenly sickened him, and it was as if, horribly, he saw, in the truth, in the cruelty of his image, what had been appointed and done. He saw the Jungle of his life and saw the lurking Beast; then, while he looked, perceived it, as by a stir of the air, rise, huge and hideous, for the leap that was to settle him. His eyes darkened—it was close; and, instinctively turning, in his hallucination, to avoid it, he flung himself, on his face, on the tomb.

NICCOLO MACHIAVELLI was born in Florence, Italy, in 1469 to a distinguished and once wealthy family. The details of his early life are uncertain, but when Machiavelli was twenty-nine, he was appointed to an important position in the chancellery of the Florentine republic. Machiavelli became a valued civil servant and a diplomat involved with the government of Florence and the Tuscan empire. He was directly concerned, also, with the relations between Florence and other European powers. The years of his life were turbulent ones for the many small, constantly warring Italian states and for the foreign nations—France, Spain, and Germany— interested in gaining control over them. When the leader of the Florentine republic was banished by a Spanish papal army in 1512 and the Medici rulers were restored to power, Machiavelli lost his prestige, his job, and his political clout. First he was accused of conspiracy and tortured; then Machiavelli retired to the country and wrote. *The Prince* (1513) and some other works were composed in the hope of regaining his chancellery appointment, but reinstatement remained a wish. Machiavelli died in 1527 in Florence.

A selection from *The Prince, A Bilingual Edition,* translated and edited by Mark Musa. Publisher: St. Martin's Press, Inc., 1964. Chapters 3, 6, 8, 9, 15–19, 21, and 23.

The Prince

On Mixed Principalities

It is with the new principality[1] that difficulties arise. First, if it is not altogether new but rather an addition (so that the two together may be called mixed), its problems originate mainly from one inherent difficulty that exists in all new principalities: men willingly change masters, believing to better themselves; and this belief makes them take up arms against their master, but in this they deceive themselves, because eventually with experience they see that things have gotten worse. Problems stem from another natural and common necessity, which is that a prince will always offend his new subjects both with his soldiers and with the many other abuses that accompany his new conquest; as a result you have made enemies of all those you offended while occupying that principality, and you are not able to keep those friends that helped to put you in power, since you are incapable of satisfying them in the way they had expected, nor can you use drastic measures against them, for you are obligated to them; because, though one may have the strongest of armies, one always needs the backing of the inhabitants to take over a province. For these reasons Louis XII, king of France, quickly occupied Milan and quickly lost it; and the first

---

[1] [Machiavelli has earlier defined new principalities as states in which a prince rules not by inheritance but by having taken over the government himself or having conquered the state and added it to his other dominions.]

time Ludovico's troops alone were enough to take it from him, because those people who had opened the gates to him, finding themselves deceived in their beliefs and in that future good they had anticipated, could not put up with the affronts of the new prince.

It is certainly true that once those lands that have rebelled are conquered a second time, they are lost with more difficulty; for the master, taking advantage of the rebellion, is less hesitant in insuring his position by punishing offenders, exposing suspects, and strengthening himself in weak spots. So that, if in order for France to lose Milan the first time, only the person of a Duke Ludovico threatening the borders was enough, in order to cause her to lose it a second time, the whole world had to oppose her and wipe out her armies or drive them out of Italy; and this came about for the reasons mentioned above. In spite of this, both the first and second time it was taken away from her.

The general reasons for the first loss have been discussed; there remains to mention those for the second, and to see what solutions there were for the king of France, and those available to one who might be in the same situation, so that he might be able to keep a better hold over his conquest than did France. I say, then, that those dominions that, once conquered, are annexed to the long-established state of the conqueror are either of the same province and language or they are not. When they are, it is very easy to hold on to them, especially so when they are not accustomed to freedom; and to possess them securely one need only to have extinguished the family line of the former prince in power, because as far as other things are concerned, so long as their old way of life is preserved and there is no difference in customs, men will live peacefully: as we have seen in the case of Burgundy, Brittany, Gascony and Normandy, which have been joined to France for so long a time; and although there is a certain dissimilarity in the language, nonetheless the customs are the same, and they have been able to get along together easily. And whoever takes possession of such lands and desires to hold on to them should keep two things in mind: the first, that the family line of the old prince must be extinguished; the other, that neither the laws nor the taxes be changed; as a result in a very short time they will become, together with the old principality, as one body.

But when dominions are acquired in a province that differs in language, customs and laws, it is here that difficulties arise; and in this case one needs a great deal of good fortune and much zeal to hold on to them. And one of the best and most effective solutions would be for the person who has taken possession to go there to live. This move would make that possession more secure and more permanent: just as the Turk did with Greece; for in spite of all the other precautions he took to hold on to that dominion, if he had not gone there to live, it would have been impossible for him to hold it. Because, living right there, one sees trouble from its start and can take care of it immediately; not living there, one hears about it when it has greatly increased and there is no longer any remedy. Besides this, the province would not be plundered by one's officials; the subjects would be satisfied in having direct recourse to the prince; this way, desiring to be good citizens, they have more reason to love him, and, desiring to be otherwise, more reason to fear him. Whatever outside force might want to invade that dominion would be more hesitant in undertaking it; so that the prince, living right there, can only with the greatest difficulty lose it.

The other and even better solution is to send colonies into one or two places that will serve as connecting links to your state; for it is imperative that either the prince do this or maintain a large cavalry and infantry. Colonies do not cost much, and at little or no cost on the part of the prince, he can send and maintain them; and he only hurts those whose fields and houses are taken and given to the new inhabitants, who are a very small part of that state; and those that he hurts, scattered and poor as they are, can never be a threat to him, and all the others remain on the one hand unharmed (and therefore they should be quiet), and on the other fearful of making a mistake, lest what happened to those who had been dispossessed might happen to them. I conclude that these colonies are not expensive, they are more faithful, and they give less trouble; and those who are hurt can pose no threat, since they are poor and scattered, as I have said. About this it should be noted that men must be either pampered or done away with, because they will revenge themselves for a slight hurt, but for serious ones they cannot; so that any hurt done to a man should be the kind that leaves no fear of revenge. But by maintaining, instead of colonies, an army of men, one spends much more, for all the revenues of that state will be used up in guarding it, so that the gain turns into a loss; and far greater injury is done, because the whole state is hurt by the prince's army changing quarters from one place to another; everyone feels this inconvenience, and everyone becomes an enemy; and they are enemies that can do harm, for they remain, though conquered, in their own home. In every respect, therefore, this kind of defense is as useless as the other kind, the founding of colonies, is useful.

Furthermore, whoever is in a province that differs from his own in the ways just mentioned should make himself the head and protector of his less powerful neighbors and do all possible to weaken those who are strong, and he should be on his guard that, for whatever reason, no foreigner as powerful as himself enter there. And it will always happen that the foreigner will be brought in by those who are dissatisfied because of either excessive ambition or fear: as was seen once when the Aetolians brought the Romans into Greece; and every other province the Romans entered, they were brought in by the inhabitants. What happens is that as soon as a powerful foreigner enters a province, all those who are less powerful cling to him, impelled by their envy of the one who has ruled over them; so that, in regard to these weaker powers, he has no difficulty whatever in winning them over, for all of them will immediately and gladly blend into the state he has taken over. He has only to beware that they do not get hold of too much power and authority; and he can very easily, with his strength and their backing, put down those who are powerful, remaining, in everything, arbiter of that province. And whoever does not follow carefully this practice will soon lose what he has acquired; and while he holds it he will find it full of infinite difficulties and troubles.

In the provinces they took over, the Romans carefully followed these practices; they sent in colonies, kept the less powerful in check without increasing their strength, put down the powerful, and did not allow powerful foreigners to gain prestige there. And I shall let the province of Greece serve as my only example: the Romans kept a friendly check on the Achaeans and the Aetolians; the kingdom of Macedonia was put down; Antiochus was driven out; nor were they ever induced by the merits of the Achaeans or the Aetolians to allow them any gain of territory; nor did the coaxing of Philip ever convince them to make him a friend without first putting him down; nor could the power of Antiochus make them consent to his holding any authority at all in that province. For the Romans did in these cases what all wise princes should do: they not only have to watch out for troubles at hand, but also for those ahead, and endeavor diligently to avoid them; for once trouble is foreseen, it can be easily remedied; however, if you wait for it to become evident, the medicine will be too late, for the disease will have become incurable. And what doctors say about a disease will apply here: that at the beginning the disease is easy to cure but difficult to recognize; but, as time goes on, not having at the start been recognized or treated, it becomes easy to recognize and difficult to cure. The same thing happens in affairs of state; for recognizing from afar (which is the gift of only a prudent ruler) the disorders that are taking form within, one can soon heal them; but when, not having been recognized, they are left to grow so that everyone recognizes them, there is no longer a remedy.

For this reason the Romans, sensing trouble from afar, always found a remedy; and they never allowed it to develop in order to avoid going to war, because they knew that war cannot be avoided but only postponed to the advantage of others; therefore, they decided to go to war with Philip and Antiochus in Greece in order not to have to fight them in Italy; and they could have, for the time being, avoided both the one and the other, but they did not want to. Nor did they ever like what is constantly on the lips of our sages today, to enjoy the benefits of the present time, but rather they enjoyed the benefits of their ingenuity and prudence; for time brings out everything, and it can bring with it the good as well as the bad and the bad as well as the good.

But let us return to France and see if she did any of the things just mentioned; and I shall talk about Louis, not Charles, and so about him whose development has been observed better because he held possession in Italy for a longer time: and you will see that he did the opposite of those things that must be done in order to maintain one's rule in a foreign country.

King Louis was brought into Italy by the ambition of the Venetians, who by his coming wanted to win for themselves half of Lombardy. I do not wish to condemn the enterprise undertaken by the king; for desiring to get a first foothold in Italy and having no friends in this country—furthermore, because of the actions of King Charles all the gates were closed to him—he was forced to make whatever friends he could; and this worthwhile enterprise would have been successful if he had not made any mistakes in his other maneuvers. The king, then, having taken over Lombardy, immediately won back that prestige which Charles had taken from him: Genoa surrendered; the Florentines became his friends; the marquis of Mantua, the duke of Ferrara, the Bentivogli, the Countess of Forlì, lords of Faenza, of Pesaro, of Rimini, of Camerino, of Piombino, the people of Lucca, Pisa, and Siena, all came to him in friendship. And then the Venetians were able to see the imprudence of the enterprise they had undertaken; in order to acquire a few cities in Lombardy, they made the king master of a third of Italy.

Now think with what little difficulty the King could have maintained his prestige in Italy if he had observed the rules mentioned above and kept safe and secure all those friends of his, who, there being a large number of them, both weak and fearful, some of the Church, others of the Venetians, were bound by necessity to stay by his side; and by means of them he could easily have protected himself from those who remained great powers. But no sooner was he in Milan than he did the opposite, helping Pope Alexander to occupy the Romagna. Nor did he realize that with this move he weakened himself, stripping himself of his friends and of those who had thrown themselves into his lap, and made the Church stronger by adding so much temporal power to the spiritual power that gives it so much authority. And having made one mistake, he was forced to continue making others; so that in order to put an end to the ambition of Alexander, that he might not become master of Tuscany, he was forced to come to Italy. He was not satisfied to have made the Church powerful and to have stripped himself of his friends, for desiring the kingdom of Naples, he divided it with the king of Spain; and, whereas at one time he was arbiter of Italy, he brought in a companion so that the ambitious and unhappy citizens of that province might have another to appeal to; and where he could have left a tributary king in charge of that kingdom, he cast him out, putting one there who could, in turn, throw him out.

The desire to acquire is truly a very natural and common thing; and whenever men who can, do so, they are praised and not condemned; but when they cannot and want to do so just the same, herein lies the mistake and the condemnation. If France, then, with her own forces could have attacked Naples, she should have done so; if she could not, she should not have divided it. And if the division of Lombardy with the Venetians deserved to be excused in that it allowed Louis to get a foothold in Italy, the other division deserves to be condemned, for there is no excuse of necessity.

Louis, therefore, had made these five mistakes: he had extinguished the weaker powers; increased the power in Italy of a powerful force; brought into that country a most powerful foreigner; did not come to live in Italy; did not bring in colonies. Nevertheless, these mistakes, if he had lived, might not have hurt him if he had not made a sixth: that of depriving the Venetians of their power; for if he had not made the Church powerful nor brought Spain into Italy, it would have been most sensible and necessary to put down the Venetians; but having taken those first steps, he never should have allowed them to be ruined; for while they remained powerful they always would have kept the others from attempting to take Lombardy, in part because the Venetians would not have allowed this unless they themselves were to become the rulers of Lombardy, and in part because the others would not have wanted to take it from France in order to give it to them, and they would not have had the courage to provoke both of them. And if someone were to say: King Louis surrendered Romagna to Alexander and the kingdom of Naples to Spain in order to avoid going to war, I would answer with the arguments expressed above: that one must never permit disorder to develop in order to avoid going to war, because one does not avoid war but rather defers it to his own disadvantage. And if some others were to cite the promise that the king had made the pope to undertake that enterprise in exchange for the annulment of his marriage and the Cardinal's hat of Rouen, I would answer with what I shall say further on concerning the promise of princes and how it should be observed.

And so, King Louis lost Lombardy by not having observed any of the precepts observed by others who have taken over provinces and wished to hold on to them. Nor is this in any way a miracle, but very natural and reasonable. . . . And through experience we have seen that the power of the Church and of Spain in Italy has been brought about by France, and that her ruin has been caused by them. From this we extract a general rule which never or rarely fails: that whoever is the cause of another's coming into power ruins himself, because that power is brought about by him either through cleverness or force; and both the one and the other of these two are suspect to the one who has come into power.

*   *   *

On New Principalities Acquired by Means of One's Own Arms and Ingenuity

No one should be surprised if, in my discussion of principalities that are completely new in respect to their prince and composition, I make use of the most outstanding examples; since men almost always walk the path made by others and conduct their affairs through imitation, although they are not altogether able to stay on the path of others nor arrive at the ingenuity of those they imitate, a prudent man should always take the path trodden by great men and imitate those who have been most outstanding; so that, if his own ingenuity does not come up to theirs, at least it will have the smell of it; and he should act like those prudent archers, who, when the target they are aiming at seems too far off, aware of the capacity of their bow, set their sight a good deal higher than the desired target, not to reach such a height with their arrow but rather to be able, with the help of aiming high, to reach their target.

I say, then, that in entirely new principalities, where there is a new prince, one will find more or less difficulty in maintaining them according to the greater or lesser ingenuity of the one who acquires them. And since this event of transition from ordinary citizen to prince presupposes either ingenuity or fortune, it would seem that either the one or the other of these two things should, to some extent, mitigate many of the difficulties; nevertheless, he who has trusted less in fortune has held on to his position best. Things are made easier also by the fact that the prince, having no other state to rule, is forced to come and live there in person. But to come to those who, by means of their own ingenuity and not by fortune, have become princes, let me say that the most outstanding are Moses, Cyrus, Romulus, Theseus and the like. And although one should not discuss Moses, for he was a mere executor of the things God had commanded, he still should be admired if only for that grace which made him worthy of speaking with God. But let us consider Cyrus and the others who acquired or founded kingdoms: you will find them all admirable; and if their particular actions and institutions are examined, they do not appear to differ from those of Moses, who had so great a preceptor. And examining their actions and lives, we see that from fortune they received nothing but the occasion; which in turn offered them the material they could then shape into whatever form they pleased; and without that occasion their very ingenuity would have been extinguished, and without that ingenuity the occasion would have come in vain.

Therefore it was necessary for Moses to find the people of Israel in Egypt slaves and oppressed by the Egyptians, so that they, in order to escape this servitude, might be disposed to following him. It was imperative that Romulus not remain in Alba and for him to be exposed at birth, so that he might become king of Rome and founder of that nation. It was requisite that Cyrus find the Persians dissatisfied with the empire of the Medes and the Medes soft and effeminate through years of peace. Theseus could not have displayed his ingenuity if he had not found the Athenians dispersed. These occasions, then, made these men successful, and their outstanding ingenuity made that occasion known to them; whereby their nations were made renowned and they became prosperous.

Those who, like these men, become princes by means of ingenuity, acquire their principality with difficulty, but hold on to it with ease; and the difficulties they encounter in acquiring the principality arise, in part, from the new institutions and methods they are forced to introduce in order to establish their state and their security. And it should be kept in mind that there is nothing more difficult to carry out nor more doubtful of success nor more dangerous to manage than to introduce a new system of things; for the introducer has as his enemies all those who benefit from the old system, and lukewarm defenders in all those who would benefit from the new system. This luke-warmness originates partly from fear of their adversaries, who have the law on their side, and partly from the incredulousness of men in general, who do not really believe something new unless they actually have had experience with it; therefore it happens that, whenever those who are enemies have the occasion to attack, they do so with the fervor of partisans, and those others come to the defense lukewarmly, so that both the prince and his friends are in danger.

It is necessary, however, if we wish to discuss this matter thoroughly, to observe whether these innovators stand on their own or are dependent on others; that is, if in order to carry out their work, they are obliged to beg, or are able to use force. In the first case, they always come to a bad end and never achieve anything; but when they depend on themselves and are able to use force, then very seldom will they find themselves in danger. From this comes the fact that the armed prophets conquered and the unarmed came to ruin. Besides what has been said, people in general are unstable; and it is easy to persuade them of something but difficult to hold them to that persuasion; and therefore things should be arranged so that, when people no longer believe, they can be made to believe by force. Had Moses, Cyrus, Theseus and Romulus been unarmed they would not have had their institutions respected by the people for very long; just as in our own times it happened to Brother Girolamo Savonarola, who was defeated by his new institutions when the multitude began not to believe in him; and he had no means of holding firm those who had believed nor of making the disbelievers believe. Therefore men such as these have great difficulty in getting ahead, and they encounter all their dangers as they advance, and they must overcome them by means of their ingenuity; but once they have overcome them and have begun to be held in veneration, and once they have done away with those who were envious of their abilities, they remain powerful, secure, honored, prosperous.

*   *   *

On Those Who Have Become Princes
Through Iniquity

But since there are still two more ways one can from an ordinary citizen become prince, which cannot be attributed altogether to fortune or ingenuity, I do not think they should be overlooked, even though one of them could be dealt with at more length in a treatise on republics. These are, when one becomes prince by some iniquitous and nefarious way, or when an ordinary citizen becomes prince of his native city with the backing of his fellow citizens. And in speaking of the first way, I shall use [an] example . . . without entering further into the merits of such a way. . . .

Agathocles the Sicilian, not only from an ordinary citizen but from low and abject status, became king of Syracuse. This man, the son of a potter, led an iniquitous life at every stage of his career; however, he coupled his iniquities with such power of mind and body that, when he turned to a military career, he rose through the ranks to become commander of Syracuse. Once elected to such a position, having given thought to becoming prince and to maintaining with violence and without any obligations to others that which had been unanimously conceded to him, and having taken into his confidence Hamilcar the Carthaginian, who was waging war with his armies in Sicily, one morning he called together the people and senators of Syracuse as if he were going to discuss the affairs of state with them; and with a prearranged gesture, he had his soldiers kill all the senators and the richest citizens; once they were dead, he occupied and maintained jurisdiction over that city without any civil strife. And although he was beaten twice by the Carthaginians and finally besieged, not only was he able to defend his city, but leaving part of his troops to defend it from besiegers, he invaded Africa with the rest, and in a short time he liberated Syracuse from the siege, and reduced the Carthaginians to dire straits: and they were forced to come to an agreement with him, to be content with possessing Africa and to leave Sicily to Agathocles.

Whoever examines, therefore, the actions and life of this man will find nothing or very little that can be attributed to fortune; for, as was said above, not with the help of others but by advancing in the military ranks, which involved a thousand hardships and dangers, he came to rule the principality which he then managed to maintain by many courageous and dangerous efforts. Yet it cannot be called ingenuity to kill one's fellow citizens, betray friends, be without faith, without pity, without religion; all of these may bring one to power, but not to glory. For if one were to consider the ingenuity of Agathocles in facing and surviving dangers, in his courageous spirit to undergo and overcome adversities, one cannot see why he should be judged inferior to any most outstanding commander; nevertheless, his vicious cruelty and inhumanity, together with his infinite iniquitous deeds, do not allow him to be counted among the most outstanding famous men. One cannot, therefore, attribute to fortune or ingenuity what was achieved by him without either of the two. . . .

One might question how Agathocles and others like him, after so many treacheries and cruelties, could live for a long time secure in their country and defend themselves from outside enemies without being conspired against by their own citizens; while many others, because of their cruelty, were unable, even in times of peace, to hold their power, not to mention the unstable times of war. I believe this depends on cruelty being badly or well used. Those cruelties can be considered well used (if it is permissible to say good about the bad) that are performed all at once, in order to assure one's position, and are not continued, but rather turned to the greatest advantage as possible for the subjects. Badly used are those cruelties that, although at first they are few, increase with time rather than disappear. Those who observe the first way can remedy their position with God and man as Agathocles did; the others will find it impossible to survive.

Whereby it should be noted that in capturing a state the conqueror should consider all the injuries he must inflict, and inflict all of them at once, so as not to have to repeat them daily, and in not repeating them to be able to give men a feeling of security and win them over with the benefits he offers. Whoever does otherwise, whether through timidity or bad advice, will always have to keep knife in hand; nor will he ever be able to count on his subjects, who, because of their fresh and continuous injuries, cannot feel secure with him. Injuries, then, should be inflicted all at once, for the less they are tasted the less they offend; benefits should be distributed little by little so they may be better tasted. And a prince should, above all, live with his subjects in such a way that no unforeseen event whether good or bad makes him change his course; for should the need to change arise because of adverse conditions, you are not in time to resort to the bad, and the good you do will gain you nothing, for it will be considered a necessary measure, and earn you no gratitude.

On the Civil Principality

But now coming to the other situation, when a private citizen, not through iniquity or any other intolerable means of violence, but with the help of his fellow citizens, becomes prince of his country (and this may be called a civil principality, the attainment of which depends neither entirely on ingenuity or fortune but rather on a combination of astuteness and luck), let me say that one attains this principality either with the help of the common people or the nobles. For these two different tendencies are found in every city and arise from the fact that the common people do not wish to be governed nor oppressed by the nobles, and the nobles wish to govern and oppress the common people; and from these two diverse desires there arise in cities one of three effects: a principality or freedom or anarchy.

A principality is created either by the common people or the nobles, depending on which of these two factions has the opportunity. For when the nobles see that they cannot hold out against the common people, they begin to build up the prestige of one of their own and make him prince in order to be able, under his protection, to satisfy their desires. The common people, in the same way, seeing they cannot hold out against the nobles, build up the prestige of one of their own and make him prince in order to have the defense of his authority. He who becomes prince with the help of the nobles sustains his position with more difficulty than he who becomes prince with the help of the common people; for he will find himself a prince surrounded by many who believe they are his equals, and for this reason he can neither govern nor handle them as he would like to. But he who is made prince with the support of the common people will find himself all alone, surrounded by no one or very few who are not ready to obey him. Besides this, it is impossible for the nobles to be satisfied in an honest way without doing harm to others, but the common people certainly can be, for the goal of the common people is more honest than that of the nobles, the latter wishing to oppress and the former wishing not to be oppressed. In addition, a prince can never be safe when the common people are his enemy, for there are so many of them; he can be safe with the nobles, for there are so few of them. The worst that a prince can expect from a hostile people is to be abandoned by them; but with the nobles as his enemies, not only must he fear their abandoning him but also their turning against him, for possessing more foresight and more shrewdness, they are always in time to save themselves and seek the favors of the side they hope will win. Furthermore, a prince must always live with the same common people; but he certainly can do without the same nobles, for he can create them and destroy them from one day to the next, as well as take away and give them their prestige as he pleases.

To clarify this part more fully, let me say that the nobles should be considered mainly in two ways: either they conduct themselves in such a way that they wholly ally themselves to your fortunes or they do not. Those who ally themselves and are not greedy should be honored and loved; those who do not ally themselves can be analyzed in two ways. They act this way out of cowardice and a natural lack of courage, in which case you should make use of them, especially of those who are wise counselors, for in times of prosperity they will bring you honor and in adverse times you have nothing to fear from them;

however, when they do not ally themselves to you for a definite reason and for ambitious purposes, it is a sign that they are thinking more about themselves than about you; and the prince should watch out for such men, and he should fear them as if they were open enemies, because in adverse times without fail they will help bring about his downfall.

One who becomes prince through the support of the common people, however, should maintain their friendship, which should be easy for him, since the only thing they ask of him is that they not be oppressed. But one who, contrary to the wishes of the common people, becomes prince with the help of nobles should, above all else, try to win over the common people, which should be easy for him once he takes them into his protection. And since all men, when they are well treated by someone they expected would treat them badly, are more bound to their bene-factor, the common people will quickly become more inclined to him than if he became prince with their help. And a prince can win over the common people in many ways, but since these ways vary according to circumstances, no fixed rules can be established, and therefore I shall not discuss them. I shall con-clude by saying only that a prince must keep on friendly terms with the common people; otherwise, in adverse times, he will find no assistance.

Nabis, prince of the Spartans, resisted the attacks of all of Greece as well as one of Rome's most victorious armies, and he defended his country and his reign against them; and when danger was imminent he had only to protect himself from very few of his subjects: but if he had had the common people against him, this would not have been enough. And let no one contradict my convictions with that trite proverb, "Who builds on the people builds on the mud"; because that holds true when a private citizen lays his foundations there and lets himself believe that the people will liberate him should he be oppressed by the enemy or by the magistrates (in this case, a man could often find himself deceived, like the Gracchi in Rome and Messer Giorgio Scali in Florence); but when the prince who lays his foundations on the people is one who is able to command, and is a man of courage who is not bewildered by adversity, and does not lack other necessities, and who by his courage and the regulations he has established is able to keep his community stimulated, he will never find himself deceived by the people; ✔ and he shall see that he has laid good foundations.

Principalities of this kind are usually in danger when they are at the point of changing from a civil to an absolute form of government. For these princes rule either on their own or by means of magistrates; in the latter case the prince's position is weaker and more dangerous for he remains entirely under the will of those citizens who are appointed magistrates: they can, especially in adverse times, very easily seize his power either by openly opposing him or by not obeying him. And in such danger the prince is no longer in time to take absolute control, because the citizens and subjects who are used to taking orders from the magistrates will not, at such crises, obey his; and in uncertain times he will always find a scarcity of people he can trust. Therefore, such a prince cannot count on what he observes during tranquil times, when the citizens need his state, for then everyone comes running, everyone makes promises, and each one is willing to give up his life for the prince, the possibility of death being so remote; but in adverse times, when the state needs its citizens, then so few are to be found. And this experiment is all the more dangerous in that it cannot be performed more than once. And so a wise prince must think of a way by which his citizens, at all times and in every kind of situation, will feel the need for the state and for himself; and then they will be forever faithful to him.

*   *   *

On Those Things for Which Men, and
Especially Princes, Are Praised or Blamed

Now there remains to be seen what ought to be the criteria and actions of a prince in dealing with his subjects and friends. And because I know that many have written about this, I am afraid, by writing about it again, that I shall be thought presumptuous, all the more so for departing, in my discussion of this material, from the procedures of others. But my intention being to write something useful for whoever understands it, it seemed to me more appropriate to pursue the effectual truth of the matter rather than its imagined one. And many have imagined republics and principalities that have never been seen or known to exist in reality; for there is such a gap between how one lives and how one should live that he who neglects what is being done for what should be done will learn his destruction rather than his preservation: for a man who wishes to profess goodness at all times must fall to ruin among so many who are not good. Whereby it is necessary for a prince who wishes to maintain his position to learn how not to be good, and to use it or not according to necessity.

Putting aside, then, the imagined things concerning a prince, and taking into account those that are true, let me say that all men, when they are spoken of, and especially princes, since they are on a higher level, are judged by some of these qualities which bring them blame or praise. And this is why some are considered to be generous, others stingy . . . some are considered givers, others graspers, some cruel, others merciful; one treacherous, another faithful; one effeminate and cowardly, another vigorous and courageous; one friendly, another haughty; one man lascivious, another pure; one sincere, another cunning; one severe, another lenient; one man serious-minded, another frivolous; one religious, another unbelieving, and the like. And I know everyone will agree that it would be a very praiseworthy thing to find in a prince all of the qualities mentioned above that are considered good; but since it is impossible to have and observe all of them, for human nature does not allow it, the prince must be prudent enough to know how to escape the infamy of those vices that would lose him his state, and be on his guard against those that will not lose it for him, if this be possible; but if it prove impossible, he need not be too troubled about foregoing them. And furthermore, he must not be concerned with incurring the infamy of those vices without which it would be difficult to save his state; because taking all carefully into account, he will discover that something that appears to be a virtue, if pursued, will result in his ruin; while some other thing that appears to be a vice, if pursued, will bring about his security and well-being.

On Generosity and Parsimony

Beginning, then, with the first of the qualities mentioned above, I say that it would be good to be thought of as generous; however, generosity employed in such a way as to give you a reputation for it harms you; yet if it is employed virtuously, and as one should employ it, it may not be recognized and you will not escape the infamy of its opposite. And so, if a man wishes to continue to be known among men as generous, he must not neglect any possible means of lavish display; so that a prince of this type will inevitably consume in such displays all his riches, and eventually it will become necessary for him, if he wishes to maintain his reputation for generosity, to burden the people with exaggerated taxes, and to do everything possible to get money. This will begin to make him hateful to his subjects, and in becoming poor, he will be respected by no one; so that, as a result of his generosity, having offended the many and rewarded the few, he will feel the effects of any slight disturbance and is likely to fall at the slightest sign of danger;

realizing this and wishing to change his ways, he immediately incurs the infamy of the miser.

A prince, therefore, unable to employ this virtue of generosity in a way that will make him known for it without endangering himself, should, if he is wise, not worry about being known as a miser; because with time he will come to be thought of as more and more generous, once the people see that because of his parsimony he finds his revenues are sufficient, he is able to defend himself from whoever wages war against them, he can carry on a campaign without burdening the people; so that he comes to be generous with all those from whom he takes nothing, and they are innumerable, and miserly with all those to whom he gives nothing, and they are few. In our own times we have not seen great things accomplished by anyone who was not considered a miser; the others were destroyed. Pope Julius II, though he did make use of his reputation for generosity in order to attain the papacy, decided then not to maintain it in order that he might be able to wage war; the present king of France waged many wars without imposing extra taxes on his people, because his long-practiced parsimony alone provided for his extra expenses; the present king of Spain, had he been considered generous, would not have carried on or won as many campaigns as he did.

Therefore a prince, in order not to have to despoil his subjects, to be able to defend himself, not to become poor and despised, not to be forced into becoming rapacious, should not be too concerned with incurring the name of miser, because it is one of those vices that allows him to reign. And if someone were to say: Caesar by means of generosity came to rule the empire, and many others, because they were generous and known to be so, eventually achieved greatness, I would answer: you are either a prince already or you are on the way to becoming one; in the first case, such generosity is harmful; in the second, it is certainly necessary to be thought of as generous. And Caesar was one of those who wished to become the ruler of Rome; but if, after having achieved this, he had lived and had not taken measures to moderate his spending, he would have destroyed that empire. And if someone were to reply: there have been many princes who with their troops have done great things, and have been considered very generous; I would answer: either a prince spends his own money and that of his subjects or he spends that of others; in the first case, he should be frugal; in the other, he should in no way hold back in his generosity. And to that prince who marches with his troops, who lives by plundering, sacking and ransom, who controls what belongs to others, such generosity is essential; otherwise, his soldiers would not follow him. And with that which does not belong to you or to your subjects you can be a more liberal giver as was Cyrus, Caesar or Alexander, because spending what belongs to others does not detract from your reputation, rather it enhances it; only spending your own is what will hurt you. And there is nothing more self-consuming than generosity, for as you use it you are losing the means for using it, and you become either poor and despicable, or, to escape poverty, rapacious and hated. And above all other things a prince must guard against being despicable and hated; and generosity leads you to both the one and the other. Consequently, it is wiser to put up with the name of miser, which gives birth to an infamy without hate, than to be obliged, because you wish to be known as generous, to incur the name of rapacious, which gives birth to an infamy with hate.

On Cruelty and Compassion and Whether It Is Better to Be Loved Than Feared or the Opposite

Moving along to the other qualities mentioned above, let me say that every prince must desire to be thought of as compassionate and not cruel; however, he must be careful not to misuse this compassion. Cesare Borgia was reputed to be cruel; none-theless, his cruelty had brought order to Romagna, united it, brought it peace and obedience. If we examine this carefully, we see that he was much more compassionate than the Florentine people who, in order to avoid the reputation of being cruel, allowed Pistoia to be destroyed. Therefore, a prince must not concern himself with the infamy of cruelty when it comes to keeping his subjects united and obedient; for, with just a few displays of cruelty, he will turn out to be more compassionate than those who, through excessive compassion, allow disorders to arise from which spring forth murder and ravaging; because these usually hurt the community in general, while those exe-cutions that come from the prince hurt one in particular. And of all princes, it is the new prince that finds it impossible to avoid the reputation of being cruel, since new states are full of dangers. And Virgil, through the mouth of Dido, says:

My difficult task and the newness of my reign make me act this way, and guard my territory on all sides.

Yet a prince must be cautious in his beliefs and in his actions, nor should he be afraid of his own shadow; and his conduct should be of a sort tempered by prudence and kindness, so that excessive confidence does not make him imprudent and excessive mistrust render him intolerable.

From this comes the question: whether it is better to be loved than feared, or the contrary. I answer that a person would like to be the one and the other; but since it is difficult to mix them together, it is much safer to be feared than loved, if one of the two must be lacking. For this can be generally said of men: they are ungrateful, fickle, liars and deceivers, avoiders of danger, greedy for profit; and as long as you serve their welfare, they are entirely yours, offering you their blood, possessions, life and children, as I mentioned earlier, when the occasion to do so is not in sight; but when you are faced with it, they turn against you. And that prince who lays his foundations on their promises alone, finding himself stripped of other preparations, falls to ruin; because friendships that are acquired with a price and not with excellence and nobility of character are bought, but they are not owned, and at the right time they cannot be spent. And men are less concerned with hurting someone who makes himself loved than one who makes himself feared, because love is held by a link of obligation, which, since men are wretched creatures, is broken every time their own interests are involved; but fear is held by a dread of punishment which will never leave you.

A prince must nevertheless make himself feared in such a way that if he does not gain love, he will avoid hate; because to be feared and not hated can go very well together; and this will always be the case so long as one abstains from the possessions of his citizens and subjects, and from their women. And should it become necessary for him to do away with someone, let him do it when there is convenient justification and manifest reason; but, above all, let him abstain from what belongs to others, for men forget more quickly about the death of their fathers than the loss of their patrimony. Furthermore, reasons for taking another's possessions are never lacking, and inevitably he who begins to live by ravaging will find reasons for taking over what belongs to others; while, on the contrary, reasons for taking a life are more scarce, and they fade away more quickly.

But when the prince is with his troops and has command of many soldiers, then it is certainly imperative that he not care about the reputation of being cruel; because without such a reputation troops can never be kept united nor prepared for any combat. Among the admirable accomplishments of Hannibal is numbered this: that, with a very large army, composed of men of all races, which he led into battle on foreign lands, there never arose any kind of dissension, neither among themselves nor against the prince, during his bad as well as good fortune. This could not have come about from anything other than that inhuman cruelty of his which, together with his many qualities, always made him revered and terrifying in the eyes of his men; and, without that, to achieve the same effect, his other qualities would not have been enough. And the writers, having reflected very little on this, on the one hand admire these accomplishments of his, and on the other they condemn the principal cause of them.

And that it is true that his other qualities would not have sufficed can be seen in the case of Scipio, a most outstanding figure not only of his own time but of all recorded time, whose troops in Spain turned against him; this came about from nothing other than his excessive leniency, which allowed his soldiers more liberty than the military code would normally provide. For this he was reproved in the Senate by Fabius Maximus, who called him corruptor of the Roman army. The people of Locri, having been ruined by one of Scipio's officers, were not avenged by him, nor was the insolence of that officer checked, all this arising from his easy-going nature; so that, someone in the Senate wishing to free him of blame, said that there were many more men who knew how not to err better than they knew how to correct errors; such a nature in time would have damaged the fame and glory of Scipio, if he had maintained it during the empire; but living under the rule of the Senate, this harmful quality of his not only hid itself, but brought him glory.

I conclude, then, returning to the question of being feared and loved, that, since men love at their own pleasure, and fear at the pleasure of the prince, a wise prince should build his foundation on what is his own, not on what belongs to others: he must strive only to avoid hatred, as has been said.

How a Prince Should Keep His Word

How praiseworthy it is for a prince to keep his word and live by honesty and not deceit, everyone knows; nevertheless we see, by what goes on in our own times, that those princes who have accomplished great things are the ones who had cared little for keeping promises and who knew how to manipulate the minds of men with shrewdness; and in the end they won out over those who founded themselves on loyalty.

You should know, then, that there are two ways of fighting: one with the law, the other with force; the first way is peculiar to man, the other to beasts; but since the first in many instances is not enough, it becomes necessary to resort to the second. Therefore, a prince must know how to make good use of the beast and the man. This role was taught to princes indirectly by the ancient writers, who wrote how Achilles and many other ancient princes were given to Chiron the Centaur to be brought up and trained under his direction. This can only mean, having as a teacher a half-beast and half-man, that a prince ought to know how to make use of both natures; and the one without the other cannot endure.

Since a prince must know how to make good use of the beast, he should choose then the fox and the lion; for the lion has no protection from traps, and the fox is defenseless against the wolves. It is necessary, therefore, to be a fox in order to know the traps, and a lion to frighten the wolves. Those who live by the lion alone do not understand matters. And so, a wise ruler cannot, nor should he, keep his word when doing so would be to his disadvantage and when the reasons that led him to make promises no longer exist. And if all men were good, this principle would not be good; but since men are a contemptible lot, and would not keep their promises to you, you too need not keep yours to them. To a prince legitimate reasons to break promises are never lacking. Of this an infinite number of present-day examples could be noted, indicating how many peace treaties, how many promises have been made null and void by the unfaithfulness of princes; and he who has known best how to use the fox has come to a better end. But one must know how to disguise this nature well, and how to be a fine liar and hypocrite; and men are so simple-minded and so dominated by their present needs that one who deceives will always find one who will allow himself to be deceived. . . .

It is not necessary, then, for a prince to have all of the qualities mentioned above, but it is certainly necessary that he appear to have them. In fact, I would go so far as to say this, that having them and observing them at all times, they are harmful; and appearing to have them, they are useful; for example, appearing to be compassionate, faithful, humane, upright, religious, and being so; but his mind should be disposed in such a way that should it become necessary not to be so, he will be able to know how to change to the contrary. And it must be understood that a prince, and in particular a new prince, cannot observe all those things by which men are considered good, for it is often necessary, in order to maintain the state, to act against your word, against charity, against kindness, against religion. And so, he must have a mind ready to turn itself according as the winds of fortune and the fluctuation of things command him, and, as I said above, he must not separate himself from the good, if he is able, but he must know how to take up evil, should it become necessary.

A prince, therefore, should take great care never to say a single thing that is not infused with the five qualities mentioned above; he should appear, when seen and heard, to be all compassion, all faithfulness, all integrity, all kindness, all religion. And nothing is more essential than to appear to have this last quality. And men, in general, judge more according to their eyes than their hands; since everyone is in a position to observe, just a few to touch. Everyone sees what you appear to be, few touch what you are; and those few do not dare oppose the opinions of the many who have the majesty of the state defending them; and with regard to the actions of all men, and especially with princes where there is no court of appeal, we must look at the final result. Let a prince, then, conquer and maintain the state; his methods will always be judged honorable and they will be praised by all; because the ordinary people are always taken by the appearance and the outcome of a thing; and in the world there is nothing but ordinary people; and there is no room for the few while the many have a place to lean on. A certain prince in our own time, whose name is better left unmentioned, preaches nothing but peace and good faith, and he is exceedingly hostile to both of them; and if he had put both of them into practice, on more than one occasion they would have lost him either his reputation or his state.

On Avoiding Being Disdained and Hated

But now that I have talked about the most important of the qualities mentioned above, I would like to discuss the others briefly in this general way: that a prince, as was mentioned in part above, should concentrate on avoiding those things that may render him hateful and contemptible; and when he has avoided this, he will have fulfilled his duties and will find no danger in his other vices. What makes him hated above all, as I have said, is being rapacious and a usurper of the property and the women belonging to his subjects: he must abstain from this; for the majority of men, so long as you do not deprive them of their possessions and honor, live happily; and you have only to contend with the ambition of a few who can be kept in check easily and in many ways. He is contemptible if he is thought of as changeable, frivolous, effeminate, cowardly, irresolute: a prince should be on his guard for these things as he would for a reef, and he should strive in such a way that in his actions will be recognized magnanimity, courageousness, seriousness, and strength; and in regard to the private affairs of his subjects, he should insist that his judgment be irrevocable; and he should be regarded in such a way that no one would think of deceiving him or cheating him.

That prince who gives such an impression of himself is highly esteemed; and it is difficult to conspire against one who is esteemed, and difficult to attack him, provided that it is understood he is an outstanding man and respected by his subjects. For a prince must have two fears: one internal, in regard to his subjects; the other external, in regard to outside powers. From the latter he can defend himself with good armed forces and good friends; and if he has good armed forces he will always have good friends; and internal affairs will always remain stabilized when those outside are stable, on condition that they have not already been disturbed by conspiracy; and even when outside conditions shift, if he is organized and has lived the way I have prescribed, if he does not lose control of himself, he will always be able to withstand every blow, just as I said the Spartan Nabis did. But in regard to his subjects, when outside affairs are not shifting, there may be fear of secret conspiracy, from which the prince best protects himself by avoiding being hated or disdained, and by maintaining the people's satisfaction with him—which is a necessary accomplishment, as was discussed above at length. And one of the most powerful remedies a prince has against conspiracies is not to be hated by the majority: for the one who conspires always thinks that by killing the prince he will satisfy the people; but when he thinks he might offend them, he has no courage to undertake such an enterprise, for the difficulties on the side of the conspirators are infinite. And experience shows that the number of conspiracies are many, but few have come to a good end; for he who conspires cannot be on his own nor can he choose companions from any if not from those whom he believes to be malcontent; and as soon as you have revealed yourself to one malcontent, you provide him with the means to become content, for in revealing this plan he can hope to have everything he wants: to the extent that, seeing that the gain is certain on the one side, while on the other it is uncertain and full of dangers, he would either have to be an unusual kind of friend indeed, or a truly sworn enemy of the prince, in order to keep faith with you. To put it briefly, let me say that on the side of the conspirator there is nothing but fear, jealousy, and the prospect of punishment that haunts him; but on the side of the prince, there is the majesty of the principality, the laws, the protection of friends, and the government to defend him: so that, with the good will of the people added to all these things, it is impossible for someone to be so rash as to conspire against him. For, where ordinarily a conspirator has to fear before he performs his evil, in this instance he has also to fear after the crime has been committed (when he has the people as his enemy), nor can he, because of this, hope to find any refuge whatsoever. . . .

I conclude, then, that a prince should not be too concerned with conspiracies, when he has the good will of the people; but when they are hostile toward him and bear him hatred, he should fear everything and everybody. And well-organized states and wise princes have in every way taken care not to infuriate the nobles, and to satisfy the common people and keep them happy; for this is one of the most important functions a prince has.

Among those kingdoms in our times that are organized and governed well is that of France: in it are found numerous good institutions upon which the freedom and safety of the king depend. Of these the first is the parliament and its authority; for he who organized that kingdom, being aware of the ambitions and arrogance of the nobles and realizing the necessity of keeping a bit in their mouths in order to restrain them, while, on the other hand, being aware of the hatred, based on fear, of the masses for the nobles, and wishing to reassure them, did not want this to be a particular obligation of the king; so that he would be relieved of that pressure which he might incur from the nobles in favoring the common people and from the common people in favoring the nobles, he established a third arbiter that might, without burdening the king, repress the nobles and favor the lower classes. There could not be a better or wiser system, nor could there be a better measure of security for the king and the kingdom. From this another noteworthy point can be drawn: that princes should delegate unpleasant obligations to others; those pleasant ones he should keep for himself. Again let me conclude by saying that a prince should respect the nobles, but not make himself hated by the people.

* * *

I shall come to the conclusion of this discourse by saying that the princes of our time have less of [the] difficulty of satisfying the soldiers in their states by inordinate means; for, though certain considerations should be shown toward them, any difficulties are quickly resolved, for none of these princes have standing armies that are connected with the government and the administration of the provinces as were the armies of the Roman Empire. And so, if at one time it was necessary to satisfy the soldiers more than the people, it was because the soldiers could do more than the people; now it is more necessary for all princes, except the Turk and the Sultan, to satisfy the people rather than the soldiers, because the people can do more than the soldiers. I make an exception of the Turk, because he always keeps around him twelve thousand foot soldiers and fifteen thousand horsemen, on whom depend the security and the strength of his realm, and it is necessary that all other considerations be secondary to that ruler's maintaining their friendship. Similarly with the realm of the Sultan which is entirely in the hands of the soldiers; he too must, without concern for the people, maintain their friendship.

* * *

How a Prince Should Act
to Acquire Esteem

Nothing makes a prince more esteemed than great enterprises and evidence of his unusual abilities. In our own times we have Ferdinand of Aragon, the present king of Spain. This man can almost be called a new prince, because he rose with fame and glory from a weak king to the foremost king of Christendom; and if you will examine his accomplishments you will find them all very great and some of them extraordinary. Early in his reign he attacked Granada, and that enterprise was the foundation of his state. At first, he carried on the campaign while things were peaceful, without fear of being impeded: he kept the minds of the barons of Castille occupied with it, and they, concentrating on that war, did not think about changes at home. And he acquired, in the meanwhile, prestige and control over them without their knowing it; he was able, with the money of the church and the people, to support troops and lay a foundation during that long war for his own army; which brought him honor later on. Besides this, to be able to undertake greater enterprises, continuing to make use of religion, he turned to a kind of holy cruelty by chasing out and clearing the Moors from his kingdom: no accomplishment could have been more pathetic or unusual. He attacked, under the same cloak, Africa; he conducted the campaign in Italy; he finally attacked France; and in this way he continuously carried out and contrived great things that always kept the minds of his subjects uncertain and amazed and occupied with the outcome of events. And one action of his would spring from another, so that between one and the other he would never allow enough time for men to work calmly against him.

It is also most helpful for a prince to furnish unusual evidence of his abilities in regard to internal politics, such as we hear told about Messer Bernabò of Milan; when the occasion arises that an individual in civil life performs some extraordinary deed, whether good or bad, he should choose a way of rewarding him or punishing him that will stimulate much discussion. And above all, a prince should strive in all his actions to give the impression of the great man of outstanding intelligence.

A prince is also esteemed when he is a true friend or a true enemy; that is when, without any reservation, he declares himself in favor of one against another. Such a policy will always be more useful than remaining neutral; because if two powerful neighbors of yours come to blows, they will be of the sort that, when one of them has won, you will either have reason to fear the victor, or you will not. In either of these two instances, it will always be more useful for you to declare yourself and fight an open war; for, in the first instance, if you do not declare yourself, you will always be the prey of the winner, to the delight and satisfaction of the one who has been defeated, and you have no excuse, nothing to defend you, nor anyone to offer you refuge; because, whoever wins does not want dubious friends that would not help him in adverse times, and whoever loses will not take you in, since you were not willing to run the risk of coming to his defense.

At the request of the Aetolians, Antiochus moved into Greece to chase out the Romans. Antiochus sent envoys to the Achaeans, who were friendly toward the Romans, to encourage them to remain neutral; and on the other hand the Romans were encouraging them to take up arms on their behalf. This matter came up for consideration in the council of the Achaeans, where the legate of Antiochus persuaded them to remain neutral; whereupon the Roman legate replied: "The advice these people give you about not getting mixed up in a war is indeed contrary to your interests; without respect, without dignity, you will be the prey of the victors."

And it will always happen that he who is not your friend will request your neutrality, and that one who is your friend will ask you to declare yourself by taking up arms. And the irresolute princes, in order to flee present dangers, most often follow the neutral road, and most often they ruin themselves. But when a prince undauntedly declares himself in favor of one side, if the one with whom you join wins, though he may be powerful and you may be left to his discretion, he is in your debt and a bond of friendship exists; and men are never so dishonest as to turn on you with such obvious ingratitude; and then, victories are never so clear-cut that the victor need not show some caution, especially with justice. But if the one with whom you join loses, you will be taken in by him; and while he is able he will assist you, and you become the companion of a fortune that may spring up again.

In the second case, when those who are fighting each other are of the caliber that you need not fear the one who wins, it is all the more wise for you to join sides, because you attend the downfall of one with the help of the other who should have saved him, if he had been wise; and in winning he is left to your discretion, and it is impossible for him with your help not to win.

And here it is to be noted that a prince should be careful never to join forces with one more powerful than himself against others unless necessity demands it, as was mentioned above, for, in winning, you are his prisoner; and princes should avoid, as much as possible, being left to the mercy of others. The Venetians joined up with France against the Duke of Milan, and they could have avoided making such an alliance, which resulted in their downfall. But when it cannot be avoided (as happened to the Florentines when the Pope and Spain led their armies in the assault against Lombardy) then a prince should join a side for the reasons mentioned above. Nor let any state ever believe that it can always adopt safe policies, rather let it think that they will all be uncertain; for this is what we find to be in the order of things: that we never try to escape one difficulty without running into another; but prudence consists in knowing how to recognize the nature of the difficulties and how to choose the least bad as good.

Furthermore, a prince should show that he is an admirer of talent by giving recognition to talented men, and honoring those who excel in a particular art. Moreover, he should encourage his subjects to enable them to pursue their trades in tranquillity, whether they be in commerce, agriculture, or any other trade a man may have; so that one man will not be afraid to enrich his possessions for fear that they will be taken from him, while another will not be afraid to engage in commerce through fear of taxes; rather he should establish awards for those who wish to do these things and for whoever seeks in any way to aggrandize his city or his state. He should, besides this, at appropriate times during the year, keep the people occupied with festivals and shows. And since every city is divided into guilds or clans, he should keep these groups in mind, meet with them at times, give evidence of his kindness and munificence, always maintaining firmly, however, the dignity of his position, for this should never be lacking in any way.

*   *   *

How Flatterers Are to Be Avoided

I do not want to skip over an important subject and an error from which princes protect themselves with difficulty, if they are not very clever, or do not make good choices. And these are the flatterers, of which courts are full; because men take such delight in their own affairs and in this way deceive themselves, that with difficulty do they defend themselves from this pestilence; and the desire to defend themselves from it brings with it the danger of becoming despised. For there is no other way to guard oneself from flatterers than by letting men know that you will not be offended by being told the truth; but when everyone is able to tell you the truth, you lose their respect. Therefore a wise prince should adopt a third means, choosing wise men for his state, and only to those should he allow the freedom to speak truthfully to him, and only concerning those matters about which he asks, and nothing else. But he should ask them about everything, and listen to their opinions, and afterward deliberate by himself, in his own way; and with these councils, and with each one of his advisers, he should act in such a way that everyone may know that the more freely he speaks, all the more he will be acceptable: aside from these, he should not want to hear any others, he should carry through what was decided and be firm in his decisions. Who does otherwise either falls prey to the flatterers, or changes his mind many times with the divergence of opinions: because of this he has little esteem.

I wish in this respect to cite a recent example. Father Luca, a follower of Maximilian, the present emperor, speaking of his majesty told how he never sought anyone's advice, yet he never did anything the way he wanted to: this arose from maintaining a position contrary to the one mentioned above. Since the emperor is a secretive man, he discusses his plans with no one, he accepts no opinions concerning them; but as they begin to be known and discovered when they are being put into effect, they begin to be contradicted by those around him; and he, easily influenced, is diverted from them. From this it comes about that things he accomplishes one day, he destroys the next, and that no one ever understands what he wishes or plans to do, and that one cannot rely on his decisions.

A prince, therefore, should always seek advice, but only when he wishes and not when others wish it; indeed, he should discourage everyone from giving him advice on any subject, unless he asks for it. Nevertheless, he should certainly be a free asker-of-questions, and afterward, about what was asked, a patient listener to the truth; moreover, if he becomes aware that anyone, for whatever reason, is not telling him the truth, he should become angry. And since many believe that any prince who gives the appearance of being clever is regarded so not because of his own merits but because of the good counselors he has around him, they are without a doubt deceiving themselves. For here is a general rule that never fails: that a prince who is not wise in his own right cannot be advised well, unless purely by chance he submitted himself to a single individual who governed him in all and who was a very wise man. In this case, he certainly could be, but it would not last long, because that governor in a short time would take his state from him. But by seeking advice from more than one, a prince who is not wise will never have consistent advice, nor will he know how to make it consistent on his own; all of the counselors will think of their own interests; he will not know how to manage or understand them. And it is not possible to find counselors who are otherwise, for men always turn out badly for you, unless by some necessity they are made to be good. And so it may be concluded that good advice, from whomever it may come, must originate from the wisdom of the prince, and not the wisdom of the prince from good advisers.

LEO TOLSTOY was born in 1828 south of Moscow in
Russia. The son of a count and a princess, Tolstoy
inherited their estate—and its seven hundred serfs—
when he was nineteen. After a youth of what he called
"vulgar licentiousness," including study, military service,
European travel, and gadding about in Moscow, Tolstoy
returned to live on his estate. He had already written
and published short stories to acclaim. Tolstoy plunged
into social reforms, establishing a school for his serfs
and publishing a controversial magazine about education. His aristocratic wife remarked: "For me he is
revolting with his peasants." In 1869, Tolstoy's first
major novel, *War and Peace,* was published; *Anna
Karenina* followed in 1877. In the late 1870s, a spiritual
crisis led Tolstoy to embrace religion and to practice—
imperfectly—chastity and vegetarianism. He translated
the Gospels, considered entering a monastery, and
corresponded with Gandhi. "Live seeking God and
then life will not exist without God," he wrote, yet also
commented in his diary: "Can't feel sorry for flies—
there's a limit." He wished to give away his personal
property. Tolstoy died at a railroad station after mysteri-
ously leaving home in 1910. He was buried on his
estate near where a green stick—containing, he believed,
the secret of life—was hidden.

From *Great Short Works of Leo Tolstoy,* translated by
Louise and Aylmer Maude. Publisher: Harper and Row,
Publishers, Inc., 1967.

The Death of Ivan Ilych

1

During an interval in the Melvinski trial in the large building of the Law Courts the members and public prosecutor met in Ivan Egorovich Shebek's private room, where the conversation turned on the celebrated Krasovski case. Fedor Vasilievich warmly maintained that it was not subject to their jurisdiction, Ivan Egorovich maintained the contrary, while Peter Ivanovich, not having entered into the discussion at the start, took no part in it but looked through the *Gazette* which had just been handed in.

"Gentlemen," he said, "Ivan Ilych has died!"

"You don't say so!"

"Here, read it yourself," replied Peter Ivanovich, handing Fedor Vasilievich the paper still damp from the press. Surrounded by a black border were the words: "Praskovya Fedorovna Golovina, with profound sorrow, informs relatives and friends of the demise of her beloved husband Ivan Ilych Golovin, Member of the Court of Justice, which occurred on February the 4th of this year 1882. The funeral will take place on Friday at one o'clock in the afternoon."

Ivan Ilych had been a colleague of the gentlemen present and was liked by them all. He had been ill for some weeks with an illness said to be incurable. His post had been kept open for him, but there had been conjectures that in case of his death Alexeev might receive his appointment, and that either Vinnikov or Shtabel would succeed Alexeev. So on receiving the

news of Ivan Ilych's death the first thought of each of the
gentlemen in that private room was of the changes and pro-
motions it might occasion among themselves or their acquaintances.

"I shall be sure to get Shtabel's place or Vinnikov's," thought
Fedor Vasilievich. "I was promised that long ago, and the pro-
motion means an extra eight hundred rubles a year for me
besides the allowance."

"Now I must apply for my brother-in-law's transfer from
Kaluga," thought Peter Ivanovich. "My wife will be very glad,
and then she won't be able to say that I never do anything for
her relations."

"I thought he would never leave his bed again," said Peter
Ivanovich aloud. "It's very sad."

"But what really was the matter with him?"

"The doctors couldn't say—at least they could, but each of
them said something different. When last I saw him I thought
he was getting better."

"And I haven't been to see him since the holidays. I always
meant to go."

"Had he any property?"

"I think his wife had a little—but something quite trifling."

"We shall have to go to see her, but they live so terribly far
away."

"Far away from you, you mean. Everything's far away from
your place."

"You see, he never can forgive my living on the other side
of the river," said Peter Ivanovich, smiling at Shebek. Then,
still talking of the distances between different parts of the city,
they returned to the Court.

Besides considerations as to the possible transfers and pro-
motions likely to result from Ivan Ilych's death, the mere fact
of the death of a near acquaintance aroused, as usual, in all who
heard of it the complacent feeling that, "it is he who is dead
and not I."

Each one thought or felt, "Well, he's dead but I'm alive!" But the more intimate of Ivan Ilych's acquaintances, his so-called friends, could not help thinking also that they would now have to fulfill the very tiresome demands of propriety by attending the funeral service and paying a visit of condolence to the widow.

Fedor Vasilievich and Peter Ivanovich had been his nearest acquaintances. Peter Ivanovich had studied law with Ivan Ilych and had considered himself to be under obligations to him.

Having told his wife at dinner-time of Ivan Ilych's death, and of his conjecture that it might be possible to get her brother transferred to their circuit, Peter Ivanovich sacrificed his usual nap, put on his evening clothes, and drove to Ivan Ilych's house.

At the entrance stood a carriage and two cabs. Leaning against the wall in the hall downstairs near the cloak-stand was a coffin-lid covered with a cloth of gold, ornamented with gold cord and tassels, that had been polished up with metal powder. Two ladies in black were taking off their fur cloaks. Peter Ivanovich recognized one of them as Ivan Ilych's sister, but the other was a stranger to him. His colleague Schwartz was just coming downstairs, but on seeing Peter Ivanovich enter he stopped and winked at him, as if to say: "Ivan Ilych has made a mess of things — not like you and me."

Schwartz's face with his Piccadilly whiskers, and his slim figure in evening dress, had as usual an air of elegant solemnity which contrasted with the playfulness of his character and had a special piquancy here, or so it seemed to Peter Ivanovich.

Peter Ivanovich allowed the ladies to precede him and slowly followed them upstairs. Schwartz did not come down but remained where he was, and Peter Ivanovich understood that he wanted to arrange where they should play bridge that evening. The ladies went upstairs to the widow's room, and Schwartz with seriously compressed lips but a playful look in his eyes, indicated by a twist of his eyebrows the room to the right where the body lay.

Peter Ivanovich, like everyone else on such occasions, entered feeling uncertain what he would have to do. All he knew was that at such times it is always safe to cross oneself. But he was not quite sure whether one should make obeisances while doing so. He therefore adopted a middle course. On entering the room he began crossing himself and made a slight movement resembling a bow. At the same time, as far as the motion of his head and arm allowed, he surveyed the room. Two young men— apparently nephews, one of whom was a high-school pupil— were leaving the room, crossing themselves as they did so. An old woman was standing motionless, and a lady with strangely arched eyebrows was saying something to her in a whisper. A vigorous, resolute Church Reader, in a frock-coat, was reading something in a loud voice with an expression that precluded any contradiction. The butler's assistant, Gerasim, stepping lightly in front of Peter Ivanovich, was strewing something on the floor. Noticing this, Peter Ivanovich was immediately aware of a faint odour of a decomposing body.

The last time he had called on Ivan Ilych, Peter Ivanovich had seen Gerasim in the study. Ivan Ilych had been particularly fond of him and he was performing the duty of a sick nurse.

Peter Ivanovich continued to make the sign of the cross slightly inclining his head in an intermediate direction between the coffin, the Reader, and the icons on the table in a corner of the room. Afterwards, when it seemed to him that this movement of his arm in crossing himself had gone on too long, he stopped and began to look at the corpse.

The dead man lay, as dead men always lie, in a specially heavy way, his rigid limbs sunk in the soft cushions of the coffin, with the head forever bowed on the pillow. His yellow waxen brow with bald patches over his sunken temples was thrust up in the way peculiar to the dead, the protruding nose seeming to press on the upper lip. He was much changed and had grown even thinner since Peter Ivanovich had last seen him, but, as is always the case with the dead, his face was handsomer and above all more dignified than when he was alive. The expression on the face said that what was necessary had been accomplished, and accomplished rightly. Besides this there was in that expression a reproach and a warning to the living. This warning seemed to Peter Ivanovich out of place, or at least not applicable to him. He felt a certain discomfort and so he hurriedly crossed himself once more and turned and went out of the door—too hurriedly and too regardless of propriety, as he himself was aware.

Schwartz was waiting for him in the adjoining room with legs spread wide apart and both hands toying with his top-hat behind his back. The mere sight of that playful, well-groomed, and elegant figure refreshed Peter Ivanovich. He felt that Schwartz was above all these happenings and would not surrender to any depressing influences. His very look said that this incident of a church service for Ivan Ilych could not be a sufficient reason for infringing the order of the session—in other words, that it would certainly not prevent his unwrapping a new pack of cards and shuffling them that evening while a footman placed four fresh candles on the table: in fact, there was no reason for supposing that this incident would hinder their spending the evening agreeably. Indeed he said this in a whisper as Peter Ivanovich passed him, proposing that they should meet for a game at Fedor Vasilievich's. But apparently Peter Ivanovich was not destined to play bridge that evening. Praskovya Fedorovna (a short, fat woman who despite all efforts to the contrary had continued to broaden steadily from her shoulders downwards and who had the same extraordinarily arched eyebrows as the lady who had been standing by the coffin), dressed all in black, her head covered with lace, came out of her own room with some other ladies, conducted them to the room where the dead body lay, and said: "The service will begin immediately. Please go in."

Schwartz, making an indefinite bow, stood still, evidently neither accepting nor declining this invitation. Praskovya Fedorovna recognizing Peter Ivanovich, sighed, went close up to

him, took his hand, and said: "I know you were a true friend
to Ivan Ilych . . ." and looked at him awaiting some suitable
response. And Peter Ivanovich knew that, just as it had been
the right thing to cross himself in that room, so what he had
to do here was to press her hand, sigh, and say, "Believe me . . ."
So he did all this and as he did it felt that the desired result
had been achieved: that both he and she were touched.

"Come with me. I want to speak to you before it begins,"
said the widow. "Give me your arm."

Peter Ivanovich gave her his arm and they went to the inner
rooms, passing Schwartz who winked at Peter Ivanovich com-
passionately.

"That does for our bridge! Don't object if we find another
player. Perhaps you can cut in when you do escape," said his
playful look.

Peter Ivanovich sighed still more deeply and despondently,
and Praskovya Fedorovna pressed his arm gratefully. When they
reached the drawing-room, upholstered in pink cretonne and
lighted by a dim lamp, they sat down at the table—she on a
sofa and Peter Ivanovich on a low pouffe, the springs of which
yielded spasmodically under his weight. Praskovya Fedorovna
had been on the point of warning him to take another seat, but
felt that such a warning was out of keeping with her present
condition and so changed her mind. As he sat down on the
pouffe Peter Ivanovich recalled how Ivan Ilych had arranged
this room and had consulted with him regarding this pink
cretonne with green leaves. The whole room was full of furniture
and knick-knacks, and on her way to the sofa the lace of the
widow's black shawl caught on the carved edge of the table.
Peter Ivanovich rose to detach it, and the springs of the pouffe,
relieved of his weight, rose also and gave him a push. The
widow began detaching her shawl herself, and Peter Ivanovich
again sat down, suppressing the rebellious springs of the pouffe
under him. But the widow had not quite freed herself and Peter

Ivanovich got up again, and again the pouffe rebelled and even creaked. When this was all over she took out a clean cambric handkerchief and began to weep. The episode with the shawl and the struggle with the pouffe had cooled Peter Ivanovich's emotions and he sat there with a sullen look on his face. This awkward situation was interrupted by Sokolov, Ivan Ilych's butler, who came to report that the plot in the cemetery that Praskovya Fedorovna had chosen would cost two hundred rubles. She stopped weeping and, looking at Peter Ivanovich with the air of a victim, remarked in French that it was very hard for her. Peter Ivanovich made a silent gesture signifying his full conviction that it must indeed be so.

"Please smoke," she said in a magnanimous yet crushed voice, and turned to discuss with Sokolov the price of the plot for the grave.

Peter Ivanovich while lighting his cigarette heard her inquiring very circumstantially into the prices of different plots in the cemetery and finally decide which she would take. When that was done she gave instructions about engaging the choir. Sokolov then left the room.

"I look after everything myself," she told Peter Ivanovich, shifting the albums that lay on the table; and noticing that the table was endangered by his cigarette-ash, she immediately passed him an ashtray, saying as she did so: "I consider it an affectation to say that my grief prevents my attending to practical affairs. On the contrary, if anything can—I won't say console me, but—distract me, it is seeing to everything concerning him." She again took out her handkerchief as if preparing to cry, but suddenly, as if mastering her feeling, she shook herself and began to speak calmly. "But there is something I want to talk to you about."

Peter Ivanovich bowed, keeping control of the springs of the pouffe, which immediately began quivering under him.

"He suffered terribly the last few days."

"Did he?" said Peter Ivanovich.

"Oh, terribly! He screamed unceasingly, not for minutes but for hours. For the last three days he screamed incessantly. It was unendurable. I cannot understand how I bore it; you could hear him three rooms off. Oh, what I have suffered!"

"Is it possible that he was conscious all that time?" asked Peter Ivanovich.

"Yes," she whispered. "To the last moment. He took leave of us a quarter of an hour before he died, and asked us to take Volodya away."

The thought of the sufferings of this man he had known so intimately, first as a merry little boy, then as a school-mate, and later as a grown-up colleague, suddenly struck Peter Ivanovich with horror, despite an unpleasant consciousness of his own and this woman's dissimulation. He again saw that brow, and that nose pressing down on the lip, and felt afraid for himself.

"Three days of frightful suffering and then death! Why, that might suddenly, at any time, happen to me," he thought, and for a moment felt terrified. But—he did not himself know how—the customary reflection at once occurred to him that this had happened to Ivan Ilych and not to him, and that it should not and could not happen to him, and that to think that it could would be yielding to depression which he ought not to do, as Schwartz's expression plainly showed. After which reflection Peter Ivanovich felt reassured, and began to ask with interest about the details of Ivan Ilych's death, as though death was an accident natural to Ivan Ilych but certainly not to himself.

After many details of the really dreadful physical sufferings that Ivan Ilych had endured (which details he learnt only from the effect those sufferings had produced on Praskovya Fedorovna's nerves) the widow apparently found it necessary to get to business.

"Oh, Peter Ivanovich, how hard it is! How terribly, terribly hard!" and she again began to weep.

Peter Ivanovich sighed and waited for her to finish blowing her nose. When she had done so he said, "Believe me . . . ," and she again began talking and brought out what was evidently her chief concern with him—namely, to question him as to how she could obtain a grant of money from the government on the occasion of her husband's death. She made it appear that she was asking Peter Ivanovich's advice about her pension, but he soon saw that she already knew about that to the minutest detail, more even than he did himself. She knew how much could be got out of the government in consequence of her husband's death, but wanted to find out whether she could not possibly extract something more. Peter Ivanovich tried to think of some means of doing so, but after reflecting for a while and, out of propriety, condemning the government for its niggardliness, he said he thought that nothing more could be got. Then she sighed and evidently began to devise means of getting rid of her visitor. Noticing this, he put out his cigarette, rose, pressed her hand, and went out into the anteroom.

In the dining-room where the clock stood that Ivan Ilych had liked so much and had bought at an antique shop, Peter Ivanovich met a priest and a few acquaintances who had come to attend the service, and he recognized Ivan Ilych's daughter, a handsome young woman. She was in black and her slim figure appeared slimmer than ever. She had a gloomy, determined, almost angry expression, and bowed to Peter Ivanovich as though he were in some way to blame. Behind her, with the same offended look, stood a wealthy young man, an examining magistrate, whom Peter Ivanovich also knew and who was her fiance, as he had heard. He bowed mournfully to them and was about to pass into the death-chamber, when from under the stairs appeared the figure of Ivan Ilych's schoolboy son, who was extremely like his father. He seemed a little Ivan Ilych, such as Peter Ivanovich remembered when they studied law together. His tear-stained eyes had in them the look that is seen in the eyes of boys of thirteen or fourteen who are not pure-minded. When he saw Peter Ivanovich he scowled morosely and shame-facedly. Peter Ivanovich nodded to him and entered the death-chamber. The service began: candles, groans, incense, tears, and sobs. Peter Ivanovich stood looking gloomily down at his feet. He did not look once at the dead man, did not yield to any depressing influence, and was one of the first to leave the room. There was no one in the anteroom, but Gerasim darted out of the dead man's room, rummaged with his strong hands among the fur coats to find Peter Ivanovich's and helped him on with it.

"Well, friend Gerasim," said Peter Ivanovich, so as to say something. "It's a sad affair, isn't it?"

"It's God's will. We shall all come to it some day," said Gerasim, displaying his teeth—the even, white teeth of a healthly peasant—and, like a man in the thick of urgent work, he briskly opened the front door, called the coachman, helped Peter Ivanovich into the sledge, and sprang back to the porch as if in readiness for what he had to do next.

Peter Ivanovich found the fresh air particularly pleasant after the smell of incense, the dead body, and carbolic acid.

"Where to, sir?" asked the coachman.

"It's not too late even now. . . . I'll call round on Fedor Vasilievich."

He accordingly drove there and found them just finishing the first rubber, so that it was quite convenient for him to cut in.

2

Ivan Ilych's life had been most simple and most ordinary and therefore most terrible.

He had been a member of the Court of Justice, and died at the age of forty-five. His father had been an official who after serving in various ministries and departments in Petersburg had made the sort of career which brings men to positions from which by reason of their long service they cannot be dismissed, though they are obviously unfit to hold any responsible position, and for whom therefore posts are specially created, which though fictitious carry salaries of from six to ten thousand rubles that are not fictitious, and in receipt of which they live on to a great age.

Such was the Privy Councillor and superfluous member of various superfluous institutions, Ilya Epimovich Golovin.

He had three sons, of whom Ivan Ilych was the second. The eldest son was following in his father's footsteps only in another department, and was already approaching that stage in the service at which a similar sinecure would be reached. The third son was a failure. He had ruined his prospects in a number of positions and was now serving in the railway department. His father and brothers, and still more their wives, not merely disliked meeting him, but avoided remembering his existence unless compelled to do so. His sister had married Baron Greff, a Petersburg official of her father's type. Ivan Ilych was *le phenix de la famille* as people said. He was neither as cold and formal as his elder brother nor as wild as the younger, but was a happy mean between them—an intelligent, polished, lively and agreeable man. He had studied with his younger brother at the School of Law, but the latter had failed to complete the course and was expelled when he was in the fifth class. Ivan Ilych finished the course well. Even when he was at the School of Law he was just what he remained for the rest of his life: a capable, cheerful, good-natured, and sociable man, though strict in the fulfilment of what he considered to be his duty: and he considered his duty to be what was so considered by those in authority. Neither as a boy nor as a man was he a toady, but from early youth was by nature attracted to people of high station as a fly is drawn to the light, assimilating their ways and views of life and establishing friendly relations with them. All the enthusiasms of childhood and youth passed without leaving much trace on him; he succumbed to sensuality, to vanity, and latterly among the highest classes to liberalism, but always within limits which his instinct unfailingly indicated to him as correct.

At school he had done things which had formerly seemed to him very horrid and made him feel disgusted with himself when he did them; but when later on he saw that such actions were done by people of good position and that they did not regard them as wrong, he was able not exactly to regard them as right, but to forget about them entirely or not be at all troubled at remembering them.

Having graduated from the School of Law and qualified for the tenth rank of the civil service, and having received money from his father for his equipment, Ivan Ilych ordered himself clothes at Scharmer's, the fashionable tailor, hung a medallion inscribed *respice finem* on his watch-chain, took leave of his professor and the prince who was patron of the school, had a farewell dinner with his comrades at Donon's first-class restaurant, and with his new and fashionable portmanteau, linen, clothes, shaving and other toilet appliances, and a travelling rug, all purchased at the best shops, he set off for one of the provinces where, through his father's influence, he had been attached to the Governor as an official for special service.

In the province Ivan Ilych soon arranged as easy and agreeable a position for himself as he had had at the School of Law. He performed his official tasks, made his career, and at the same time amused himself pleasantly and decorously. Occasionally he paid official visits to country districts, where he behaved with dignity both to his superiors and inferiors, and performed the duties entrusted to him, which related chiefly to the sectarians, with an exactness and incorruptible honesty of which he could not but feel proud.

In official matters, despite his youth and taste for frivolous gaiety, he was exceedingly reserved, punctilious, and even severe; but in society he was often amusing and witty, and always good-natured, correct in his manner, and *bon enfant,* as the Governor and his wife—with whom he was like one of the family—used to say of him.

In the province he had an affair with a lady who made advances to the elegant young lawyer, and there was also a milliner; and there were carousals with aides-de-camp who visited the district, and after-supper visits to a certain outlying street of doubtful reputation; and there was too some obsequiousness to his chief and even to his chief's wife, but all this was done with such a tone of good breeding that no hard names could be applied to it. It all came under the heading of the French saying: *"Il faut que jeunesse se passe."* It was all done with clean hands, in clean linen, with French phrases, and above all among people of the best society and consequently with the approval of people of rank.

So Ivan Ilych served for five years and then came a change in his official life. The new and reformed judicial institutions were introduced, and new men were needed. Ivan Ilych became such a new man. He was offered the post of Examining Magistrate, and he accepted it though the post was in another province and obliged him to give up the connections he had formed and to make new ones. His friends met to give him a send-off; they had a group-photograph taken and presented him with a silver cigarette-case, and he set off to his new post.

As examining magistrate Ivan Ilych was just as *comme il faut* and decorous a man, inspiring general respect and capable of separating his official duties from his private life, as he had been when acting as an official on special service. His duties now as examining magistrate were far more interesting and attractive than before. In his former position it had been pleasant to wear an undress uniform made by Scharmer, and to pass through the crowd of petitioners and officials who were timorously awaiting an audience with the governor, and who envied him as with free and easy gait he went straight into his chief's private room to have a cup of tea and a cigarette with him. But not many people had then been directly dependent on him—only police officials and the sectarians when he went on special missions— and he liked to treat them politely, almost as comrades, as if he were letting them feel that he who had the power to crush them was treating them in this simple, friendly way. There were then but few such people. But now, as an examining magistrate, Ivan Ilych felt that everyone without exception, even the most important and self-satisfied, was in his power, and that he need only write a few words on a sheet of paper with a certain heading, and this or that important, self-satisfied person would be brought before him in the role of an accused person or a witness, and if he did not choose to allow him to sit down, would have to stand before him and answer his questions. Ivan Ilych never abused his power; he tried on the contrary to soften its expression, but the consciousness of it and of the possibility of softening its effect, supplied the chief interest and attraction of his office. In his work itself, especially in his examinations, he very soon acquired a method of eliminating all considerations irrelevant to the legal aspect of the case, and reducing even the most complicated case to a form in which it would be presented on paper only in its externals, completely excluding his personal opinion of the matter, while above all observing every prescribed formality. The work was new and Ivan Ilych was one of the first men to apply the new Code of 1864.

On taking up the post of examining magistrate in a new town, he made new acquaintances and connections, placed himself on a new footing, and assumed a somewhat different tone. He took up an attitude of rather dignified aloofness towards the provincial authorities, but picked out the best circle of legal gentlemen and wealthy gentry living in the town and assumed a tone of slight dissatisfaction with the government, of moderate liberalism, and of enlightened citizenship. At the same time, without at all altering the elegance of his toilet, he ceased shaving his chin and allowed his beard to grow as it pleased.

Ivan Ilych settled down very pleasantly in this new town. The society there, which inclined towards opposition to the Governor, was friendly, his salary was larger, and he began to play *vint* (a form of bridge), which he found added not a little to the pleasure of life, for he had a capacity for cards, played good-humouredly, and calculated rapidly and astutely, so that he usually won.

After living there for two years he met his future wife, Praskovya Fedorovna Mikhel, who was the most attractive, clever, and brilliant girl of the set in which he moved, and among other amusements and relaxations from his labours as examining magistrate, Ivan Ilych established light and playful relations with her.

While he had been an official on special service he had been accustomed to dance, but now as an examining magistrate it was exceptional for him to do so. If he danced now, he did it as if to show that though he served under the reformed order of things, and had reached the fifth official rank, yet when it came to dancing he could do it better than most people. So at the end of an evening he sometimes danced with Praskovya Fedorovna, and it was chiefly during these dances that he captivated her. She fell in love with him. Ivan Ilych had at first no definite intention of marrying, but when the girl fell in love with him he said to himself: "Really, why shouldn't I marry?"

Praskovya Fedorovna came of a good family, was not bad looking, and had some little property. Ivan Ilych might have aspired to a more brilliant match, but even this was good. He had his salary, and she, he hoped, would have an equal income. She was well connected, and was a sweet, pretty and thoroughly correct young woman. To say that Ivan Ilych married because he fell in love with Praskovya Fedorovna and found that she sympathized with his views of life would be as incorrect as to say that he married because his social circle approved of the match. He was swayed by both these considerations: the marriage gave him personal satisfaction, and at the same time it was considered the right thing by the most highly placed of his associates.

So Ivan Ilych got married.

The preparations for marriage and the beginning of married life, with its conjugal caresses, the new furniture, new crockery, and new linen, were very pleasant until his wife became pregnant—so that Ivan Ilych had begun to think that marriage would not impair the easy, agreeable, gay and always decorous character of his life, approved of by society and regarded by himself as natural, but would even improve it. But from the first months of his wife's pregnancy, something new, unpleasant, depressing, and unseemly, and from which there was no way of escape, unexpectedly showed itself.

His wife, without any reason—*de gâieté de coeur* as Ivan Ilych expressed it to himself—began to disturb the pleasure and propriety of their life. She began to be jealous without any cause, expected him to devote his whole attention to her, found fault with everything, and made coarse and ill-mannered scenes.

At first Ivan Ilych hoped to escape from the unpleasantness of this state of affairs by the same easy and decorous relation to life that had served him heretofore: he tried to ignore his wife's disagreeable moods, continued to live in his usual easy and pleasant way, invited friends to his house for a game of cards, and also tried going out to his club or spending his evenings with friends. But one day his wife began upbraiding him so vigorously, using such coarse words, and continued to abuse him every time he did not fulfil her demands, so resolutely and with such evident determination not to give way till he submitted—that is, till he stayed at home and was bored just as she was—that he became alarmed. He now realized that matrimony—at any rate with Praskovya Fedorovna—was not always conducive to the pleasures and amenities of life but on the contrary often infringed both comfort and propriety, and that he must therefore entrench himself against such infringement. And Ivan Ilych began to seek the means of doing so. His official duties were the one thing that imposed upon Praskovya Fedorovna, and by means of his official work and the duties attached to it he began struggling with his wife to secure his own independence.

With the birth of their child, the attempts to feed it and the various failures in doing so, and with the real and imaginary illnesses of mother and child, in which Ivan Ilych's sympathy was demanded but about which he understood nothing, the need of securing for himself an existence outside his family life became still more imperative.

As his wife grew more irritable and exacting and Ivan Ilych transferred the centre of gravity of his life more and more to his official work, so did he grow to like his work better and became more ambitious than before.

Very soon, within a year of his wedding, Ivan Ilych had realized that marriage, though it may add some comforts to life, is in fact a very intricate and difficult affair towards which in order to perform one's duty, that is, to lead a decorous life approved of by society, one must adopt a definite attitude just as towards one's official duties.

And Ivan Ilych evolved such an attitude towards married life. He only required of it those conveniences—dinner at home, housewife, and bed—which it could give him, and above all that propriety of external forms required by public opinion. For the rest he looked for light-hearted pleasure and propriety, and was very thankful when he found them, but if he met with antagonism and querulousness he at once retired into his separate fenced-off world of official duties, where he found satisfaction.

Ivan Ilych was esteemed a good official, and after three years was made Assistant Public Prosecutor. His new duties, their importance, the possibility of indicting and imprisoning anyone he chose, the publicity his speeches received, and the success he had in all these things, made his work still more attractive.

More children came. His wife became more and more quer- ulous and ill-tempered, but the attitude Ivan Ilych had adopted towards his home life rendered him almost impervious to her grumbling.

After seven years' service in that town he was transferred to another province as Public Prosecutor. They moved, but were short of money and his wife did not like the place they moved to. Though the salary was higher the cost of living was greater, besides which two of their children died and family life became still more unpleasant for him.

Praskovya Fedorovna blamed her husband for every inconvenience they encountered in their new home. Most of the conversations between husband and wife, especially as to the children's education, led to topics which recalled former disputes, and those disputes were apt to flare up again at any moment. There remained only those rare periods of amorousness which still came to them at times but did not last long. These were islets at which they anchored for a while and then again set out upon that ocean of veiled hostility which showed itself in their aloofness from one another. This aloofness might have grieved Ivan Ilych had he considered that it ought not to exist, but he now regarded the position as normal, and even made it the goal at which he aimed in family life. His aim was to free himself more and more from those unpleasantnesses and to give them a semblance of harmlessness and propriety. He attained this by spending less and less time with his family, and when obliged to be at home he tried to safeguard his position by the presence of outsiders. The chief thing however was that he had his official duties. The whole interest of his life now centered in the official world and that interest absorbed him. The consciousness of his power, being able to ruin anybody he wished to ruin, the importance, even the external dignity of his entry into court, or meetings with his subordinates, his success with superiors and inferiors, and above all his masterly handling of cases, of which he was conscious—all this gave him pleasure and filled his life, together with chats with his colleagues, dinners, and bridge. So that on the whole Ivan Ilych's life continued to flow as he considered it should do—pleasantly and properly.

So things continued for another seven years. His eldest daughter was already sixteen, another child had died, and only one son was left, a schoolboy and a subject of dissension. Ivan Ilych wanted to put him in the School of Law, but to spite him Praskovya Fedorovna entered him at the High School. The daughter had been educated at home and had turned out well; the boy did not learn badly either.

3

So Ivan Ilych lived for seventeen years after his marriage. He was already a Public Prosecutor of long standing, and had declined several proposed transfers while awaiting a more desirable post, when an unanticipated and unpleasant occurrence quite upset the peaceful course of his life. He was expecting to be offered the post of presiding judge in a University town, but Happe somehow came to the front and obtained the appointment instead. Ivan Ilych became irritable, reproached Happe, and quarrelled both with him and with his immediate superiors—who became colder to him and again passed him over when other appointments were made.

This was in 1880, the hardest year of Ivan Ilych's life. It was then that it became evident on the one hand that his salary was insufficient for them to live on, and on the other that he had been forgotten, and not only this, but that what was for him the greatest and most cruel injustice appeared to others a quite ordinary occurrence. Even his father did not consider it his duty to help him. Ivan Ilych felt himself abandoned by everyone, and that they regarded his position with a salary of 3,500 rubles (about £350) as quite normal and even fortunate. He alone knew that with the consciousness of the injustices done him, with his wife's incessant nagging, and with the debts he had contracted by living beyond his means, his position was far from normal.

In order to save money that summer he obtained leave of absence and went with his wife to live in the country at her brother's place.

In the country, without his work, he experienced *ennui* for the first time in his life, and not only *ennui* but intolerable depression, and he decided that it was impossible to go on living like that, and that it was necessary to take energetic measures.

Having passed a sleepless night pacing up and down the veranda, he decided to go to Petersburg and bestir himself, in order to punish those who had failed to appreciate him and to get transferred to another ministry.

Next day, despite many protests from his wife and her brother, he started for Petersburg with the sole object of obtaining a post with a salary of five thousand rubles a year. He was no longer bent on any particular department, or tendency, or kind of activity. All he now wanted was an appointment to another post with a salary of five thousand rubles, either in the administration, in the banks, with the railways, in one of the Empress Marya's Institutions, or even in the customs—but it had to carry with it a salary of five thousand rubles and be in a ministry other than that in which they had failed to appreciate him.

And this quest of Ivan Ilych's was crowned with remarkable and unexpected success. At Kursk an acquaintance of his, F. I. Ilyin, got into the first-class carriage, sat down beside Ivan Ilych, and told him of a telegram just received by the Governor of Kursk announcing that a change was about to take place in the ministry: Peter Ivanovich was to be superseded by Ivan Semenovich.

The proposed change, apart from its significance for Russia, had a special significance for Ivan Ilych, because by bringing forward a new man, Peter Petrovich, and consequently his friend Zachar Ivanovich, it was highly favourable for Ivan Ilych, since Zachar Ivanovich was a friend and colleague of his.

In Moscow this news was confirmed, and on reaching Petersburg Ivan Ilych found Zachar Ivanovich and received a definite promise of an appointment in his former Department of Justice.

A week later he telegraphed to his wife: "Zachar in Miller's place. I shall receive appointment on presentation of report."

Thanks to this change of personnel, Ivan Ilych had unexpectedly obtained an appointment in his former ministry which placed him two stages above his former colleagues besides giving him five thousand rubles salary and three thousand five hundred rubles for expenses connected with his removal. All his ill humour towards his former enemies and the whole department vanished, and Ivan Ilych was completely happy.

He returned to the country more cheerful and contented than he had been for a long time. Praskovya Fedorovna also cheered up and a truce was arranged between them. Ivan Ilych told of how he had been feted by everybody in Petersburg, how all those who had been his enemies were put to shame and now fawned on him, how envious they were of his appointment, and how much everybody in Petersburg had liked him.

Praskovya Fedorovna listened to all this and appeared to believe it. She did not contradict anything, but only made plans for their life in the town to which they were going. Ivan Ilych saw with delight that these plans were his plans, that he and his wife agreed, and that, after a stumble, his life was regaining its due and natural character of pleasant lightheartedness and decorum.

Ivan Ilych had come back for a short time only, for he had to take up his new duties on the 10th of September. Moreover, he needed time to settle into the new place, to move all his belongings from the province, and to buy and order many additional things: in a word, to make such arrangements as he had resolved on, which were almost exactly what Praskovya Fedorovna too had decided on.

Now that everything had happened so fortunately, and that he and his wife were at one in their aims and moreover saw so little of one another, they got on together better than they had done since the first years of marriage. Ivan Ilych had thought of taking his family away with him at once, but the insistence of his wife's brother and her sister-in-law, who had suddenly become particularly amiable and friendly to him and his family, induced him to depart alone.

So he departed, and the cheerful state of mind induced by his success and by the harmony between his wife and himself, the one intensifying the other, did not leave him. He found a delightful house, just the thing both he and his wife had dreamt of. Spacious, lofty reception rooms in the old style, a convenient and dignified study, rooms for his wife and daughter, a study for his son—it might have been specially built for them. Ivan Ilych himself superintended the arrangements, chose the wall-papers, supplemented the furniture (preferably with antiques which he considered particularly *comme il faut*), and supervised the upholstering. Everything progressed and progressed and approached the ideal he had set himself: even when things were only half completed they exceeded his expectations. He saw what a refined and elegant character, free from vulgarity, it would all have when it was ready. On falling asleep he pictured to himself how the reception-room would look. Looking at the yet unfinished drawing-room he could see the fireplace, the screen, the what-not, the little chairs dotted here and there, the dishes and plates on the walls, and the bronzes, as they would be when everything was in place. He was pleased by the thought of how his wife and daughter, who shared his taste in this matter, would be impressed by it. They were certainly not expecting as much. He had been particularly successful in finding, and buying cheaply, antiques which gave a particularly aristocratic character to the whole place. But in his letters he intentionally understated everything in order to be able to surprise them. All this so absorbed him that his new duties—though he liked his official work—interested him less than he had expected. Sometimes he even had moments of absent-mindedness during the Court Sessions, and would consider whether he should have straight or curved cornices for his curtains. He was so interested in it all that he often did things himself, rearranging the furniture, or rehanging the curtains. Once when mounting a stepladder to show the upholsterer, who did not understand, how he wanted the hangings draped, he made a false step and slipped, but being a strong and agile man he clung on and only knocked his side against the knob of the window frame. The bruised place was painful but the pain soon passed, and he felt particularly bright and well just then. He wrote: "I feel fifteen years younger." He thought he would have everything ready by September, but it dragged on till mid-October. But the result was charming not only in his eyes but to everyone who saw it.

In reality it was just what is usually seen in the houses of people of moderate means who want to appear rich, and therefore succeed only in resembling others like themselves: there were damasks, dark wood, plants, rugs, and dull and polished bronzes—all the things people of a certain class have in order to resemble other people of that class. His house was so like the others that it would never have been noticed, but to him it all seemed to be quite exceptional. He was very happy when he met his family at the station and brought them to the newly furnished house all lit up, where a footman in a white tie opened the door into the hall decorated with plants, and when they went on into the drawing-room and the study uttering exclamations of delight. He conducted them everywhere, drank in their praises eagerly, and beamed with pleasure. At tea that evening, when Praskovya Fedorovna among other things asked him about his fall, he laughed, and showed them how he had gone flying and had frightened the upholsterer.

"It's a good thing I'm a bit of an athlete. Another man might have been killed, but I merely knocked myself, just here; it hurts when it's touched, but it's passing off already—it's only a bruise."

So they began living in their new home—in which, as always happens, when they got thoroughly settled in they found they were just one room short—and with the increased income, which as always was just a little (some five hundred rubles) too little, but it was all very nice.

Things went particularly well at first, before everything was finally arranged and while something had still to be done: this thing bought, that thing ordered, another thing moved, and something else adjusted. Though there were some disputes between husband and wife, they were both so well satisfied and had so much to do that it all passed off without any serious quarrels. When nothing was left to arrange it became rather dull and something seemed to be lacking, but they were then making acquaintances, forming habits, and life was growing fuller.

Ivan Ilych spent his mornings at the law courts and came home to dinner, and at first he was generally in a good humour, though he occasionally became irritable just on account of his house. (Every spot on the tablecloth or the upholstery, and every broken windowblind string, irritated him. He had devoted so much trouble to arranging it all that every disturbance of it distressed him.) But on the whole his life ran its course as he believed life should do: easily, pleasantly, and decorously.

He got up at nine, drank his coffee, read the paper, and then put on his undress uniform and went to the law courts. There the harness in which he worked had already been stretched to fit him and he donned it without a hitch: petitioners, inquiries at the chancery, the chancery itself, and the sittings public and administrative. In all this the thing was to exclude everything fresh and vital, which always disturbs the regular course of official business, and to admit only official relations with people, and then only on official grounds. A man would come, for instance, wanting some information. Ivan Ilych, as one in whose sphere the matter did not lie, would have nothing to do with him: but if the man had some business with him in his official capacity, something that could be expressed on officially stamped paper, he would do everything, positively everything he could within the limits of such relations, and in doing so would maintain the semblance of friendly human relations, that is, would observe the courtesies of life. As soon as the official relations ended, so did everything else. Ivan Ilych possessed this capacity to separate his real life from the official side of affairs and not mix the two, in the highest degree, and by long practice and natural aptitude had brought it to such a pitch that sometimes, in the manner of a virtuoso, he would even allow himself to let the human and official relations mingle. He let himself do this just because he felt that he could at any time he chose resume the strictly official attitude again and drop the human relation. And he did it all easily, pleasantly, correctly, and even artistically. In the intervals between the sessions he smoked, drank tea, chatted a little about politics, a little about general topics, a little about cards, but most of all about official appointments. Tired, but with the feelings of a virtuoso—one of the first violins who has played his part in an orchestra with precision—he would return home to find that his wife and daughter had been out paying calls, or had a visitor, and that his son had been to school, had done his homework with his tutor, and was duly learning what is taught at High School. Everything was as it should be. After dinner, if they had no visitors, Ivan Ilych sometimes read a book that was being much discussed at the time, and in the evening settled down to work, that is, read official papers, compared the depositions of witnesses, and noted paragraphs of the Code applying to them. This was neither dull nor amusing. It was dull when he might have been playing bridge, but if no bridge was available it was at any rate better than doing nothing or sitting with his wife. Ivan Ilych's chief pleasure was giving little dinners to which he invited men and women of good social position, and just as his drawing-room resembled all other drawing-rooms so did his enjoyable little parties resemble all other such parties.

Once they even gave a dance. Ivan Ilych enjoyed it and everything went off well, except that it led to a violent quarrel with his wife about the cakes and sweets. Praskovya Fedorovna had made her own plans, but Ivan Ilych insisted on getting everything from an expensive confectioner and ordered too many cakes, and the quarrel occurred because some of those cakes were left over and the confectioner's bill came to forty-five rubles. It was a great and disagreeable quarrel. Praskovya Fedorovna called him "a fool and an imbecile," and he clutched at his head and made angry allusions to divorce.

But the dance itself had been enjoyable. The best people were there, and Ivan Ilych had danced with Princess Trufonova, a sister of the distinguished founder of the Society "Bear my Burden."

The pleasures connected with his work were pleasures of ambition; his social pleasures were those of vanity; but Ivan Ilych's greatest pleasure was playing bridge. He acknowledged that whatever disagreeable incident happened in his life, the pleasure that beamed like a ray of light above everything else was to sit down to bridge with good players, not noisy partners, and of course to four-handed bridge (with five players it was annoying to have to stand out, though one pretended not to mind), to play a clever and serious game (when the cards allowed it) and then to have supper and drink a glass of wine. After a game of bridge, especially if he had won a little (to win a large sum was unpleasant), Ivan Ilych went to bed in specially good humour.

So they lived. They formed a circle of acquaintances among the best people and were visited by people of importance and by young folk. In their views as to their acquaintances, husband, wife and daughter were entirely agreed, and tacitly and unan-imously kept at arm's length and shook off the various shabby friends and relations who, with much show of affection, gushed into the drawing-room with its Japanese plates on the walls. Soon these shabby friends ceased to obtrude themselves and only the best people remained in the Golovins' set.

Young men made up to Lisa, and Petrishchev, an examining magistrate and Dmitri Ivanovich Petrishchev's son and sole heir, began to be so attentive to her that Ivan Ilych had already spoken to Praskovya Fedorovna about it, and considered whether they should not arrange a party for them, or get up some private theatricals.

So they lived, and all went well, without change, and life flowed pleasantly.

4

They were all in good health. It could not be called ill health if Ivan Ilych sometimes said that he had a queer taste in his mouth and felt some discomfort in his left side.

But this discomfort increased and, though not exactly painful, grew into a sense of pressure in his side accompanied by ill humour. And his irritability became worse and worse and began to mar the agreeable, easy, and correct life that had established itself in the Golovin family. Quarrels between husband and wife became more and more frequent, and soon the ease and amenity disappeared and even the decorum was barely maintained. Scenes again became frequent, and very few of those islets remained on which husband and wife could meet without an explosion. Praskovya Fedorovna now had good reason to say that her hus-band's temper was trying. With characteristic exaggeration she said he had always had a dreadful temper, and that it had needed all her good nature to put up with it for twenty years. It was true that now the quarrels were started by him. His bursts of temper always came just before dinner, often just as he began to eat his soup. Sometimes he noticed that a plate or dish was chipped, or the food was not right, or his son put his elbow on the table, or his daughter's hair was not done as he liked it, and for all this he blamed Praskovya Fedorovna. At first she retorted and said disagreeable things to him, but once or twice he fell into such a rage at the beginning of dinner that she realized it was due to some physical derangement brought on by taking food, and so restrained herself and did not answer, but only hurried to get the dinner over. She regarded this self-restraint as highly praiseworthy. Having come to the conclusion that her husband had a dreadful temper and made her life miserable, she began to feel sorry for herself, and the more she pitied herself the more she hated her husband. She began to wish he would die; yet she did not want him to die because then his salary would cease. And this irritated her against him still more. She considered herself dreadfully unhappy just because not even his death could save her, and though she concealed her exasperation, that hidden exasperation of hers increased his irritation also.

After one scene in which Ivan Ilych had been particularly unfair and after which he had said in explanation that he certainly was irritable but that it was due to his not being well, she said that if he was ill it should be attended to, and insisted on his going to see a celebrated doctor.

He went. Everything took place as he had expected and as it always does. There was the usual waiting and the important air assumed by the doctor, with which he was so familiar (resembling that which he himself assumed in court), and the sounding and listening, and the questions which called for answers that were foregone conclusions and were evidently unnecessary, and the look of importance which implied that "if only you put yourself in our hands we will arrange everything —we know indubitably how it has to be done, always in the same way for everybody alike." It was all just as it was in the law courts. The doctor put on just the same air towards him as he himself put on towards an accused person.

The doctor said that so-and-so indicated that there was so-and-so inside the patient, but if the investigation of so-and-so did not confirm this, then he must assume that and that. If he assumed that and that, then . . . and so on. To Ivan Ilych only one question was important: was his case serious or not? But the doctor ignored that inappropriate question. From his point of view it was not the one under consideration; the real question was to decide between a floating kidney, chronic catarrh, or appendicitis. It was not a question of Ivan Ilych's life or death, but one between a floating kidney and appendicitis. And that question the doctor solved brilliantly, as it seemed to Ivan Ilych, in favour of the appendix, with the reservation that should an examination of the urine give fresh indications the matter would be reconsidered. All this was just what Ivan Ilych had himself brilliantly accomplished a thousand times in dealing with men on trial. The doctor summed up just as brilliantly, looking over his spectacles triumphantly and even gaily at the accused. From the doctor's summing up Ivan Ilych concluded that things were bad, but that for the doctor, and perhaps for everybody else, it was a matter of indifference, though for him it was bad. And this conclusion struck him painfully, arousing in him a great feeling of pity for himself and of bitterness towards the doctor's indifference to a matter of such importance.

He said nothing of this, but rose, placed the doctor's fee on the table, and remarked with a sigh: "We sick people probably often put inappropriate questions. But tell me, in general, is this complaint dangerous, or not? . . ."

The doctor looked at him sternly over his spectacles with one eye, as if to say: "Prisoner, if you will not keep to the questions put to you, I shall be obliged to have you removed from the court."

"I have already told you what I consider necessary and proper. The analysis may show something more." And the doctor bowed.

Ivan Ilych went out slowly, seated himself disconsolately in his sledge, and drove home. All the way home he was going over what the doctor had said, trying to translate those complicated, obscure, scientific phrases into plain language and find in them an answer to the question: "Is my condition bad? Is it very bad? Or is there as yet nothing much wrong?" And it seemed to him that the meaning of what the doctor had said was that it was very bad. Everything in the streets seemed depressing. The cabmen, the houses, the passers-by, and the shops, were dismal. His ache, this dull gnawing ache that never ceased for a moment, seemed to have acquired a new and more serious significance from the doctor's dubious remarks. Ivan Ilych now watched it with a new and oppressive feeling.

He reached home and began to tell his wife about it. She listened, but in the middle of his account his daughter came in with her hat on, ready to go out with her mother. She sat down reluctantly to listen to this tedious story, but could not stand it long, and her mother too did not hear him to the end.

"Well, I am very glad," she said. "Mind now to take your medicine regularly. Give me the prescription and I'll send Gerasim to the chemist's." And she went to get ready to go out.

While she was in the room Ivan Ilych had hardly taken time to breath, but he sighed deeply when she left it.

"Well," he thought, "perhaps it isn't so bad after all."

He began taking his medicine and following the doctor's directions, which had been altered after the examination of the urine. But then it happened that there was a contradiction between the indications drawn from the examination of the urine and the symptoms that showed themselves. It turned out that what was happening differed from what the doctor had told him, and that he had either forgotten, or blundered, or hidden something from him. He could not, however, be blamed for that, and Ivan Ilych still obeyed his orders implicitly and at first derived some comfort from doing so.

From the time of his visit to the doctor, Ivan Ilych's chief occupation was the exact fulfilment of the doctor's instructions regarding hygiene and the taking of medicine, and the observation of his pain and his excretions. His chief interests came to be people's ailments and people's health. When sickness, deaths, or recoveries, were mentioned in his presence, especially when the illness resembled his own, he listened with agitation which he tried to hide, asked questions, and applied what he heard to his own case.

The pain did not grow less, but Ivan Ilych made efforts to force himself to think that he was better. And he could do this so long as nothing agitated him. But as soon as he had any unpleasantness with his wife, any lack of success in his official work, or held bad cards at bridge, he was at once acutely sensible of his disease. He had formerly borne such mischances, hoping soon to adjust what was wrong, to master it and attain success, or make a grand slam. But now every mischance upset him and plunged him into despair. He would say to himself: "There now, just as I was beginning to get better and the medicine had begun to take effect, comes this accursed misfortune, or unpleasantness . . . " And he was furious with the mishap, or with the people who were causing the unpleasantness and killing him, for he felt that this fury was killing him but could not restrain it. One would have thought that it should have been clear to him that this exasperation with circumstances and people aggravated his illness, and that he ought therefore to ignore unpleasant occurrences. But he drew the very opposite conclusion: he said that he needed peace, and he watched for everything that might disturb it and became irritable at the slightest infringement of it. His condition was rendered worse by the fact that he read medical books and consulted doctors. The progress of his disease was so gradual that he could deceive himself when comparing one day with another—the difference was so slight. But when he consulted the doctors it seemed to him that he was getting worse, and even very rapidly. Yet despite this he was continually consulting them.

That month he went to see another celebrity, who told him almost the same as the first had done but put his questions rather differently, and the interview with this celebrity only increased Ivan Ilych's doubts and fears. A friend of a friend of his, a very good doctor, diagnosed his illness again quite differently from the others, and though he predicted recovery, his questions and suppositions bewildered Ivan Ilych still more and increased his doubts. A homeopathist diagnosed the disease in yet another way, and prescribed medicine which Ivan Ilych took secretly for a week. But after a week, not feeling any improvement and having lost confidence both in the former doctor's treatment and in this one's, he became still more despondent. One day a lady acquaintance mentioned a cure effected by a wonder-working icon. Ivan Ilych caught himself listening attentively and beginning to believe that it had occurred. This incident alarmed him. "Has my mind really weakened to such an extent?" he asked himself. "Nonsense! It's all rubbish. I mustn't give way to nervous fears but having chosen a doctor must keep strictly to his treatment. That is what I will do. Now it's all settled. I won't think about it, but will follow the treatment seriously till summer, and then we shall see. From now there must be no more of this wavering!" This was easy to say but impossible to carry out. The pain in his side oppressed him and seemed to grow worse and more incessant, while the taste in his mouth grew stranger and stranger. It seemed to him that his breath had a disgusting smell, and he was conscious of a loss of appetite and strength. There was no deceiving himself: something terrible, new, and more important than anything before in his life, was taking place within him of which he alone was aware. Those about him did not understand or would not understand it, but thought everything in the world was going on as usual. That tormented Ivan Ilych more than anything. He saw that his household, especially his wife and daughter who were in a perfect whirl of visiting, did not understand anything of it and were annoyed that he was so depressed and so exacting, as if he were to blame for it. Though they tried to disguise it he saw that he was an obstacle in their path, and that his wife had adopted a definite line in regard to his illness and kept to it regardless of anything he said or did. Her attitude was this: "You know," she would say to her friends, "Ivan Ilych can't do as other people do, and keep to the treatment prescribed for him. One day he'll take his drops and keep strictly to his diet and go to bed in good time, but the next day unless I watch him he'll suddenly forget his medicine, eat sturgeon— which is forbidden—and sit up playing cards till one o'clock in the morning."

"Oh, come, when was that?" Ivan Ilych would ask in vexation. "Only once at Peter Ivanovich's."

"And yesterday with Shebek."

"Well, even if I hadn't stayed up, this pain would have kept me awake."

"Be that as it may you'll never get well like that, but will always make us wretched."

Praskovya Fedorovna's attitude to Ivan Ilych's illness, as she expressed it both to others and to him, was that it was his own fault and was another of the annoyances he caused her. Ivan Ilych felt that this opinion escaped her involuntarily—but that did not make it easier for him.

At the law courts, too, Ivan Ilych noticed, or thought he noticed, a strange attitude towards himself. It sometimes seemed to him that people were watching him inquisitively as a man whose place might soon be vacant. Then again, his friends would suddenly begin to chaff him in a friendly way about his low spirits, as if the awful, horrible, and unheard-of thing that was going on within him, incessantly gnawing at him and irresistibly drawing him away, was a very agreeable subject for jests. Schwartz in particular irritated him by his jocularity, vivacity, and *savoir faire*, which reminded him of what he himself had been ten years ago.

Friends came to make up a set and they sat down to cards. They dealt, bending the cards to soften them, and he sorted the diamonds in his hand and found he had seven. His partner said "No trumps" and supported him with two diamonds. What more could be wished for? It ought to be jolly and lively. They would make a grand slam. But suddenly Ivan Ilych was conscious of that gnawing pain, that taste in his mouth, and it seemed ridiculous that in such circumstances he should be pleased to make a grand slam.

He looked at his partner Mikhail Mikhaylovich, who rapped the table with his strong hand and instead of snatching up the tricks pushed the cards courteously and indulgently towards Ivan Ilych that he might have the pleasure of gathering them up without the trouble of stretching out his hand for them. "Does he think I am too weak to stretch out my arm?" thought Ivan Ilych, and forgetting what he was doing he over-trumped his partner, missing the grand slam by three tricks. And what was most awful of all was that he saw how upset Mikhail Mikhaylovich was about it but did not himself care. And it was dreadful to realize why he did not care.

They all saw that he was suffering, and said: "We can stop if you are tired. Take a rest." Lie down? No, he was not at all tired, and he finished the rubber. All were gloomy and silent. Ivan Ilych felt that he had diffused this gloom over them and could not dispel it. They had supper and went away, and Ivan Ilych was left alone with the consciousness that his life was poisoned and was poisoning the lives of others, and that this poison did not weaken but penetrated more and more deeply into his whole being.

With this consciousness, and with physical pain besides the terror, he must go to bed, often to lie awake the greater part of the night. Next morning he had to get up again, dress, go to the law courts, speak, and write; or if he did not go out, spend at home those twenty-four hours a day each of which was a torture. And he had to live thus all alone on the brink of an abyss, with no one who understood or pitied him.

5

So one month passed and then another. Just before the New Year his brother-in-law came to town and stayed at their house. Ivan Ilych was at the law courts and Praskovya Fedorovna had gone shopping. When Ivan Ilych came home and entered his study he found his brother-in-law there—a healthy, florid man—unpacking his portmanteau himself. He raised his head on hearing Ivan Ilych's footsteps and looked up at him for a moment without a word. That stare told Ivan Ilych everything. His brother-in-law opened his mouth to utter an exclamation of surprise but checked himself, and that action confirmed it all.

"I have changed, eh?"

"Yes, there is a change."

And after that, try as he would to get his brother-in-law to return to the subject of his looks, the latter would say nothing about it. Praskovya Fedorovna came home and her brother went out to her. Ivan Ilych locked the door and began to examine himself in the glass, first full face, then in profile. He took up a portrait of himself, taken with his wife, and compared it with what he saw in the glass. The change in him was immense. Then he bared his arms to the elbow, looked at them, drew the sleeves down again, sat down on an ottoman, and grew blacker than night.

"No, no, this won't do!" he said to himself, and jumped up, went to the table, took up some law papers and began to read them, but could not continue. He unlocked the door and went into the reception-room. The door leading to the drawing-room was shut. He approached it on tiptoe and listened.

"No, you are exaggerating!" Praskovya Fedorovna was saying.

"Exaggerating! Don't you see it? Why, he's a dead man! Look at his eyes—there's no light in them. But what is it that is wrong with him?"

"No one knows. Nikolaevich (that was another doctor) said something, but I don't know what. And Leshchetitsky (this was the celebrated specialist) said quite the contrary . . ."

Ivan Ilych walked away, went to his own room, lay down, and began musing: "The kidney, a floating kidney." He recalled all the doctors had told him of how it detached itself and swayed about. And by an effort of imagination he tried to catch that kidney and arrest it and support it. So little was needed for this, it seemed to him. "No, I'll go to see Peter Ivanovich again." (That was the friend whose friend was a doctor.) He rang, ordered the carriage, and got ready to go.

"Where are you going, Jean?" asked his wife, with a specially sad and exceptionally kind look.

This exceptionally kind look irritated him. He looked morosely at her.

"I must go to see Peter Ivanovich."

He went to see Peter Ivanovich, and together they went to see his friend, the doctor. He was in, and Ivan Ilych had a long talk with him.

Reviewing the anatomical and physiological details of what in the doctor's opinion was going on inside him, he understood it all.

There was something, a small thing, in the vermiform appendix. It might all come right. Only stimulate the energy of one organ and check the activity of another, then absorption would take place and everything would come right. He got home rather late for dinner, ate his dinner, and conversed cheerfully, but could not for a long time bring himself to go back to work in his room. At last, however, he went to his study and did what was necessary, but the consciousness that he had put something aside—an important, intimate matter which he would revert to when his work was done—never left him. When he had finished his work he remembered that this intimate matter was the thought of his vermiform appendix. But he did not give himself up to it, and went to the drawing-room for tea. There were callers there, including the examining magistrate who was a desirable match for his daughter, and they were conversing, playing the piano, and singing. Ivan Ilych, as Praskovya Fedorovna remarked, spent that evening more cheerfully than usual, but he never for a moment forgot that he had postponed the important matter of the appendix. At eleven o'clock he said good-night and went to his bedroom. Since his illness he had slept alone in a small room next to his study. He undressed and took up a novel by Zola, but instead of reading it he fell into thought, and in his imagination that desired improvement in the vermiform appendix occurred. There was the absorption and evacuation and the re-establishment of normal activity. "Yes, that's it!" he said to himself. "One need only assist nature, that's all." He remembered his medicine, rose, took it, and lay down on his back watching for the beneficent action of the medicine and for it to lessen the pain. "I need only take it regularly and avoid all injurious influences. I am already feeling better, much better." He began touching his side: it was not painful to the touch. "There, I really don't feel it. It's much better already." He put out the light and turned on his side . . . "The appendix is getting better, absorption is occurring." Suddenly he felt the old, familiar, dull, gnawing pain, stubborn and serious. There was the same familiar loathsome taste in his mouth. His heart sank and he felt dazed. "My God! My God!" he muttered. "Again, again! And it will never cease." And suddenly the matter presented itself in a quite different aspect. "Vermiform appendix! Kidney!" he said to himself. "It's not a question of appendix or kidney, but of life and . . . death. Yes, life was there and now it is going, going and I cannot stop it. Yes. Why deceive myself? Isn't it obvious to everyone but me that I'm dying, and that it's only a question of weeks, days . . . it may happen this moment. There was light and now there is darkness. I was here and now I'm going there! Where?" A chill came over him, his breathing ceased, and he felt only the throbbing of his heart.

"When I am not, what will there be? There will be nothing. Then where shall I be when I am no more? Can this be dying? No, I don't want to!" He jumped up and tried to light the candle, felt for it with trembling hands, dropped candle and candlestick on the floor, and fell back on his pillow.

"What's the use? It makes no difference," he said to himself, staring with wide-open eyes into the darkness. "Death. Yes, death. And none of them know or wish to know it, and they have no pity for me. Now they are playing." (He heard through the door the distant sound of a song and its accompaniment.) "It's all the same to them, but they will die too! Fools! I first, and they later, but it will be the same for them. And now they are merry . . . the beasts!"

Anger choked him and he was agonizingly, unbearably miserable. "It is impossible that all men have been doomed to suffer this awful horror!" He raised himself.

"Something must be wrong. I must calm myself—must think it all over from the beginning." And he again began thinking. "Yes, the beginning of my illness: I knocked my side, but I was still quite well that day and the next. It hurt a little, then rather more. I saw the doctors, then followed despondency and anguish, more doctors, and I drew nearer to the abyss. My strength grew less and I kept coming nearer and nearer, and now I have wasted away and there is no light in my eyes. I think of the appendix—but this is death! I think of mending the appendix, and all the while here is death! Can it really be death?" Again terror seized him and he gasped for breath. He leant down and began feeling for the matches, pressing with his elbow on the stand beside the bed. It was in his way and hurt him, he grew furious with it, pressed on it still harder, and upset it. Breathless and in despair he fell on his back, expecting death to come immediately.

Meanwhile the visitors were leaving. Praskovya Fedorovna was seeing them off. She heard something fall and came in.

"What has happened?"

"Nothing. I knocked it over accidentally."

She went out and returned with a candle. He lay there panting heavily, like a man who has run a thousand yards, and stared upwards at her with a fixed look.

"What is it, Jean?"

"No . . . o . . . thing. I upset it." ("Why speak of it? She won't understand," he thought.)

And in truth she did not understand. She picked up the stand, lit his candle, and hurried away to see another visitor off. When she came back he still lay on his back, looking upwards.

"What is it? Do you feel worse?"

"Yes."

She shook her head and sat down.

"Do you know, Jean, I think we must ask Leshchetitsky to come and see you here."

This meant calling in the famous specialist, regardless of expense. He smiled malignantly and said "No." She remained a little longer and then went up to him and kissed his forehead.

While she was kissing him he hated her from the bottom of his soul and with difficulty refrained from pushing her away.

"Good-night. Please God you'll sleep."

"Yes."

6

Ivan Ilych saw that he was dying, and he was in continual despair.

In the depth of his heart he knew he was dying, but not only was he not accustomed to the thought, he simply did not and could not grasp it.

The syllogism he had learnt from Kiezewetter's Logic: "Caius is a man, men are mortal, therefore Caius is mortal," had always seemed to him correct as applied to Caius, but certainly not as applied to himself. That Caius—man in the abstract—was mortal, was perfectly correct, but he was not Caius, not an abstract man, but a creature quite quite separate from all others. He had been little Vanya, with a mamma and a papa, with Mitya and Volodya, with the toys, a coachman and a nurse, afterwards with Katenka and with all the joys, griefs, and delights of childhood, boyhood, and youth. What did Caius know of the smell of that striped leather ball Vanya had been so fond of? Had Caius kissed his mother's hand like that, and did the silk of her dress rustle so for Caius? Had he rioted like that at school when the pastry was bad? Had Caius been in love like that? Could Caius preside at a session as he did? "Caius really was mortal, and it was right for him to die; but for me, little Vanya, Ivan Ilych, with all my thoughts and emotions, it's altogether a different matter. It cannot be that I ought to die. That would be too terrible."

Such was his feeling.

"If I had to die like Caius I should have known it was so. An inner voice would have told me so, but there was nothing of the sort in me and I and all my friends felt that our case was quite different from that of Caius. And now here it is!" he said to himself. "It can't be. It's impossible! But here it is. How is this? How is one to understand it?"

He could not understand it, and tried to drive this false, incorrect, morbid thought away and to replace it by other proper and healthy thoughts. But that thought, and not the thought only but the reality itself, seemed to come and confront him.

And to replace that thought he called up a succession of others, hoping to find in them some support. He tried to get back into the former current of thoughts that had once screened the thought of death from him. But strange to say, all that had formerly shut off, hidden, and destroyed, his consciousness of death, no longer had that effect. Ivan Ilych now spent most of his time in attempting to re-establish that old current. He would say to himself: "I will take up my duties again—after all I used to live by them." And banishing all doubts he would go to the law courts, enter into conversation with his colleagues, and sit carelessly as was his wont, scanning the crowd with a thoughtful look and leaning both his emaciated arms on the arms of his oak chair; bending over as usual to a colleague and drawing his papers nearer he would interchange whispers with him, and then suddenly raising his eyes and sitting erect would pronounce certain words and open the proceedings. But suddenly in the midst of those proceedings the pain in his side, regardless of the stage the proceedings had reached, would begin its own gnawing work. Ivan Ilych would turn his attention to it and try to drive the thought of it away, but without success. *It* would come and stand before him and look at him, and he would be petrified and the light would die out of his eyes, and he would again begin asking himself whether *It* alone was true. And his colleagues and subordinates would see with surprise and distress that he, the brilliant and subtle judge, was becoming confused and making mistakes. He would shake himself, try to pull himself together, manage somehow to bring the sitting to a close, and return home with the sorrowful consciousness that his judicial labours could not as formerly hide from him what he wanted them to hide, and could not deliver him from *It*. And what was worst of all was that *It* drew his attention to itself not in order to make him take some action but only that he should look at *It,* look it straight in the face: look at it and without doing anything, suffer inexpressibly.

And to save himself from this condition Ivan Ilych looked for consolations—new screens—and new screens were found and for a while seemed to save him, but then they immediately fell to pieces or rather became transparent, as if *It* penetrated them and nothing could veil *It*.

In these latter days he would go into the drawing-room he had arranged—that drawing-room where he had fallen and for the sake of which (how bitterly ridiculous it seemed) he had sacrificed his life—for he knew that his illness originated with that knock. He would enter and see that something had scratched the polished table. He would look for the cause of this and find that it was the bronze ornamentation of an album, that had got bent. He would take up the expensive album which he had lovingly arranged, and feel vexed with his daughter and her friends for their untidiness—for the album was torn here and there and some of the photographs turned upside down. He would put it carefully in order and bend the ornamentation back into position. Then it would occur to him to place all those things in another corner of the room, near the plants. He would call the footman, but his daughter or wife would come to help him. They would not agree, and his wife would contradict him, and he would dispute and grow angry. But that was all right, for then he did not think about *It. It* was invisible.

But then, when he was moving something himself, his wife would say: "Let the servants do it. You will hurt yourself again." And suddenly *It* would flash through the screen and he would see it. It was just a flash, and he hoped it would disappear, but he would involuntarily pay attention to his side. "It sits there as before, gnawing just the same!" And he could no longer forget *It*, but could distinctly see it looking at him from behind the flowers. "What is it all for?"

"It really is so! I lost my life over that curtain as I might have done when storming a fort. Is that possible? How terrible and how stupid. It can't be true! It can't, but it is."

He would go to his study, lie down, and again be alone with *It*: face to face with *It*. And nothing could be done with *It* except to look at it and shudder.

7

How it happened it is impossible to say because it came about step by step, unnoticed, but in the third month of Ivan Ilych's illness, his wife, his daughter, his son, his acquaintances, the doctors, the servants, and above all he himself, were aware that the whole interest he had for other people was whether he would soon vacate his place, and at last release the living from the discomfort caused by his presence and be himself released from his sufferings.

He slept less and less. He was given opium and hypodermic injections of morphine, but this did not relieve him. The dull depression he experienced in a somnolent condition at first gave him a little relief, but only as something new, afterwards it became as distressing as the pain itself or even more so.

Special foods were prepared for him by the doctor's orders, but all those foods became increasingly distasteful and disgusting to him.

For his excretions also special arrangements had to be made, and this was a torment to him every time—a torment from the uncleanliness, the unseemliness, and the smell, and from knowing that another person had to take part in it.

But just through this most unpleasant matter, Ivan Ilych obtained comfort. Gerasim, the butler's young assistant, always come in to carry the things out. Gerasim was a clean, fresh peasant lad, grown stout on town food and always cheerful and bright. At first the sight of him, in his clean Russian peasant costume, engaged on that disgusting task embarrassed Ivan Ilych.

Once when he got up from the commode too weak to draw up his trousers, he dropped into a soft armchair and looked with horror at his bare, enfeebled thighs with the muscles so sharply marked on them.

Gerasim, with a firm light tread, his heavy boots emitting a pleasant smell of tar and fresh winter air, came in wearing a clean Hessian apron, the sleeves of his print shirt tucked up over his strong bare young arms; and refraining from looking at his sick master out of consideration for his feelings, and restraining the joy of life that beamed from his face, went up to the commode.

"Gerasim!" said Ivan Ilych in a weak voice.

Gerasim started, evidently afraid he might have committed some blunder, and with a rapid movement turned his fresh, kind, simple young face which just showed the first downy signs of a beard.

"Yes, sir?"

"That must be very unpleasant for you. You must forgive me. I am helpless."

"Oh, why, sir," and Gerasim's eyes beamed and he showed his glistening white teeth, "what's a little trouble? It's a case of illness with you, sir."

And his deft strong hands did their accustomed task, and he went out of the room stepping lightly. Five minutes later he as lightly returned.

Ivan Ilych was still sitting in the same position in the arm-chair.

"Gerasim," he said when the latter had replaced the freshly-washed utensil. "Please come here and help me." Gerasim went up to him. "Lift me up. It is hard for me to get up, and I have sent Dmitri away."

Gerasim went up to him, grasped his master with his strong arms deftly but gently, in the same way that he stepped—lifted him, supported him with one hand, and with the other drew up his trousers and would have set him down again, but Ivan Ilych asked to be led to the sofa. Gerasim, without an effort and without apparent pressure, led him, almost lifting him, to the sofa and placed him on it.

"Thank you. How easily and well you do it all!"

Gerasim smiled again and turned to leave the room. But Ivan Ilych felt his presence such a comfort that he did not want to let him go.

"One thing more, please move up that chair. No, the other one—under my feet. It is easier for me when my feet are raised."

Gerasim brought the chair, set it down gently in place, and raised Ivan Ilych's legs on to it. It seemed to Ivan Ilych that he felt better while Gerasim was holding up his legs.

"It's better when my legs are higher," he said. "Place that cushion under them."

Gerasim did so. He again lifted the legs and placed them, and again Ivan Ilych felt better while Gerasim held his legs. When he set them down Ivan Ilych fancied he felt worse.

"Gerasim," he said. "Are you busy now?"

"Not at all, sir," said Gerasim, who had learnt from the townsfolk how to speak to gentlefolk.

"What have you still to do?"

"What have I to do? I've done everything except chopping the logs for to-morrow."

"Then hold my legs up a bit higher, can you?"

"Of course I can. Why not?" And Gerasim raised his master's legs higher and Ivan Ilych thought that in that position he did not feel any pain at all.

"And how about the logs?"

"Don't trouble about that, sir. There's plenty of time."

Ivan Ilych told Gerasim to sit down and hold his legs, and began to talk to him. And strange to say it seemed to him that he felt better while Gerasim held his legs up.

After that Ivan Ilych would sometimes call Gerasim and get him to hold his legs on his shoulders, and he liked talking to him. Gerasim did it all easily, willingly, simply, and with a good nature that touched Ivan Ilych. Health, strength, and vitality in other people were offensive to him, but Gerasim's strength and vitality did not mortify but soothed him.

What tormented Ivan Ilych most was the deception, the lie, which for some reason they all accepted, that he was not dying but was simply ill, and that he only need keep quiet and undergo a treatment and then something very good would result. He however knew that do what they would nothing would come of it, only still more agonizing suffering and death. This deception tortured him—their not wishing to admit what they all knew and what he knew, but wanting to lie to him concerning his terrible condition, and wishing and forcing him to participate in that lie. Those lies—lies enacted over him on the eve of his death and destined to degrade this awful, solemn act to the level of their visitings, their curtains, their sturgeon for dinner —were a terrible agony for Ivan Ilych. And strangely enough, many times when they were going through their antics over him he had been within a hairbreadth of calling out to them: "Stop lying! You know and I know that I am dying. Then at least stop lying about it!" But he had never had the spirit to do it. The awful, terrible act of his dying was, he could see, reduced by those about him to the level of a casual, unpleasant, and almost indecorous incident (as if someone entered a drawing-room diffusing an unpleasant odour) and this was done by that very decorum which he had served all his life long. He saw that no one felt for him, because no one even wished to grasp his position. Only Gerasim recognized it and pitied him. And so Ivan Ilych felt at ease only with him. He felt comforted when Gerasim supported his legs (sometimes all night long) and re-fused to go to bed, saying: "Don't you worry, Ivan Ilych. I'll get sleep enough later on," or when he suddenly became familiar and exclaimed: "If you weren't sick it would be another matter, but as it is, why should I grudge a little trouble?" Gerasim alone did not lie; everything showed that he alone understood the facts of the case and did not consider it necessary to disguise them, but simply felt sorry for his emaciated and enfeebled master. Once when Ivan Ilych was sending him away he even said straight out: "We shall all of us die, so why should I grudge a little trouble?"—expressing the fact that he did not think his work burdensome, because he was doing it for a dying man and hoped someone would do the same for him when his time came.

Apart from this lying, or because of it, what most tormented Ivan Ilych was that no one pitied him as he wished to be pitied. At certain moments after prolonged suffering he wished most of all (though he would have been ashamed to confess it) for someone to pity him as a sick child is pitied. He longed to be petted and comforted. He knew he was an important functionary, that he had a beard turning grey, and that therefore what he longed for was impossible, but still he longed for it. And in Gerasim's attitude towards him there was something akin to what he wished for, and so that attitude comforted him. Ivan Ilych wanted to weep, wanted to be petted and cried over, and then his colleague Shebek would come, and instead of weeping and being petted, Ivan Ilych would assume a serious, severe, and profound air, and by force of habit would express his opinion on a decision of the Court of Cassation and would stubbornly insist on that view. This falsity around him and within him did more than anything else to poison his last days.

8

It was morning. He knew it was morning because Gerasim had gone, and Peter the footman had come and put out the candles, drawn back one of the curtains, and begun quietly to tidy up. Whether it was morning or evening, Friday or Sunday, made no difference, it was all just the same: the gnawing, unmitigated, agonizing pain, never ceasing for an instant, the consciousness of life inexorably waning but not yet extinguished, that approach of that ever dreaded and hateful Death which was the only reality, and always the same falsity. What were days, weeks, hours, in such a case?

"Will you have some tea, sir?"

"He wants things to be regular, and wishes the gentlefolk to drink tea in the morning," thought Ivan Ilych, and only said "No."

"Wouldn't you like to move onto the sofa, sir?"

"He wants to tidy up the room, and I'm in the way. I am uncleanliness and disorder," he thought, and said only:

"No, leave me alone."

The man went on bustling about. Ivan Ilych stretched out his hand. Peter came up, ready to help.

"What is it, sir?"

"My watch."

Peter took the watch which was close at hand and gave it to his master.

"Half-past eight. Are they up?"

"No sir, except Vladimir Ivanich" (the son) "who has gone to school. Praskovya Fedorovna ordered me to wake her if you asked for her. Shall I do so?"

"No, there's no need to." "Perhaps I'd better have some tea," he thought, and added aloud: "Yes, bring me some tea."

Peter went to the door but Ivan Ilych dreaded being left alone. "How can I keep him here? Oh yes, my medicine." "Peter, give me my medicine." "Why not? Perhaps it may still do me some good." He took a spoonful and swallowed it. "No, it won't help. It's all tomfoolery, all deception," he decided as soon as he became aware of the familiar, sickly, hopeless taste. "No, I can't believe in it any longer. But the pain, why this pain? If it would only cease just for a moment!" And then he moaned. Peter turned towards him. "It's all right. Go and fetch me some tea."

Peter went out. Left alone Ivan Ilych groaned not so much with pain, terrible though that was, as from mental anguish. Always and forever the same, always these endless days and nights. If only it would come quicker! If only *what* would come quicker? Death, darkness? . . . No, no! Anything rather than death!

When Peter returned with the tea on a tray, Ivan Ilych stared at him for a time in perplexity, not realizing who and what he was. Peter was disconcerted by that look and his embarrassment brought Ivan Ilych to himself.

"Oh, tea! All right, put it down. Only help me to wash and put on a clean shirt."

And Ivan Ilych began to wash. With pauses for rest, he washed his hands and then his face, cleaned his teeth, brushed his hair, and looked in the glass. He was terrified by what he saw, especially by the limp way in which his hair clung to his pallid forehead.

While his shirt was being changed he knew that he would be still more frightened at the sight of his body, so he avoided looking at it. Finally he was ready. He drew on a dressing-gown, wrapped himself in a plaid, and sat down in the armchair to take his tea. For a moment he felt refreshed, but as soon as he began to drink the tea he was again aware of the same taste, and the pain also returned. He finished it with an effort, and then lay down stretching out his legs, and dismissed Peter.

Always the same. Now a spark of hope flashes up, then a sea of despair rages, and always pain; always pain, always despair, and always the same. When alone he had a dreadful and distressing desire to call someone, but he knew beforehand that with others present it would be still worse. "Another dose of morphine—to lose consciousness. I will tell him, the doctor, that he must think of something else. It's impossible, impossible, to go on like this."

An hour and another pass like that. But now there is a ring at the door bell. Perhaps it's the doctor? It is. He comes in fresh, hearty, plump, and cheerful, with that look on his face that seems to say: "There now, you're in a panic about something, but we'll arrange it all for you directly!" The doctor knows this expression is out of place here, but he has put it on once for all and can't take it off—like a man who has put on a frock-coat in the morning to pay a round of calls.

The doctor rubs his hands vigorously and reassuringly.

"Brr! How cold it is! There's such a sharp frost: just let me warm myself!" he says, as if it were only a matter of waiting till he was warm, and then he would put everything right.

"Well now, how are you?"

Ivan Ilych feels that the doctor would like to say: "Well, how are our affairs?" but that even he feels that this would not do, and says instead: "What sort of a night have you had?"

Ivan Ilych looks at him as much as to say: "Are you really never ashamed of lying?" But the doctor does not wish to understand this question, and Ivan Ilych says: "Just as terrible as ever. The pain never leaves me and never subsides. If only something . . ."

"Yes, you sick people are always like that. . . . There, now I think I am warm enough. Even Praskovya Fedorovna, who is so particular, could find no fault with my temperature. Well, now I can say good-morning," and the doctor presses his patient's hand.

Then, dropping his former playfulness, he begins with a most serious face to examine the patient, feeling his pulse and taking his temperature, and then begins the sounding and auscultation.

Ivan Ilych knows quite well and definitely that all this is nonsense and pure deception, but when the doctor, getting down on his knee, leans over him, putting his ear first higher then lower, and performs various gymnastic movements over him with a significant expression on his face, Ivan Ilych submits to it all as he used to submit to the speeches of the lawyers, though he knew very well that they were all lying and why they were lying.

The doctor, kneeling on the sofa, is still sounding him when Praskovya Fedorovna's silk dress rustles at the door and she is heard scolding Peter for not having let her know of the doctor's arrival.

She comes in, kisses her husband, and at once proceeds to prove that she has been up a long time already, and only owing to a misunderstanding failed to be there when the doctor arrived.

Ivan Ilych looks at her, scans here all over, sets against her the whiteness and plumpness and cleanness of her hands and neck, the gloss of her hair, and the sparkle of her vivacious eyes. He hates her with his whole soul. And the thrill of hatred he feels for her makes him suffer from her touch.

Her attitude towards him and his disease is still the same. Just as the doctor had adopted a certain relation to his patient which he could not abandon, so had she formed one towards him—that he was not doing something he ought to do and was himself to blame, and that she reproached him lovingly for this—and she could not now change that attitude.

"You see he doesn't listen to me and doesn't take his medicine at the proper time. And above all he lies in a position that is no doubt bad for him—with his legs up."

She described how he made Gerasim hold his legs up.

The doctor smiled with a contemptuous affability that said: "What's to be done? These sick people do have foolish fancies of that kind, but we must forgive them."

When the examination was over the doctor looked at his watch, and then Praskovya Fedorovna announced to Ivan Ilych that it was of course as he pleased, but she had sent to-day for a celebrated specialist who would examine him and have a consultation with Michael Danilovich (their regular doctor).

"Please don't raise any objections. I am doing this for my own sake," she said ironically, letting it be felt that she was doing it all for his sake and only said this to leave him no right to refuse. He remained silent, knitting his brows. He felt that he was so surrounded and involved in a mesh of falsity that it was hard to unravel anything.

Everything she did for him was entirely for her own sake, and she told him she was doing for herself what she actually was doing for herself, as if that was so incredible that he must understand the opposite.

At half-past eleven the celebrated specialist arrived. Again the sounding began and the significant conversations in his presence and in another room, about the kidneys and the appendix, and the questions and answers, with such an air of importance that again, instead of the real question of life and death which now alone confronted him, the question arose of the kidney and appendix which were not behaving as they ought to and would now be attacked by Michael Danilovich and the specialist and forced to amend their ways.

The celebrated specialist took leave of him with a serious though not hopeless look, and in reply to the timid question Ivan Ilych, with eyes glistening with fear and hope, put to him as to whether there was a chance of recovery, said that he could not vouch for it but there was a possibility. The look of hope with which Ivan Ilych watched the doctor out was so pathetic that Praskovya Fedorovna, seeing it, even wept as she left the room to hand the doctor his fee.

The gleam of hope kindled by the doctor's encouragement did not last long. The same room, the same pictures, curtains, wall-paper, medicine bottles, were all there, and the same aching suffering body, and Ivan Ilych began to moan. They gave him a subcutaneous injection and he sank into oblivion.

It was twilight when he came to. They brought him his dinner and he swallowed some beef tea with difficulty, and then everything was the same again and night was coming on.

After dinner, at seven o'clock, Praskovya Fedorovna came into the room in evening dress, her full bosom pushed up by her corset, and with traces of powder on her face. She had reminded him in the morning that they were going to the theatre. Sarah Bernhardt was visiting the town and they had a box, which he had insisted on their taking. Now he had forgotten about it and her toilet offended him, but he concealed his vexation when he remembered that he had himself insisted on their securing a box and going because it would be an instructive and aesthetic pleasure for the children.

Praskovya Fedorovna came in, self-satisfied but yet with a rather guilty air. She sat down and asked how he was but, as he saw, only for the sake of asking and not in order to learn about it, knowing that there was nothing to learn—and then went on to what she really wanted to say: that she would not on any account have gone but that the box had been taken and Helen and their daughter were going, as well as Petrishchev (the examining magistrate, their daughter's fiance) and that it was out of the question to let them go alone; but that she would have much preferred to sit with him for a while; and he must be sure to follow the doctor's orders while she was away.

"Oh, and Fedor Petrovich" (the fiance) "would like to come in. May he? And Lisa?"

"All right."

Their daughter came in in full evening dress, her fresh young flesh exposed (making a show of that very flesh which in his own case caused so much suffering), strong, healthy, evidently in love, and impatient with illness, suffering, and death, because they interfered with her happiness.

Fedor Petrovich came in too, in evening dress, his hair curled *à la Capoul,* a tight stiff collar round his long sinewy neck, an enormous white shirt-front and narrow black trousers tightly stretched over his strong thighs. He had one white glove tightly drawn on, and was holding his opera hat in his hand.

Following him the schoolboy crept in unnoticed, in a new uniform, poor little fellow, and wearing gloves. Terribly dark shadows showed under his eyes, the meaning of which Ivan Ilych knew well.

His son had always seemed pathetic to him, and now it was dreadful to see the boy's frightened look of pity. It seemed to Ivan Ilych that Vasya was the only one besides Gerasim who understood and pitied him.

They all sat down and again asked how he was. A silence followed. Lisa asked her mother about the opera-glasses, and there was an altercation between mother and daughter as to who had taken them and where they had been put. This occasioned some unpleasantness.

Fedor Petrovich inquired of Ivan Ilych whether he had ever seen Sarah Bernhardt. Ivan Ilych did not at first catch the question, but then replied: "No, have you see her before?"

"Yes, in *Adrienne Lecouvreur.*"

Praskovya Fedorovna mentioned some roles in which Sarah Bernhardt was particularly good. Her daughter disagreed. Conversation sprang up as to the elegance and realism of her acting—the sort of conversation that is always repeated and is always the same.

In the midst of the conversation Fedor Petrovich glanced at Ivan Ilych and became silent. The others also looked at him and grew silent. Ivan Ilych was staring with glittering eyes straight before him, evidently indignant with them. This had to be rectified, but it was impossible to do so. The silence had to be broken, but for a time no one dared to break it and they all became afraid that the conventional deception would suddenly become obvious and the truth become plain to all. Lisa was the first to pluck up courage and break that silence, but by trying to hide what everybody was feeling, she betrayed it.

"Well, if we are going it's time to start," she said, looking at her watch, a present from her father, and with a faint and significant smile at Fedor Petrovich relating to something known only to them. She got up with a rustle of her dress.

They all rose, said good-night, and went away.

When they had gone it seemed to Ivan Ilych that he felt better; the falsity had gone with them. But the pain remained—that same pain and that same fear that made everything monotonously alike, nothing harder and nothing easier. Everything was worse.

Again minute followed minute and hour followed hour. Everything remained the same and there was no cessation. And the inevitable end of it all became more and more terrible.

"Yes, send Gerasim here," he replied to a question Peter asked.

9

His wife returned late at night. She came in on tiptoe, but he heard her, opened his eyes, and made haste to close them again. She wished to send Gerasim away and to sit with him herself, but he opened his eyes and said: "No, go away."

"Are you in great pain?"

"Always the same."

"Take some opium."

He agreed and took some. She went away.

Till about three in the morning he was in a state of stupefied misery. It seemed to him that he and his pain were being thrust into a narrow, deep black sack, but though they were pushed further and further in they could not be pushed to the bottom. And this, terrible enough in itself, was accompanied by suffering. He was frightened yet wanted to fall through the sack, he struggled but yet co-operated. And suddenly he broke through, fell, and regained consciousness. Gerasim was sitting at the foot of the bed dozing quietly and patiently, while he himself lay with his emaciated stockinged legs resting on Gerasim's shoulders; the same shaded candle was there and the same unceasing pain.

"Go away, Gerasim," he whispered.

"It's all right, sir. I'll stay a while."

"No. Go away."

He removed his legs from Gerasim's shoulders, turned sideways onto his arm, and felt sorry for himself. He only waited till Gerasim had gone into the next room and then restrained himself no longer but wept like a child. He wept on account of his helplessness, his terrible loneliness, the cruelty of man, the cruelty of God, and the absence of God.

"Why hast Thou done all this? Why hast Thou brought me here? Why, why dost Thou torment me so terribly?"

He did not expect an answer and yet wept because there was no answer and could be none. The pain again grew more acute, but he did not stir and did not call. He said to himself: "Go on! Strike me! But what is it for? What have I done to Thee? What is it for?"

Then he grew quiet and not only ceased weeping but even held his breath and became all attention. It was as though he were listening not to an audible voice but to the voice of his soul, to the current of thoughts arising within him.

"What is it you want?" was the first clear conception capable of expression in words, that he heard.

"What do you want? What do you want?" he repeated to himself.

"What do I want? To live and not to suffer," he answered.

And again he listened with such concentrated attention that even his pain did not distract him.

"To live? How?" asked his inner voice.

"Why, to live as I used to—well and pleasantly."

"As you lived before, well and pleasantly?" the voice repeated.

And in imagination he began to recall the best moments of his pleasant life. But strange to say none of these best moments of his pleasant life now seemed at all what they had then seemed—none of them except the first recollections of childhood. There, in childhood, there had been something really pleasant with which it would be possible to live if it could return. But the child who had experienced that happiness existed no longer, it was like a reminiscence of somebody else.

As soon as the period began which had produced the present Ivan Ilych, all that had then seemed joys now melted before his sight and turned into something trivial and often nasty.

And the further he departed from childhood and the nearer he came to the present the more worthless and doubtful were the joys. This began with the School of Law. A little that was really good was still found there—there was light-heartedness, friendship, and hope. But in the upper classes there had already been fewer of such good moments. Then during the first years of his official career, when he was in the service of the Governor, some pleasant moments again occurred: they were the memories of love for a woman. Then all became confused and there was still less of what was good; later on again there was still less that was good, and the further he went the less there was. His marriage, a mere accident, then the disenchantment that followed it, his wife's bad breath and the sensuality and hypocrisy: then that deadly official life and those preoccupations about money, a year of it, and two, and ten, and twenty, and always the same thing. And the longer it lasted the more deadly it became. "It is as if I had been going downhill while I imagined I was going up. And that is really what it was. I was going up in public opinion, but to the same extent life was ebbing away from me. And now it is all done and there is only death."

"Then what does it mean? Why? It can't be that life is so senseless and horrible. But if it really has been so horrible and senseless, why must I die and die in agony? There is something wrong!"

"Maybe I did not live as I ought to have done," it suddenly occurred to him. "But how could that be, when I did everything properly?" he replied, and immediately dismissed from his mind this, the sole solution of all the riddles of life and death, as something quite impossible.

"Then what do you want now? To live? Live how? Live as you lived in the law courts when the usher proclaimed 'The judge is coming!' The judge is coming, the judge!" he repeated to himself. "Here he is, the judge. But I am not guilty!" he exclaimed angrily. "What is it for?" And he ceased crying, but turning his face to the wall continued to ponder on the same question: Why, and for what purpose, is there all this horror? But however much he pondered he found no answer. And whenever the thought occurred to him, as it often did, that it all resulted from his not having lived as he ought to have done, he at once recalled the correctness of his whole life and dismissed so strange an idea.

10

Another fortnight passed. Ivan Ilych now no longer left his sofa. He would not lie in bed but lay on the sofa, facing the wall nearly all the time. He suffered ever the same unceasing agonies and in his loneliness pondered always on the same insoluble question: "What is this? Can it be that it is Death?" And the inner voice answered: "Yes, it is Death."

"Why these sufferings?" And the voice answered, "For no reason—they just are so." Beyond and besides this there was nothing.

From the very beginning of his illness, ever since he had first been to see the doctor, Ivan Ilych's life had been divided between two contrary and alternating moods: now it was despair and the expectation of this uncomprehended and terrible death, and now hope and an intently interested observation of the functioning of his organs. Now before his eyes there was only a kidney or an intestine that temporarily evaded its duty, and now only that incomprehensible and dreadful death from which it was impossible to escape.

These two states of mind had alternated from the very beginning of his illness, but the further it progressed the more doubtful and fantastic became the conception of the kidney, and the more real the sense of impending death.

He had but to call to mind what he had been three months before and what he was now, to call to mind with what regularity he had been going downhill, for every possibility of hope to be shattered.

Latterly during that loneliness in which he found himself as he lay facing the back of the sofa, a loneliness in the midst of a populous town and surrounded by numerous acquaintances and relations but that yet could not have been more complete anywhere—either at the bottom of the sea or under the earth —during that terrible loneliness Ivan Ilych had lived only in memories of the past. Pictures of his past rose before him one after another. They always began with what was nearest in time and then went back to what was most remote—to his childhood—and rested there. If he thought of the stewed prunes that had been offered him that day, his mind went back to the raw shrivelled French plums of his childhood, their peculiar flavour and the flow of saliva when he sucked their stones, and along with the memory of that taste came a whole series of memories of those days: his nurse, his brother, and their toys. "No, I mustn't think of that. . . . It is too painful," Ivan Ilych said to himself, and brought himself back to the present—to the button on the back of the sofa and the creases in its morocco. "Morocco is expensive, but it does not wear well: there had been a quarrel about it. It was a different kind of quarrel and a different kind of morocco that time when we tore father's portfolio and were punished, and mamma brought us some tarts. . . ." And again his thoughts dwelt on his childhood, and again it was painful and he tried to banish them and fix his mind on something else.

Then again together with that chain of memories another series passed through his mind—of how his illness had progressed and grown worse. There also the further back he looked the more life there had been. There had been more of what was good in life and more of life itself. The two merged together. "Just as the pain went on getting worse and worse so my life grew worse and worse," he thought. "There is one bright spot there at the back, at the beginning of life, and afterwards all becomes blacker and blacker and proceeds more and more rapidly—in inverse ratio to the square of the distance from death," thought Ivan Ilych. And the example of a stone falling downwards with increasing velocity entered his mind. Life, a series of increasing sufferings, flies further and further towards its end—the most terrible suffering. "I am flying. . . ." He shuddered, shifted himself, and tried to resist, but was already aware that resistance was impossible, and again with eyes weary of gazing but unable to cease seeing what was before them, he stared at the back of the sofa and waited—awaiting that dreadful fall and shock and destruction.

"Resistance is impossible!" he said to himself. "If I could only understand what it is all for! But that too is impossible. An explanation would be possible if it could be said that I have not lived as I ought to. But it is impossible to say that," and he remembered all the legality, correctitude, and propriety of his life. "That at any rate can certainly not be admitted," he thought, and his lips smiled ironically as if someone could see that smile and be taken in by it. "There is no explanation! Agony, death. . . . What for?"

11

Another two weeks went by in this way and during that fortnight an event occurred that Ivan Ilych and his wife had desired. Petrishchev formally proposed. It happened in the evening. The next day Praskovya Fedorovna came into her husband's room considering how best to inform him of it, but that very night there had been a fresh change for the worse in his condition. She found him still lying on the sofa but in a different position. He lay on his back, groaning and staring fixedly straight in front of him.

She began to remind him of his medicines, but he turned his eyes towards her with such a look that she did not finish what she was saying; so great an animosity, to her in particular, did that look express.

"For Christ's sake let me die in peace!" he said.

She would have gone away, but just then their daughter came in and went up to say good morning. He looked at her as he had done at his wife, and in reply to her inquiry about his health said dryly that he would soon free them all of himself. They were both silent and after sitting with him for a while went away.

"Is it our fault?" Lisa said to her mother. "It's as if we were to blame! I am sorry for papa, but why should we be tortured?"

The doctor came at his usual time. Ivan Ilych answered "Yes" and "No," never taking his angry eyes from him, and at last said: "You know you can do nothing for me, so leave me alone."

"We can ease your sufferings."

"You can't even do that. Let me be."

The doctor went into the drawing-room and told Praskovya Fedorovna that the case was very serious and that the only resource left was opium to allay her husband's sufferings, which must be terrible.

It was true, as the doctor said, that Ivan Ilych's physical sufferings were terrible, but worse than the physical sufferings were his mental sufferings which were his chief torture.

His mental sufferings were due to the fact that that night, as he looked at Gerasim's sleepy, good-natured face with its prominent cheek-bones, the question suddenly occurred to him: "What if my whole life has really been wrong?"

It occurred to him that what had appeared perfectly impossible before, namely that he had not spent his life as he should have done, might after all be true. It occurred to him that his scarcely perceptible attempts to struggle against what was considered good by the most highly placed people, those scarcely noticeable impulses which he had immediately suppressed, might have been the real thing, and all the rest false. And his professional duties and the whole arrangement of his life and of his family, and all his social and official interests, might all have been false. He tried to defend all those things to himself and suddenly felt the weakness of what he was defending. There was nothing to defend.

"But if that is so," he said to himself, "and I am leaving this life with the consciousness that I have lost all that was given me and it is impossible to rectify it—what then?"

He lay on his back and began to pass his life in review in quite a new way. In the morning when he saw first his footman, then his wife, then his daughter, and then the doctor, their every word and movement confirmed to him the awful truth that had been revealed to him during the night. In them he saw himself—all that for which he had lived—and saw clearly that it was not real at all, but a terrible and huge deception which had hidden both life and death. This consciousness intensified his physical suffering tenfold. He groaned and tossed about, and pulled at his clothing which choked and stifled him. And he hated them on that account.

He was given a large dose of opium and became unconscious, but at noon his sufferings began again. He drove everybody away and tossed from side to side.

His wife came to him and said:

"Jean, my dear, do this for me. It can't do any harm and often helps. Healthy people often do it."

He opened his eyes wide.

"What? Take communion? Why? It's unnecessary! However. . . ."

She began to cry.

"Yes, do, my dear. I'll send for our priest. He is such a nice man."

"All right. Very well," he muttered.

When the priest came and heard his confession, Ivan Ilych was softened and seemed to feel a relief from his doubts and consequently from his sufferings, and for a moment there came a ray of hope. He again began to think of the vermiform appendix and the possibility of correcting it. He received the sacrament with tears in his eyes.

When they laid him down again afterwards he felt a moment's ease, and the hope that he might live awoke in him

again. He began to think of the operation that had been suggested to him. "To live! I want to live!" he said to himself.

His wife came in to congratulate him after his communion,
and when uttering the usual conventional words she added:

"You feel better, don't you?"

Without looking at her he said "Yes."

Her dress, her figure, the expression of her face, the tone of
her voice, all revealed the same thing. "This is wrong, it is not
as it should be. All you have lived for and still live for is falsehood
and deception, hiding life and death from you." And as soon
as he admitted that thought, his hatred and his agonizing physical suffering again sprang up, and with that suffering a consciousness of the unavoidable, approaching end. And to this was
added a new sensation of grinding shooting pain and a feeling
of suffocation.

The expression of his face when he uttered that "yes" was
dreadful. Having uttered it, he looked her straight in the eyes,
turned on his face with a rapidity extraordinary in his weak
state and shouted:

"Go away! Go away and leave me alone!"

12

From that moment the screaming began that continued for three
days, and was so terrible that one could not hear it through two
closed doors without horror. At the moment he answered his
wife he realized that he was lost, that there was no return, that
the end had come, the very end, and his doubts were still
unsolved and remained doubts.

"Oh! Oh! Oh!" he cried in various intonations. He had begun
by screaming "I won't!" and continued screaming on the letter
"o."

For three whole days, during which time did not exist for
him, he struggled in that black sack into which he was being
thrust by an invisible, resistless force. He struggled as a man

condemned to death struggles in the hands of the executioner, knowing that he cannot save himself. And every moment he felt that despite all his efforts he was drawing nearer and nearer to what terrified him. He felt that his agony was due to his being thrust into that black hole and still more to his not being able to get right into it. He was hindered from getting into it by his conviction that his life had been a good one. That very justification of his life held him fast and prevented his moving forward, and it caused him most torment of all.

Suddenly some force struck him in the chest and side, making it still harder to breathe, and he fell through the hole and there at the bottom was a light. What had happened to him was like the sensation one sometimes experiences in a railway carriage when one thinks one is going backwards while one is really going forwards and suddenly becomes aware of the real direction.

"Yes, it was all not the right thing," he said to himself, "but that's no matter. It can be done. But what *is* the right thing?" he asked himself, and suddenly grew quiet.

This occurred at the end of the third day, two hours before his death. Just then his schoolboy son had crept softly in and gone up to the bedside. The dying man was still screaming desperately and waving his arms. His hand fell on the boy's head, and the boy caught it, pressed it to his lips, and began to cry.

At that very moment Ivan Ilych fell through and caught sight of the light, and it was revealed to him that though his life had not been what it should have been, this could still be rectified. He asked himself, "What *is* the right thing?" and grew still, listening. Then he felt that someone was kissing his hand. He opened his eyes, looked at his son, and felt sorry for him. His wife came up to him and he glanced at her. She was gazing at him open-mouthed, with undried tears on her nose and cheek and a despairing look on her face. He felt sorry for her too.

"Yes, I am making them wretched," he thought. "They are sorry, but it will be better for them when I die." He wished to say this but had not the strength to utter it. "Besides, why speak? I must act," he thought. With a look at his wife he indicated his son and said: "Take him away . . . sorry for him . . . sorry for you too. . . ." He tried to add, "forgive me," but said "forego" and waved his hand, knowing that He whose understanding mattered would understand.

And suddenly it grew clear to him that what had been oppressing him and would not leave him was all dropping away at once from two sides, from ten sides, and from all sides. He was sorry for them, he must act so as not to hurt them: release them and free himself from these sufferings. "How good and how simple!" he thought. "And the pain?" he asked himself. "What has become of it? Where are you, pain?"

He turned his attention to it.

"Yes, here it is. Well, what of it? Let the pain be."

"And death . . . where is it?"

He sought his former accustomed fear of death and did not find it. "Where is it? What death?" There was no fear because there was no death.

In place of death there was light.

"So that's what it is!" he suddenly exclaimed aloud. "What joy!"

To him all this happened in a single instant, and the meaning of that instant did not change. For those present his agony continued for another two hours. Something rattled in his throat, his emaciated body twitched, then the gasping and rattle became less and less frequent.

"It is finished!" said someone near him.

He heard these words and repeated them in his soul.

"Death is finished," he said to himself. "It is no more!"

He drew in a breath, stopped in the midst of a sigh, stretched out, and died.